THE MILITARY AND THE MEDIA

This book is dedicated to my wife, Jan.

The views expressed in this book are those of the author and are not necessarily those of the Ministry of Defence.

The Military and the Media

ALAN HOOPER
Serving Officer in the
Royal Marines

Gower

Published by

Gower Publishing Company Limited,
Gower House, Croft Road,
Aldershot, Hants GU11 3HR, England

British Library Cataloguing in Publication Data

Hooper, Alan
 The military and the media.
 1. Armed forces in mass media
 I. Title
 355.00941   P96.A7
 ISBN 0-566-00610-3

Printed and bound in Great Britain by
Biddles Ltd, Guildford and King's Lynn

Contents

Figures and tables

Foreword

There is a story told of the famous American reporter and columnist, Westbrook Pegler, about his arrival in France in 1917 as a correspondent for United Press. Pegler, young and enthusiastic, told his older colleagues he proposed to interview General Pershing, commander of the US Forces in France. Pershing, as the older journalists knew, gave no press interviews, no press conferences: he 'didn't believe' in war reporting. So they awaited with some interest Pegler's return from GHQ where, he had declared, he was 'going to interview General Pershing'.

When he got back, Pegler began typing furiously. Unable to contain himself for another second, one of his colleagues asked Pegler what Pershing had said. Pegler took the paper out of his typewriter: it read 'This correspondent had an interview with General Pershing today. The General said "Pegler, get the hell out of my office"'.

It is a matter of dismay, if not alarm, to journalists to discover that Pershing's World War One attitude to reporters and the media persists in some areas, and there are still, in all the armed services, Blimps who consistently (deliberately?) fail to recognise the change in the nature of society, not least the development of the concepts of accountability and communication. The services are, of course, not alone in this.

For the British Army, its involvement in Northern Ireland was a watershed in its relations with the media. In the first two years, there were several public information 'own goals': there was even a disastrous attempt to inject propaganda into its dealings with the media. The reappraisal that followed was led by a series of outstanding senior officers who recognised the particular tensions and pitfalls of the Irish dimension; the Army's public information machine was over-hauled, redirected, and revitalised with the result that the Public Information group at HQNI in Lisburn became (and remains) a valued, trusted and accurate source of information for journalists. It achieved that by being honest, as open as it could be without hazarding operations, above all because it demonstrated its willingness to communicate. It is unnecessary to underline to what degree that credibility enhanced the status of the Army, not only in Northern Ireland but wherever the Army serves.

The other services have been slow to learn the lessons of Northern Ireland. But they are lessons that must be learned, and, in the wake of the Falklands conflict, learned swiftly and effectively.

We live in a free society, with a free press. It is the journalist's right to ask questions: he accepts he has no divine right to receive an answer. My experience, from the media and the military sides of the matter, convinces me it is invariably better to give an answer — and that the response must be accurate and truthful. Explanation prevents specu-lation: explanation guarantees understanding.

There is no need for journalists and military men to be at logger-heads: for the greater part of the time, they are not at war with each other. This book is important in that it makes a significant contribution to the understanding of the media by the military. It explores attitudes, describes editorial processes, examines the methodology. It confirms what journalists have always said about their trade: lots of technique — and no mystique.

I believe this book should be required reading for all military officers and NCOs. It deserves to become a standard textbook at our cadet schools and staff colleges. And journalists, too, would benefit from reading it, for the insight it gives into our business through an outsider's eyes.

Its author, Major Alan Hooper, is a distinguished Royal Marines officer, who has demonstrated his academic capabilities. His book shows perception, understanding and substantial reporting skills.

The greatest compliment I can pay him is that if he wasn't a Marine, he'd make a very fine journalist!

Alan Protheroe MBE, TD, FBIM.
Assistant Director General,
British Broadcasting Corporation

Preface

'It's War!' This was the dramatic headline on the front page of the *Sun* newspaper on 3 April 1982, the day after Argentina invaded the Falkland Islands. This event dominated the news in subsequent weeks to an extent not experienced in Britain since the Suez crisis. Since there was virtually no warning of the Argentinian invasion and few people were aware of the issues involved, the media became the fundamental source of information both for up-to-the-minute news, for analysis and for background data. It also thrust the Armed Services into the spotlight (especially the Royal Navy and the Royal Marines in the critical early days) as the details of the Battles of Port Stanley and Grytviken, South Georgia were pieced together, the fleet mobilised for action over a hectic weekend, and the subsequent actions in the South Atlantic became subjected to constant daily media coverage. This in turn stressed once again the importance of the relationship between the military and the media and served to underline the fact that the reporting of armed conflict by the media is now almost an everyday occurrence.

This book is a study of that relationship and it is the first work to be devoted specifically to the subject. The study has been largely based on first-hand research consisting of personal observation of the news process in the press, radio and television, interviews with various personalities in the military and the media, and visits to a number of military establishments to see what they teach about the media.

In trying to acquire a better understanding about the relationship between the two professions, the book includes case studies of the news process in newspaper offices, in television news, and in radio news and current affairs programmes; a review of the current depth of knowledge which each profession possesses of the other; an analysis of the portrayal of the military on television; and a study of the reporting of conflict (including an examination of some examples from the Vietnam war, Northern Ireland and the Falklands crisis).

The research has revealed that there is considerable misunderstanding and mutual ignorance between military officers and journalists; and yet the characteristics of the military and the media are surprisingly similar. It is probable that this affinity has not been recognised before because, up until now, no researcher has had enough knowledge of the one profession and been allowed sufficient access to the other, to be able to analyse and compare the characteristics. The overall conclusion of the book is that both the military and the media would gain considerable mutual benefit by learning more about the other's work, and that the key to a better understanding lies in education.

Acknowledgements

A considerable amount of research for this book was carried out whilst I was at the University of Exeter as a Defence Fellow. I am grateful to the Ministry of Defence for awarding me a Defence Fellowship and for sponsoring my research during my time at university. I am also grateful to Professor Maurice Goldsmith, Dr Bob Dowse and to all members of the Department of Politics, University of Exeter for their helpful assistance throughout my time in the Department.

I owe an inestimable debt of gratitude to Dr Richard Clutterbuck, my supervisor at Exeter, who guided my research with untiring enthusiasm, wisdom and encouragement and who has provided invaluable advice ever since.

I wish to thank Alan Protheroe, the Assistant Director General of the BBC, for the compliment he has paid me by writing the Foreword to my book. I also wish to thank Louise Perry for preparing the Index so diligently.

My thanks are also due to all those people who spared the time to talk to me. This book would not have been possible without their unprecedented co-operation. I would also like to acknowledge the access granted to me by all those departments of the media which I visited. Any list of thanks, inevitably, is incomplete, but I would like to mention the following: Mr Martin Bell, Mr Alastair Burnet, Mr Tony Brooks, Mr Michael Charlton, Mr Michael Cockerell, General Sir Timothy Creasy, Mrs Edna Cutler, Sir Robin Day, Mr William Deedes, Mr John Dekker, Mr Christopher Duttson,

Major General Martin Farndale, Mr Ken Goudie, Rear Admiral Wilfred Graham, Professor James Halloran, Mr Andrew Hutchinson, Miss Gail Joughin, Major Dougie Keelan, General Sir Frank Kitson, Sir Larry Lamb, Mr John Ledlie, Mr Christopher Lee, Mr Colin Leslie, Mr Innes Lloyd, Mr Bob Moore, Mr Ron Neil, Mr David Nicholas, Mr James Omerod, Mr Peter Pagnamenta, Major General Patrick Palmer, Mr Julian Pettifer, Mr David Phillips, Mr Nigel Pope, Mr Charles Potts, Lieutenant General Sir Steuart Pringle, Mr John Purdie, Brigadier David Ramsbotham, Colonel David Slater, Mr Henry Stanhope, Mr Colin Strong, Brigadier Maurice Tugwell, Mr Christopher Wain, Mr Joe Waters, Mr John Wilson, Major Brian Woodham, Mr John Wright. The usual disclaimer applies.

Finally I would like to thank my wife, Jan, for her patience, understanding and considerable assistance with the preparation of this book.

Alan Hooper
Exeter, 1982

PART I

INTRODUCTION

1 A Turbulent Relationship

*There can be few professions more ready to misunderstand
each other than journalists and soldiers.*

S.F. Crozier[1]

Introduction

The shape of peoples' lives all over the world is still being constantly
redirected by the results of armed conflict and despite his increasing
knowledge man is apparently unable to solve many of his problems by
peaceful means. In the first half of 1982 alone, the trouble spots
include Iran—Iraq, Afghanistan, Poland, El Salvador, Belize, Israel,
Lebanon and the Falkland Islands. Whilst at home, the same year saw
the thirteenth anniversary of the British Army's struggle to keep the
peace in Northern Ireland. Some of these events have involved bitter
fighting, others contain the dormant potential to erupt into armed
conflict at a moment's notice. It was estimated that on 21 March 1982
701,600,000 people were involved in some kind of war throughout the
world (this represents one-sixth of the total world population).[2] Just
after that statistic was recorded the long standing dispute between
Argentina and Great Britain over the Falkland Islands suddenly
escalated into open conflict with subsequent world-wide implications.
This event was a timely reminder of the inherent dangers of armed
conflict in the missile age.

For good or ill, events such as this are pursued by newsmen, investi-

---

1 S.F. Crozier, 'The Press and the Army', *Army Quarterly*, vol.68, no.2, July 1954, p.214.
2 *The Sunday Times*, 21 March 1982.

gative reporters and the television cameras. A random glance at the newspaper headlines or at the list of TV news items in any period of a month leaves no doubt about the enormous proportion of the journalists' output which has a military setting. There is also little doubt about the public interest which these news stories arouse. As so often happens, the contemporary scene is reflected by television and therefore over the last few years there have also been an increasing number of television documentaries about the military, as well as plays and series which have a military setting. The spotlight is on the British military as never before and it covers a broad spectrum of defence issues such as the debate on Trident and Cruise missiles, the proposed reduction of the Navy's surface fleet, the economics of defence, the Falklands crisis, and it includes such documentaries as *Fighter Pilot*.

This media interest in the military is necessary and healthy. A free press is fundamental to the survival of democracy. Autocratic and totalitarian states may have spectacular short term successes but they have a poor survival record compared with constitutions which permit the free expression of opinion. Democracies have a longer survival record. For example, Britain has not suffered violent constitutional change for nearly 300 years, and the United States for over 200 years. By comparison, the longest lived totalitarian state (where the media report only what the government wishes its people to know) is the Soviet Union which celebrates its 66th birthday in 1983. The Nazis, despite their professionalism at both suppression of opinion and propaganda, lasted only 12 years.

It follows that the relationship between the military and the media is a vital one. Both sides have much to learn about each other, and they are likely to suffer accordingly if they fail to do so.

A turbulent relationship

Television is new. The investigative reporter is not, and it is he who has, over the years, laid the foundations of this relationship and its associated problems. So let us first of all look at the original war correspondents. Although William Howard Russell has been acknowledged as the 'father' of war correspondents, he was not the first. Henry Crabb Robinson of *The Times* is generally considered to be the original British war correspondent. He reported Napoleon's victory over the Russians at Friedland in 1807, and he went out to Corunna the following year to cover the arrival of Sir David Baird's division which had been sent out to reinforce Sir John Moore. He does not appear to have been a very industrious correspondent however, for although the battle of Friedland was fought on 14 June 1807, Robinson, who was residing in Altona, did not receive the news until 20 June.[3] Similarly, he was not actually at the battle of Corunna on 16 January 1809.[4] The first British correspondent to give eye-witness accounts of battles was Charles Lewis Cruneisen of the *Morning Post*. He covered the Spanish Civil War of 1835–37 and for a time was attached to Don Carlos' headquarters. Indeed, he was decorated by Don Carlos for bravery and was actually captured by Queen Isabella's forces, to be saved from being shot as a spy only by the intervention of Lord Palmerston, the British Foreign Secretary.[5]

From these early days in the first half of the nineteenth century until the present day, correspondents have covered all the major battles throughout the world — and right from the outset there have been examples of strained relations between the journalists and the military. On 21 November 1809, the Duke of Wellington wrote to Lord Liverpool from Badajoz:

> I beg to draw your Lordship's attention to the frequent paragraphs in the English Newspapers describing the position, the numbers, the objects, the means of attaining them possessed by the armies in Spain and Portugal. In some instances the English newspapers have accurately stated, not only the regiments occupying a position, but the number of men fit for duty of which each regiment was composed; and this intelligence must have reached the enemy at the same time as it did me, at a moment at which it was most important that he should not receive it.[6]

The American Civil War also contains examples of indiscretions by newspapers, both from the North and the South, which provided useful intelligence for the other side. General Lee complained to the Secretary of War about this, whilst General Sherman banished newspaper correspondents from his lines and threatened summary punishment for anyone who published information about his force.[7]

Genuine concern for the non-disclosure of information that would be useful to the enemy was an inevitable area of conflict between the journalist and the soldier right from the beginning and this had led to

3 Lauriston Bullard, *Famous War Correspondents*, Pitman, London 1914, p.7.
4 Ibid, pp. 7–8; see also A.E. Sullivan, 'Getting the Story, Some Facts about War Correspondents', *Army Quarterly*, vol.81, no.2, January 1961, p.204.
5 Bullard, op.cit., pp. 8–9; see also Sullivan, op.cit., p.204.
6 S.T. Sheppard, 'In Memoriam: William Howard Russell', *The United Service Magazine*, no.940, March 1907, p.571.
7 F.J. Hudleston, *Use of Newspapers to the Enemy Intelligence Service* (concocted for DMI by the Librarian of the General Staff Section, War Office Library, 21 May 1917), p.4. See also Sheppard, op.cit., p.571.

various forms of censorship being applied since the end of the Crimea War.[8] However it was Russell's attack on the incompetence of the higher command in that particular war, and his disclosures about the suffering of the troops and the senior officers' lack of concern for their pitiful condition, which led to a new low ebb in the relationship between the two professions. The high command did not take at all kindly to his criticism. He was ignored by Lord Raglan, the Commander-in-Chief, and ostracised by his officers. The subsequent criticism about the scandalous lack of medical facilities by Russell, Thomas Chenery also of *The Times*, and Edwin Larence Godkin of the *London Daily News*, strained relations even further. For the first time the actions and decisions of British commanders in the field were being subjected to censure by outsiders as a result of the journalistic insistence that the public 'had a right to know'. The revelations from the Crimea have led to an uneasy relationship ever since, neither side quite being sure where they stand, and the resulting mistrust had periodically exploded into the limelight during the last 100 years:

'If I were you I should go away! I would indeed!' (Senior British officers to Russell during the Crimea).[9]

'I trust the Army will lynch *The Times* correspondent' (Sidney Herbert, the former Secretary for War, referring to Russell after his criticism of Lord Raglan following the failure of the attack on Sebastopol)[10]

'Get out of my way, you drunken swabs!' (Lord Kitchener to the assembled war correspondents before the battle of Omdurman, 1898).[11]

'The BBC is an enemy within the gates, doing more harm than good.' (Winston Churchill's private remark to Lord Reith during World War Two).[12]

'It may well be that between press and officials there is an inherent, built-in conflict of interest. There is something to be said for both sides, but when the nation is at war and men's lives are at stake, there should be no ambiguity.' (General Westmoreland, writing about the Vietnam War).[13]

---

8 Phillip Knightley, *The First Casualty*, André Deutsch, London 1975, p.16. See also UK Public Record Office, W.O.28/131.
9 Phillip Knightley, op.cit., p.12.
10 Ibid., p.15.
11 Philip Magnus, *Kitchener*, John Murray, London 1958, p.134.
12 Sir Michael Swann, *On Disliking the Media*, lecture at the University of Salford, 7 November 1978; BBC 1978, p.7.
13 General William C. Westmoreland, *A Soldier Reports*, Doubleday, New York 1976, p.422.

Writing in the *Army Quarterly* in 1954, Major S.F. Crozier (the Assistant Editor of *The Field*) said: 'There can be few professions more ready to misunderstand each other than journalists and soldiers'[14] and he singled out mutual ignorance as a primary reason for this misunderstanding. Even in battle, where the soldier and the reporter share the discomforts together, that very closeness divides them because the one is there as a participant, compelled to remain through discipline, whereas the other is there as an observer, free to leave when he wants, compelled to remain only through self-discipline.[15] The soldier owes his loyalty to superiors, the officer to his subordinates; the reporter owes his loyalty to his editor, the editor to his public.

In peacetime, the media become the watchdog of the taxpayer and keep an eye on the military. They also keep an eye on the Government on behalf of the apolitical Armed Forces. The media have one other vital role to play in peacetime and that is to provide the link between the Services and the public by keeping them in touch with each other and by ensuring that the British people have a realistic view of defence.

The link between the military and the public is more important today than ever before. Not only has a completely new generation grown up without any experience of war, but since the ending of National Service in 1962, fewer and fewer people have had any direct contact with the Forces. Therefore the need to keep people in touch with changing attitudes in the Services, with the rapid developments in military technology, and abreast of defence strategic thinking is now an educational requirement. This link is best established via the media, and yet the vast majority of those working in newspapers, radio or television are themselves ignorant about the Forces. In their turn the Services need to be aware of the implications of the speed of modern communications which can transmit television pictures via satellite from the battlefield to a mass audience more quickly than information can be passed over the military communications net. Advances in technology have dramatically altered the influence of television and it is important that the Armed Forces learn to live with the speed and impact of modern communications.

It follows that an understanding of the relationship between the military and the media is important not only in itself but also in the context of the rapport between the public and the Services. Furthermore, during the last 35 years there has been no world war and yet the

---

14 S.F. Crozier, op.cit., p.214.
15 One notable exception to the freedom of choice about leaving a battle concerns those journalists on board ships during a naval action.

British Armed Forces have been involved continuously in low level conflict, including 13 years in Northern Ireland.[16] The reporting of armed conflict by the media is now almost a constant requirement and therefore accurate and informed coverage is a matter of public importance. The aim of this book, therefore, is to study the relationship between the military and the media in order to acquire a better understanding of that relationship.

Outline of the book

The remaining four parts of the book are designed so that a logical theme runs throughout but each is self-contained to enable the busy reader to concentrate on a specific topic which is of particular interest.

Part II is about news and current affairs. The first chapter in this part (chapter 2) considers the 'facts of life' about the media so that the reader has a clear understanding of the restraints and problems associated with producing newspapers, and radio and television broadcasts. This scene-setter is followed by three case studies based on personal observation which follow the news process of a national daily newspaper, television news, and a daily radio news and current affairs programme. Throughout these chapters comparison is drawn between the characteristics of the military and the media and this is summarised in chapter 6 in order to assess whether there is any affinity between the professions.

The military has proved to be an attractive topic for television documentaries and drama. In Part III the author reviews some of these programmes and analyses the relevance of the portrayal of the military on television in keeping the public in touch with the reality of life in today's Armed Forces.

The lack of mutual understanding has already been discussed in this introductory chapter by reference to past experiences between soldiers and journalists. Part IV is concerned with present day attitudes. Chapters 9—11 are concerned with the study of the reporting of conflict. The aim of this section is to discover whether there are any inherent problems associated with war reporting, the advance knowledge of which may help to reduce the tension between the military and the media at the beginning of any future conflict. This includes an examination of the Vietnam war, the Northern Ireland conflict, the Iranian Embassy siege in London in April 1980 and the Falklands

16 Since 1945 the only year when British forces were not on active service was 1968.

Islands crisis in 1982 to see what lessons have emerged which may be used in future to illuminate each profession about the other's problems. This study of conflict is followed by two further chapters in which the author explores the current depth of knowledge which each possesses about the other and discusses whether they could benefit from more education about the other's profession.

Part V contains the conclusion of the book, draws together the relevant deductions from the other sections and makes observations about the current relationship between the military and the media. This final chapter also takes a brief look into the future by considering the problems which might be encountered in a general war scenario and makes firm recommendations about ways of improving the relationship between the military and the media.

PART II

NEWS AND CURRENT AFFAIRS

At first sight there would appear to be little in common between the military and media professions. A closer inspection, however, suggests that there might be certain similarities between, for instance, the pressures associated with a journalist working to deadlines and a military commander required to assess 'hot' intelligence and then prepare and give his orders for an attack all in a matter of hours.

The constant demand of reporting daily news and producing reflective comment about current events inevitably imposes strain on those working for newspapers, radio and television news and current affairs programmes, and provides particular stress on those responsible for making the decisions. Therefore, a study of this side of the media is likely to provide an interesting comparison with equivalent military organisations which have to operate under similar pressure. The first three chapters of Part II are based on case studies of the news process of daily newspapers (*The Daily Telegraph* and the *Sun*), a television news programme (ITN's *5.45 News*) and a radio news and current affairs programme (BBC Radio's *Today*).

Each chapter includes comparisons with the military where appropriate as well as an analysis of the characteristics of the process of news in these three different categories of the media. In chapter 6 the characteristics of the military and the media are compared in order to discover how much is common to the two professions.

2 The Facts of Life about the Media

Ultimately, what goes out in the press, radio and television is the result of decisions taken by reporters, sub-editors and editors. They are subjected to pressure both from the outside, by the very nature of their work, and from the inside, through the inevitable personal conflicts which occur when decisions have to be made against the clock. The public are unaware of these pressures as they read their morning newspapers over breakfast, listen to the radio news whilst driving to work, or viewing the evening news on television. But it is important to comprehend certain 'facts of life' about the news media so that the reader, listener or viewer can appreciate the conditions under which they receive information. For instance, there is much debate within the newspaper business surrounding the fundamental process of decision making. Many claim that the editor has the right to decide what he publishes, just as the captain of a ship has the right to decide what course to steer. Others, including some trade union leaders, challenge that right. They contend that a group of workers, be they journalists or technicians, have the right to withhold their labour from contributing to the publication of anything with which they disagree or which they consider should not be published. This can occasionally cause internal disruption of which the public are unaware.

This chapter is concerned with the fundamentals of the press and broadcasting. We shall look at the sources of news, at some of the facts of life about the newspaper business, broadcasting, the news and current affairs dilemma, investigative journalism, and the pressures under which the news media have to operate. These functions will be viewed largely through the eyes of the journalists themselves, for it is important for the layman to understand how the professionals view the ethics of their craft. This chapter also contains information which provides the essential foundation for the case studies which are considered in the other chapters in Part II. But first of all, we need to consider the definition of 'news'.

What is news?

In a programme entitled *What is News?* broadcast on BBC Radio 4 in February 1979, Michael Charlton asked four editors to define news:[1]

'News is the unusual. It is the unusual which will attract people's interests, attract people's attention. News is not what other people want to be published, nor as some people cynically put it, is news what people don't want to be published. I just stick to the one word — news is the unusual.'

William Deedes, Editor of *The Daily Telegraph*

'. . . As Northcliffe said, news was something someone did not want to read and all the rest was advertising. So one person's news is another person's gossip . . . '

Michael Malloy, Editor of *The Daily Mirror*

'It is really something that is of interest to people. It is a combination of gossip, of fact, of information. It is the exceptional.'

Alan Protheroe, Editor, BBC TV News

'I don't think you can define what news is. I think you have to adopt the methods of scientists and try to describe its properties rather than to seek a definition. There is one description by an American newspaper tycoon who said that news is something that somebody doesn't want you to print; all the rest is propaganda. And there is another description, given by an old lady who was asked what she considered to be news and she said, "What do we know today that we did not know yesterday".'

David Nicholas, Editor ITN

1 *What is News?* introduced by Michael Charlton, broadcast on BBC Radio 4, 20 February 1979.

Sources of news

If the definitions of 'news' are varied, so are the sources. Let us start with the official news agencies. Home news is provided by the Press Association (PA) which is the British national agency. It is owned by the provincial newspapers in Britain and Eire and was originally founded in 1868 to share the costs amongst the newspapers. PA employs 250 journalists and 77 reporters (of whom 15 are specialists, including a Defence and Energy correspondent). The Association obtains its information from a number of different sources: from full time staff men located around the country and at the most likely sources of news such as the Law Courts and the House of Commons (where there are 30 PA staff), from 2,500 freelance journalists or 'stringers', from government departments, from information telexed in by business companies, and from members of the public. The Exchange Telegraph, founded four years after the Press Association, provided a similar service for many years but it now concentrates on finance and sport. The London-based Reuters is the main source of foreign news and it is owned by the newspapers of Britain, Australia and New Zealand through the press associations of those three countries (PA owns 41 per cent of Reuters). Foreign news is also provided by Associated Press (AP) and United Press International (UPI).

The broadcasting organisations are able to supplement these agencies with their own sources: 'the television news organisations are able to rely fairly heavily on their own regional structures, which are likely to employ specialist correspondents, staff and freelance reporters and camera crews. Material originated regionally can be pumped into the network news line or recorded onto videotape for replaying later on. In the BBC's case there are eight television newsrooms in provincial England plus others in Scotland, Wales and Northern Ireland, all of which are partly in business for the purpose of providing the national news with items deserving wider than purely local coverage. . . . In addition, the BBC controls four national radio networks centred on Broadcasting House in London, twenty local radio stations dotted about the country,[2] and Bush House, headquarters of external service broadcasts. There is also a BBC internal organisation, the General News Service, which evaluates all incoming news material from its own and news agency sources and relays a digest by teleprinter link from the Central newsroom at Broadcasting House in London. A particular

---

2 Now increased to 29 local radio stations.

part of the GNS Service, known as "Rip 'n' Read"[3] makes complete national radio news summaries available for immediate broadcast by local and regional BBC stations'.[4]

Although Independent Television News has links with the other 15 commercial TV companies it tends to rely very much on its own resources for coverage of both home and foreign news. In 1967, ITN formed a partnership with UPI to create the newsfilm agency UPITN which joined the other two newsfilm agencies. These are Visnews (owned jointly by the BBC, Reuters and several broadcasting organisations from the Commonwealth), and CBS News (which is part of the American network organisations). These agencies now provide over half the visual material available for the Eurovision News Exchange network.[5]

The news and newsfilm agencies provide a ceaseless flow of information which inundates newsrooms all day long. Another constant source of information is the diary stories. These are the events which are noted in newsroom diaries as a result of various items of interest which are forwarded by public relations organisations, government departments, various firms and organisations. As Ivor Yorke notes:

> To this rich harvest [of publicity handouts] can be added 'house' and trade magazines, official statistics, advance copies of speeches, invitations to exhibitions, trade fairs inaugurations, openings, closings, the laying of foundation stones and other ceremonies of varying importance. Well-established fixtures — Parliamentary sessions, Court sittings, State visits, sports events and anniversaries of all types — join the queue with scores of other public and semi-public events which are carefully weighed for their potential interest. Those surviving the first hurdle are noted in diaries of future events for more serious consideration nearer the day. These so-called 'diary' stories or their immediate consequences (follow-ups) probably account for the majority of new stories which appear on television and in the newspapers.[6]

3 The author observed this part of the GNS service in operation when he visited BBC Radio News in February 1979. It requires considerable skill under pressure in order to provide the news summaries for the regular news bulletins on the hour and half-hour, from 6 am to midnight. Ideally, the news items are selected 40 minutes before the bulletin is due, the bulletin is dictated to the teleprinter operator by the sub-editor. There is no means of correcting 'copy' on the teleprinter.
4 Ivor Yorke, *The Techniques of Television News*, Focal Press, London 1978, pp. 17—18.
5 The European News Exchange allows members of the European Broadcasting Union to share visual material of mutual interest. The network is open three times a day for the 'exchange' (at 11 am, 4 pm and 5.55 pm GMT) for transmission either by satellite or landline. The European news co-ordinator (one of nine individuals who form the co-ordinators' roster) makes the selection for each transmission, and each subscribing news organisation has the opportunity to view, and cost, the transmission before deciding whether they want to use it, or not. A telex list of the items included in the transmission is issued at midday.
6 Ivor York, op.cit., p.15.

The inevitable long term planning and careful 'staff work' which all this involves would be very familiar to a battalion adjutant or the first lieutenant of a Royal Navy ship. Good administration is also relevant to the maintenance of the extensive libraries of press cuttings and photographs held by agencies, newspapers and broadcasting news organisations; and also to the photographs, slides and film archives of the television news departments. All these records contain an immense wealth of information which has been painstakingly collected and arranged for quick and easy reference.

Another source of information within the news organisation is the specialist correspondents. As their name implies, these specialists (be they diplomatic, industrial, political, foreign or defence) are acknowledged as the experts in their field by their colleagues and a general reporter engaged on a story in a specialist field, or someone in the newsroom requiring confirmation of a fact or figure, will rely on the expertise of the relevant correspondent. This 'expertise' will have been built up over the years as a result of concentrating on a specific subject and by cultivating several influential contacts which result in the receipt of privileged information from 'off the record' conversations and briefings. Specialist correspondents can indeed become a mine of information.

Like correspondents, 'stringers' also rely on good contacts for their information. Ivor Yorke considers that it is the stringers who provide much of the basic news: 'Journalists working either for themselves or for other publications offer suggestions (for which they expect to be paid) on a fairly regular basis. Freelances or "stringers" they are called, and there are whole networks of them, wooed by news editors against the day that a really major story breaks in their area. With good contacts among local police, politicians and businessmen, they are usually first on the scene of a big story in their community, and are swift to pass on the information to their larger brethren'.[7]

To the multitude of sources already mentioned can be added the telephoned 'tip off' by a member of the public (be they an interested party or an alert observer). So it is clear that there is no shortage of news sources whichever definition of 'news' offered by the editors at the beginning of this chapter is preferred. It is also clear that the media as a whole often share the same sources and therefore, although a 'scoop' can be achieved in some instances, for the most part the various media reflect each other's news items. This results in a familiar pattern of news each day which is reinforced further by the fact that newspapers, television and radio are complementary to each other. What

---

7   Ibid., p.16.

happens to all this news copy when it is received by the copy-taster? The vast majority is rejected. In the words of John Wilson, Deputy Editor, BBC Radio News: 'Only about 10 per cent of information from all sources are used — and of that, only 5 per cent actually gets used undiluted'.[8]

Sources of information are also fundamental to the military. A commander in battle relies on intelligence and information to feed him with the necessary data on which he can base his subsequent decisions. He also requires this information to be regularly updated, especially on the enemy's positions and intentions. Like the news editor, the reliability of his sources is crucial and he is faced with the problem of assessing what to accept, and what to discard (many critical decisions in war have depended upon this assessment). Unlike the editor, however, the military commander never has enough sources of information.

Having considered the sources of news, we shall now turn to the facts of life about the news media, commencing with newspapers.

Newspapers: a commercial business

'Newspapers have objectives entirely different from objectives of other institutions — they are a commercial business . . . they are not in business to champion other people's causes.'[9] That is how William Deedes, Editor of *The Daily Telegraph*, defines the objectives of newspapers. The commercial interest of newspapers is evident through the space given to advertising (the allocation of pages, and space on those pages, is most relevant), the style of the newspaper which is aimed to attract the readers it is trying to cultivate, and the constant conflict between the editorial and commercial requirements. This conflict affects the relationship between the manager and editor of a newspaper and although each newspaper will vary as much as the individuality of the personalities involved, this quote from Lord Thomson of Fleet gives us an insight into the problem. In 1967 he said:

> How can the editor with responsibility for editorial content only — no responsibility for getting advertising, circulation, management, buying newsprint and making deals — rate ahead of the manager? The editor is no longer the top man in any viable newspaper. That is an old concept.[10]

8 Interview with the author, 6 February 1979. John Wilson has since been appointed the Editor, BBC Radio News.
9 Interview with author, 10 October 1978.
10 Charles Wintour, *Pressures on the Press*, André Deutsch, London 1972, p.24.

Whatever professional conflict may exist between a manager and an editor both are concerned with circulation figures and therefore the newspaper is designed for a specific and clearly defined market. This has a circular effect in that the paper is styled for a certain readership, and readers who identify with the style and politics of a certain newspaper tend to read that one in preference to the alternatives. Lord Beaverbrook admitted to the 1948 Royal Commission on the Press that he used his newspaper to promote political aims and that he 'ran his papers purely for propaganda and with no other purpose'.[11] William Deedes puts it this way: 'the selection of news and prominence given to it is a form of editorial comment. If the reader does not like it, he has the choice to change his newspaper'.[12] In reality most people do not change their newspaper without careful thought because over the years they have identified with a particular paper, and because they know very little about the alternatives. The editor's loyalty to his readers is often equalled by theirs to a specific newspaper, even if it changes its political policy. Charles Wintour, talking about *The Guardian's* shift in political allegiance noted:

> A newspaper will have a political policy when he [the Editor] comes to the chair and any change is likely to be as gradual as *The Guardian's* transference of its allegiance from the Liberal to the Labour Party. (Since the allegiance was never absolute, but one of continuing sympathy from an independent standpoint, there are no doubt some readers in remote Celtic fringes who have hardly noticed the change anyway.)[13]

So people who rely solely on newspapers for their news are being exposed to a slanted view of events which is often blatant in the editorials and feature articles, and usually more subtle in terms of news selection. As Chapman Pincher, the *Daily Express* correspondent, noted about his former editor-in-chief, Lord Beaverbrook: 'he claimed that he did not influence the presentation of the news but, of course, it was inevitable that he did so. His editor tended to give prominence to what would please him and, for the most part, they thought the way he did anyway. They, in turn, influenced the journalists they hired and trained'.[14]

11 Chapman Pincher, *Inside Story*, Sidgwick & Jackson, London 1978, p.210.
12 Interview with the author, 10 October 1978.
13 Charles Wintour, op.cit., p.24.
14 Chapman Pincher, op.cit., p.221.

Broadcasting news and current affairs

In contrast to the press, the broadcasting authorities are required to be impartial and not to express their own opinion. 'The basic principle of BBC News is that a mature democracy is an informed (not a guided) democracy. The BBC takes for granted that the parliamentary democracy evolved in this country is a work of national genius to be upheld and preserved. The BBC's primary constitutional role is that of a supplier of new and true information. . . . It shares the role with a free press, but with one important difference, in that a newspaper has a point of view and a place of its own in the political spectrum. The BBC has none.'[15] This restriction on broadcasting is enshrined in the regulations governing the activities of both the BBC and the IBA: Clause 13(4) of the BBC Licence requires the BBC 'to refrain from expressing its own opinion on current affairs or on matters of public policy', and Section 4 of the Independent Broadcasting Authority Act, 1973 states that 'it shall be the duty of the Authority to secure the exclusion from the programmes broadcast by them of all expressions of their own opinion as to . . . matters of political or industrial controversy or relating to current public policy'.

However, the requirement not to express 'their own' opinion does not mean that a current affairs programme cannot express 'an opinion', or that impartiality has to be maintained within a single programme. By the very nature of a current affairs programme it will most likely have a bias about an issue, and this will be evident to the viewer by the way the subject is presented in a programme. As far as the BBC is concerned, the problem of 'balance' in current affairs is specifically referred to in the Constitution:

> A former Director General, Sir Hugh Greene, said: 'We have to balance different points of view in our programmes but not necessarily within each individual programme. Nothing is more stultifying than current affairs programmes in which all opposing opinions cancel each other out. Sometimes one has to use that method but in general it makes for greater liveliness and impact if the balance can be achieved over a period, perhaps within a series of related programmes'. The policy so described is that of the BBC today.[16]

Peter Pagnamenta, the former Head of Current Affairs, Thames Television, also justifies the lack of balance within an individual programme by expressing the view that 'the viewer is more intelligent and discerning

15 *The Task of Broadcasting News*, BBC, London 1976, p.10.
16 *BBC Handbook 1979*, BBC, London 1979, p.262.

20

than he is often given credit for'.[17] A view which is also shared by the BBC.[18]

The news and current affairs dilemma has been debated for a long time and is still not resolved. The requirement is for the broadcaster to present fact and comment on radio and television in such a way that there is no doubt to the audience which is which. Compared with the press, both radio and television are severely handicapped by inherent problems; there is no recall facility which equates to re-reading a column in a newspaper so the style of communication for broadcasting has to be such that the audience can easily comprehend what is being said first time: a three-minute radio bulletin is limited to approximately 600 words (200 words per minute); a ten-minute television news bulletin equates approximately to one column in *The Times*. These restrictions have handicapped the broadcaster in his desire to report facts and to provide analysis in order to increase the public's understanding of important current issues. Most of the critics (be they academics, journalists or the ordinary citizen) are agreed that there is a requirement to provide a news analysis of some sort, but there is considerable disagreement about the format. In their three articles in *The Times* in 1975 John Birt, then Head of Current Affairs, London Weekend Television, and Peter Jay then a presenter on *Weekend World* and the Economics Editor of *The Times*, developed a thesis which criticised television journalism for failing 'to tell the citizenry at large what is happening to the world and the society in which they live'.[19] This first article also gave rise to the accusation that there was a 'bias in television journalism. It is not against any particular party or point of view. It is a bias against understanding'. The subsequent articles expressed the opinion that the separation of news and current affairs was a mistake and recommended that the long news bulletins should be replaced by brief bulletins of facts and that each weekday there should be an hour long 'flagship' programme which would consist of the news headlines followed by analysis of the major news stories of the day. These would be supplemented with a weekly one-hour programme to put the week's main news into perspective, a monthly 90-minute programme on the continuing issues of our time, and a range of feature programmes. This thesis generated considerable debate amongst journalists and within the BBC, and the interest that was aroused was probably as important as the fact that the BBC rejected

17 Interview with the author, 23 November 1978.
18 *The Task of Broadcasting News*, op.cit., p.16.
19 The three articles appeared in *The Times* on 28 February, 30 September and 1 October 1975.

the Birt and Jay proposals. In its rejection the BBC had this to say:

> To merge news and current affairs under one roof and departmental control would muddy the waters, not clarify them . . . . The proper place for it [an item of news] is a news bulletin. The proper place for exhaustive discussion of issues arising from the news is a programme.[20]

The same year that the Birt and Jay article appeared in *The Times* Robin Day's book *Day by Day* was published. He remarked, 'I think there is a growing feeling that the balance of television journalism should be redressed in favour of reason and understanding, with the aim of counteracting those tendencies inherent in this visual medium to over-emphasize the sensational and the violent'. He noted that John Birt had echoed his concern but remarked that 'there may be less agreement on the remedy than on the diagnosis'.[21] Robin Day's proposal was to extend the news to an hour programme: 'television news should be lengthened, deepened and changed in character, so as to include the analysis and explanation in which it is at present too deficient'.[21] In an interview with the author in November 1978 he re-affirmed his belief that news and current affairs should be integrated and pointed out that 'facts about the news often need interpretation for them to be meaningful'.[22]

The debate continues today and various options are tried by both BBC and ITV to test what is acceptable to the audience: ITN's *News at Ten* includes an analysis of the news, as does BBC TV's 9 o'clock news; BBC Radio combines news and current affairs in such programmes as *The World at One* and *Today*, as does BBC TV's *Newsnight*. The crucial point for both the BBC and ITV is the acceptance by the public that they are satisfied with the differentiation between fact and comment, whichever format is used. The point is also crucial for the public because a generally receptive and passive audience rely on a minute proportion of the population for news and views of current events. In such circumstances it is important that people can immediately distinguish between fact and comment. This emphasises how much the public place their trust in the professional integrity of the broadcasters.

Similarities between the press and broadcasting

'Addicts of conspiracy theories in history and politics are apt to believe

---

20 *The Task of Broadcasting News*, op.cit., p.17.
21 Robin Day, *Day by Day*, William Kimber, London 1975, p.73.
22 Interview with the author, 8 November 1978.

that the contents of a newspaper show traces of a carefully calculated plot to subvert the forces of truth, justice and human liberty. I begin therefore by giving a sketch of the speed at which decisions have to be taken. There is not much time for plotting.'[23] In this introduction to chapter one of his book *Pressures on the Press*, Charles Wintour, Editor of the *Evening Standard*, accurately reflects the cynicism of many critics of Fleet Street. In describing the pressures of the clock in his first chapter he remarks that 'of all the pressures operating on the editor of a morning or evening newspaper the heaviest is the shortage of time. There are too many people to see, too many telephone calls to be initiated and taken, too many decisions to make'.[24] Elaborating on this pressure he goes on to say: 'It is essential for newspaper editors to be concerned with accuracy. For newspapers are produced so rapidly that some errors are bound to creep in. These must be kept to a minimum'.[25]

The acknowledgement of the realities of trying to achieve accuracy within the constraints of time is a common problem to both the press and broadcasting. Every journalist whom the author interviewed, whether an editor, a correspondent or a reporter, stressed the overriding importance of accuracy and there is little doubt that the vast majority of professional journalists honestly report the facts as they see them — and editors insist on a high standard: 'Accuracy, accuracy above all else'.[26] Yet despite the intention to report an incident objectively and accurately both the press and broadcasters have often been accused of distortion by the public. We have seen Charles Wintour's explanation of the problem of the pressure of time and the case studies in the other chapters in Part II will demonstrate how the process of obtaining, collating and processing news is susceptible to inaccuracies. Then there are the problems of human error by the journalist and the prejudices of the public. Past experience suggests that there will always be suspicion about some of the claims of journalism and perhaps that is as important for society as the journalists' right to ask questions on behalf of society. The following comment by Chapman Pincher gives an interesting insight into the problem of accuracy as seen from the journalist's point of view:

> It is a common misbelief that journalists distort and even fake their reports to make them more sensational. I have found little truth in this. Certainly in *The Daily Express* there has never been

23 Charles Wintour, op.cit., introduction to chapter one.
24 Ibid., p.3.
25 Ibid., p.6.
26 Alan Protheroe, then Editor of BBC Television News, interview with the author, 6 December 1978.

any enduring kudos to be gained by inaccuracy. Almost invariably someone complains and though editors 'stand by' their reporters there is usually an internal row and the offending writer quickly becomes branded as dangerous.

It cannot be denied, however, that many newspaper reports are inaccurate when judged by those who know something about the issue being discussed. Some degree of inaccuracy is inevitable by the very nature of daily journalism, and this is particularly true about reports involving anything technical. The requirement to give the information in potted form, understandable to every reader, involves also — simplification. The story has to be told in limited space, which rules out the kind of qualification and development any expert on the subject would expect. So he tends to damn the whole report though it may have communicated the essential truth of the story to millions. A complete report is sometimes condemned as inaccurate and may even be the subject of a libel action simply because the critic has concentrated on the headline. The public should have more sympathy for headline writers, for they have to give the nub of a report in very few words and these have to be of such a length that they fit the page. The fact that so many excellent headlines are conjured up sometimes within a few minutes has always been a source of wonder to me and to others who have tried to write them.

Another source of inaccuracy is the reporter's difficulty in discovering what the truth really is. Any journalist is only as good as his sources and these, however eminent, are sometimes misleading, occasionally deliberately so.[27]

Perhaps the area of journalism which has generated the most concern about the accuracy and objectivity is the practice of investigative reporting. This type of journalism became fashionable in the 1960s at a time when television had just become firmly established in this country. The physical intrusion of television cameras, lights and cables emphasised the invasion of privacy that such television reporting involved, but the press reporter with only his notebook, and perhaps a camera, was no less effective in revealing shady practices. There is little doubt that investigative journalism has provided a service for society in revealing a number of malpractices, such as fraud and corruption, and in exposing 'offences' which the police have been unable to deal with due to the inadequacies of the law. The justification for this practice is that it is 'in the public interest' but what has concerned a number of people

27 Chapman Pincher, op.cit., pp. 210–11.

is the means by which the information has been obtained.

In 1972 the Committee on Privacy under Sir Kenneth Younger published its report. The Younger Committee had been set up partly as a result of pressure from a number of backbenchers about the right of individual privacy. The Committee was very much concerned with journalistic intrusion and eventually decided against recommending a new law providing a general right of privacy. It recognised the inevitable conflict between the right for privacy and 'the right to speak and publish the truth', and recommended that no new legislation was required:

> On balance we have come to be more impressed with the risk involved in propounding a rather general law, the scope of whose impact upon other important rights seems uncertain, than we are either with the seriousness of the residual wrongs which might thereby be righted or the effectiveness of the legal remedy proposed.[28]

The dilemma of investigative reporting in broadcasting is clearly expounded in the BBC's own study into broadcasting news:

> Then there is investigatory journalism, which some consider an essential part of a free press, and others view with great distaste. Should the BBC become involved in investigatory journalism at all? Editors reply that such journalism is valid, provided it is done responsibly and solely in order to serve the public; other people argue that it can never be justified. The over-riding concern must always be whether the public interest is best served by publishing this kind of story, and that will always be a matter of editorial judgement.[29]

Investigative journalism is now an unarguable reality in today's society and it would seem that all of us will have to continue to rely on editoral judgement and responsible reporting.

Pressures

Another similarity between the press and broadcasting is the pressures to which both are subjected. These include the pressure of time, legal pressures (such as libel, contempt of court, breach of privilege and

---

28 Report of the Committee on Privacy, Cmnd. 5012, paragraph 43.
29 *The Task of Broadcasting News*, op.cit., p.7.

the Official Secrets Act), the pressure of advertisers (newspapers and ITV), and the pressure of competition, be it circulation figures or ratings. These 'pressures on the press' are lucidly explained by Charles Wintour and these words provide the apt title of his book (1972). He also expounds on two general areas of leverage which are symptoms of the modern age: the advance in technology, and the challenge to authority. Both of these influence industrial relations and are therefore vital to the two industries which are so dependent upon the goodwill of their employees.

Both television and the press have had recent experience of the disruption caused by the introduction of new technology. For television the cause of the disagreement was the proposed introduction of Electronic News Gathering (ENG) equipment for Britain's television news services. ENG consists of a lightweight electronic camera and compact video tape recorder. It can relay pictures to the news studio for immediate transmission or record them on videotape which can then be replayed instantly. The delay and cost involved in film processing is eliminated and the system provides material of a superior technical quality. ENG has been used by American television networks for a number of years and almost every major television organisation in Europe has now gone over to the system. Both BBC and ITN were very keen to use this equipment full time from the outset but its introduction was complicated by disagreements between management and the unions. In October 1978 the BBC had to suspend their experiment after a year and they only achieved final agreement with the unions in November 1980. It took ITN almost three years' negotiations to get their technicians' union to agree to a six-month trial period in May 1979 and exactly a year later ITN was blacked out for a week before achieving a settlement with the Association of Cinematograph, Television and Allied Technicians (ACTT). During the period of dispute the frustrations to management created by these delays were summed up by Alan Protheroe, then Editor of BBC TV News (1979):

> We have had to rely on other people's pictures during the Royal visit to the Arab States. In America, our resident film crew face an almost daily problem trying to find commercial laboratories to process their film. American TV Studios just don't have film labs any more. If we don't get ENG on the road again soon, we could have a situation where a fire at Harrods might reach British screens via a US Satellite more quickly than our own coverage could make it.[30]

---

30 *The Daily Telegraph*, 27 February 1979.

As far as the press is concerned the confrontation over the introduction of new technology centred on the long running dispute at *The Times* newspaper. The difficulties arose in 1978 and both management and the unions were vitally interested in the outcome because many saw it as a proxy battle fought on behalf of other newspapers who wanted to introduce the new technology. 'Other newspapers are watching it. If we were to concede the principle of direct input it would mean a reduction by half in the composing rooms throughout the newspaper industry.'[31] The topicality of the crisis meant there was not only a vested interest in the dispute by the media — there was also a journalistic interest. And so the public were provided with a good deal of information about the realities of Fleet Street by, amongst others, *The Sunday Times* article of 26 November 1978, written by Will Ellsworth-Jones, Stephen Fray, Eric Jacobs and Phillip Knightley, and the BBC TV *Panorama* programme on *The Times* presented by Michael Cockerell on 20 November 1979.

The Sunday Times article summed up the dispute thus: 'The confrontation is between a management which believes it must restore its right to manage, and Unions which believe they are being used to concede too much, too quickly, for too little. The issues dividing them are continuous production, lower manning levels, and the introduction of new production methods'.[32] Joe Wade, General Secretary of the NGA, claimed that the deadline was unrealistic. '*The Times* management wants to go from Caxton to computer virtually overnight;'[33] Times Newspapers Limited (TNL) retorted that they had no alternative; 'We suspended publishing because, in the end, throughout 1977 we had lost 7 million copies of our papers. In just the first quarter of 1978, we lost nearly 8 million copies and at 30 November over 13 million copies. In every case, the losses were caused by unofficial strikes and restrictions. If existing disputes procedures had been observed our readers and advertisers would not have lost a single copy'.[34] *The Times* duly ceased production on 30 November 1978 and was not to re-emerge on the newspaper stands for almost a year.

At least there *was* agreement about the significance of the technological step and the inevitable disruption it would cause to relations between management and unions: 'The electronic revolution in print is

31 Joe Wade, General Secretary of the National Graphical Association, in *The Sunday Times*, 26 November 1978.
32 Ibid.
33 Ibid.
34 Advertisement by Times Newspapers Ltd, *The Daily Telegraph*, 5 March 1979. It is interesting to note that in a letter to the Editor of *The Daily Telegraph* on 6 March 1979 Mr J. Mitchell, Branch Secretary, London Machine Branch, NATSOPA, challenged a number of statements in the TNL advertisement but he did *not* dispute the reasons given for the loss of so many newspapers.

more significant than the electronic revolution in the transmission of images which has given us television. This is because complex modern societies need the details of the fine print to understand their environment and advance their civilisation. . . . They [the newspapers] could no more resist the electronic advance than the monks writing books could resist hand-set type and the hand-setters could resist the advent of the Lynotype'. In the same article, Sir Denis Hamilton (Chairman and Editor-in-Chief, TNL) went on to express his understanding of the dismay and outrage experienced by those working in the old technology 'at the thought that they and their hard-learned craft should be swept away. In practice, of course, individuals cannot and should not be swept away . . .'.[35]

In reporting *The Times* dispute the other newspapers were able to highlight a problem which affected them all. The key issue was centred on the question, who runs the newspapers? It is reported that when the late Lord Thomson went round the various departments of *The Sunday Times* after he had just bought it, he introduced himself to one of the union leaders of the men who run the presses by saying, 'How do you do, I'm Roy Thomson, the new owner of this paper', to which the union leader replied, 'You may own it, Mr Thomson, but I run it'.[36]

Both the press and the broadcasting authorities experienced a considerable amount of industrial unrest and increasing challenge to editorial freedom in 1978 and 1979. Even before *The Times* closed in 1978, the national press had lost over 100 million copies through labour disputes in the first 9½ months of that year, and *The Daily Telegraph* ceased publication for three weeks in October over a pay dispute with the NGA (until then the longest stoppage ever of any national newspaper with the exception of the closure of the entire London press for four weeks in 1955). Then in December the NUJ instructed its 9,000 provincial journalists to go on strike for more pay. This strike lasted seven weeks and demonstrated the bitterness and entrenched attitudes which were symptomatic of the newspaper industry at that time.

Industrial unrest has continued to dog *The Times* and *The Sunday Times*. Rupert Murdoch took over management of both newspapers in February 1981 but by late summer he found himself embroiled in a differential pay dispute between two unions. He took a tough line, threatened to close the newspapers and won a temporary breathing space. However, industrial problems have rumbled on into 1982.

---

35 Article by Sir Denis Hamilton in *The Sunday Times*, 26 November 1978.
36 Ibid.

Summary

These disputes have shown that the press and broadcasting have been affected by the industrial unrest, and by the concern for the effect on jobs created by the introduction of new technology, which has afflicted British society as a whole in the late 1970s and early 1980s. The reporters and commentators have themselves become part of 'the news' and as a result the public have learnt a great deal more about these problems, and about the functions of the media, than would otherwise have been the case. Indeed, the public have received this information because the disputes were considered newsworthy by the journalists themselves. The fact that it was their own industry that was making the headlines has not prevented them from reporting.

The realisation by the layman of the difficulties being experienced by the media is important, because inevitably the problems affected the means by which he normally receives news and comment. For instance, those readers who usually relied on *The Times* for their information had to look elsewhere during its closure. The same applied to television audiences who normally relied on ITN for their news during the ITV strike in 1979 and the ITN blackout in 1980. Therefore an awareness of the realities of these internal troubles is as relevant to the understanding of the facts of life about the media as is the comprehension of the relevance of the growth of investigative journalism.

In this chapter we have looked at some of the fundamentals of the media. We have seen how some of the professionals view their own craft, considered the differences and similarities between the press and broadcasting, and also looked at some of the pressures to which both may be subjected. This background knowledge provides a sound foundation for the case studies given in the following chapters. These studies will enable us to examine how news is processed in newsrooms and daily current affairs programmes so that we may appreciate the problems and difficulties involved. The examination includes examples from newspapers, radio and television so that a comparison of the characteristics of the news media as a whole can be made with those of the military.

3 Newspapers: The News Process

Although each newspaper has its own idiosyncrasies, the basic functions are similar and therefore a study of one or two newspapers will serve to illustrate the fundamental points. In order to explain how news is processed in a national daily newspaper the author has chosen *The Daily Telegraph* to explain the 'process' of news, and the *Sun* to illustrate the task of the sub-editor.

The news process at *The Daily Telegraph*

Before looking at the news process at *The Daily Telegraph* in detail it is first of all necessary to consider briefly the relationship between the Proprietor, the Editor and the Managing Editor.[1] There is constant liaison between the three (the Editor sees the Managing Editor at 1 pm and the Proprietor at 6 pm every evening), and beneath the Proprietor the management is functionally defined into two divisions: editorial policy, leading articles and features which are the responsibility of the Editor; and administration and control of news, the responsibility of the Managing Editor. In talking about his role as Editor, William Deedes stressed that he was responsible, along with his editorial team, for

---

1 The Proprietor is the Editor in Chief of *The Daily Telegraph*. This is the only remaining national daily newspaper which is privately owned.

trying to retain continuity with the accepted standards and tone of *The Telegraph* as it had developed over the years. He was open to new ideas but was very conscious of the past and he expressed an absolute loyalty to his readers: 'The readers are sovereign'.[2] He is consulted all day long, has access to proof pages and copy, vets every leading article and makes all the cuts himself (both in manuscript and proof copies). In overall terms the Editor is responsible for everything to do with the paper although this does not mean that he takes a personal decision on every occasion. Nevertheless he takes the kicks as well as the praises. The acceptance of total responsibility expressed in this last comment will be familiar to everyone who has experienced military command, and was echoed by every editor whom the author interviewed. Sir Larry Lamb, the former Editor of the *Sun*, put it this way: 'My role is similar to that of a ship's captain. I am responsible for everything in the *Sun* — I'm the one who goes to jail'.[3]

As opposed to editorial control much of the functional control of news, the responsibility of the Managing Editor, is delegated to the Night Editor. This delegation is important and necessary, for if he did not have the freedom to decide on whether, for instance, a piece of late news should be included or not (but instead had to refer upwards for a decision), that news item might well miss the publication deadline. This principle of delegated responsibility is also used by the military particularly in circumstances where speed of decision is important.

As the position of the Night Editor is crucial to the news process his appointment is the best focal point around which to describe the working of *The Daily Telegraph*. He normally arrives at Fleet Street at about 3.30 pm and immediately looks at the layout of the pages of the paper and at the photographs which are contenders for possible inclusion. The layout of the newspaper is in the form of a 'dummy' paper which commences life the previous night and whose shape develops throughout the day. The layout is outlined in pencil and the advertisements, which determine how much space is available, are positioned first. News lists are produced at 11 am by the News Editor (Home) and the Foreign Editor. The news lists are discussed with the Managing Editor during the morning. So by the time the Night Editor arrives at the office the outline of the paper is well advanced. It is important to note at this stage that the layout is initially governed by the placing of advertisements and to realise that, once the allocated areas for these have been blanked off on the 'dummy', it immediately

---

2 Interview with the author, 10 October 1978.
3 Interview with the author, 12 December 1978.

dictates the shape and size of the columns available for news items. The selection of photographs is also dependent, to a certain extent, on the shape of the gaps left on the page once the advertisements have been placed. More often than not this has as much to do with the choice of photograph as any positive decision to include a particular picture.

Having brought himself up to date, the Night Editor goes through to the Managing Editor's office at approximately 4 pm. The two of them run through the news lists and discuss possible contenders for the front page.[4] Thirty minutes later they are joined by the rest of the senior members of the team for the 4.30 pm meeting. This is the formal change-over between Day and Night News and Foreign Editors and the meeting is chaired by the Managing Editor. The News and Foreign Editors each run through their respective news lists in turn, summarising each item. Once this has been done, everybody departs except the original two who now digest the news lists.

Once this is over the Night Editor goes back to his desk in the Sub-Editors' office. The Subs' office is the focal point of the journalistic news effort; it is compact and functional. The layout is illustrated in Figure 3.1 and it will be seen that the Night Editor has the key appointments around him on the 'back bench': The Home and Foreign copy-tasters (who assess all incoming 'copy'); the Deputy Night Editor (responsible for page one and the back page); the Chief Sub (responsible for the news items on the inside pages – this can be up to twelve pages); and the Revise Sub-Editor (whose job it is to check the copy submitted from the Subs' table before it goes forward to the Composing Room). The Night Editor's Assistant is also located close to the back bench. It is his job to check the proofs for libel and content before the Night Editor sees them for approval.

At approximately 5.15 pm the Deputy Night Editor arrives and he is briefed by the Night Editor about the likely stories to be included on the first page. His experience is such that he usually anticipates these correctly and by now both of them are able to see what the evening papers have led on (the Night Editor checks through each edition of the London evening newspapers). The inside pages are already being put together by the Chief Sub; this is a continual process which also involves the copy-taster because they discuss with the Chief Sub the relative importance, shape and length of various stories.

At about 6 pm the Night Editor sees the editorial and features list. This indicates whether there are any areas of overlap from the editorial

---

4 As an example of the number of items which may be included on a news list, on 9 November 1978 there were 39 on the Home News List and 41 on the Foreign News List.

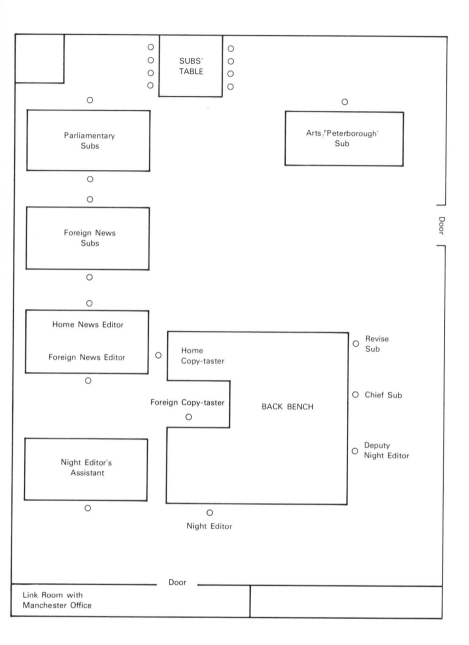

Figure 3.1   The sub-editors' office at *The Daily Telegraph*

NOTE: This diagram represents the arrangement in the sub-editors' office during the time of the visit to *The Daily Telegraph* by the author. Since then the office has been moved. The layout, however, is essentially the same.

side which may conflict with his news columns. He also gets a chance to glance at the readers' letters which accompany the list. During the author's visit he also received at about this time one of the many deliveries of news agency copy which continued at irregular intervals throughout the evening. At times he was inundated with copy, most of which was rejected and cast into an exceptionally large waste-bin, which appeared to be specifically designed for the anticipated 90 per cent wastage. The deliveries of copy reminded the author of the tapes and signals received by a busy military operational headquarters. Both the military and the media 'operations' rooms are subjected to a constant stream of communications most of which are irrelevant. The trick is to pick out the important 10 per cent.

During this early evening period the Subs' office has a general air of quiet industry and there are no obvious signs of pressure as the copy-tasters continue to digest news, subs work away refining copy and the back bench mould the paper into shape. But the pressures were there because time is all important in the production of a newspaper. Deadlines have to be set for each page and each edition and this is dependent upon the contribution of all those involved in the process — the journalists, the linotype operators, the compositors, those on the press floor, and those involved with distribution. As soon as the copy has been checked by the back bench it passes through to the Composing Room (where the compositors make up the paper), from there to the Stereo (where cardboard copies are made of the pages), and then to the foundry in the Machine Room on the Press Floor. *The Daily Telegraph* aims for four editions each day and the timings are dictated by the train departure times to the various areas thus: the first edition (to Devon, Cornwall and South Wales) should start printing at 10.40 pm, the second edition (to Wessex) at 11.45 pm, the third edition (to the outer Home Counties) at 12.50 am, and the fourth (to the inner Home Counties and London) at 02.15 am.[5]

In order to achieve these timings, deadlines have to be strictly adhered to; for instance the first edition casts should be ready by 9.50 pm and the presses should start to run at 10.30 pm. A hold-up in the system has a cumulative effect which can mean a reduction in the circulation figures. These hold-ups can vary between a delay in the process of the paper going forward to the press floor, due to a journalistic attempt to achieve perfection; to mechanical failures with the presses due to an electrical or mechanical fault; a bad 'run', or bad feeding of paper.

---

5   Copies for the North of England, Scotland, Northern Ireland and North Wales are produced from *The Daily Telegraph*'s office in Manchester.

The aim is to achieve a constant flow through the whole building all the time. This flow depends on initiation from the back bench and the production of the 'dummy' helps to get the flow started. The production of a newspaper calls for co-operation, appreciation of the various specialisations by the other 'specialists', and teamwork. Each department is virtually dependent upon the other and production must contend with the conflict between the journalistic requirements, what the machines can achieve in the time available, and the goodwill of the work force. These conflicts become more evident in the preparations for the later editions.

The conflict between the journalistic requirement and the capability of the machine rooms mirrors that other constant struggle faced by the journalist — the battle of the clock. The constant pressure of time often affects the journalist's attempts to report events accurately. These conflicts are inherent in the newspaper system and therefore they can affect the information which the reader obtains from his newspaper each day.

The role of the sub-editor at the *Sun*

The role of the sub-editor is a critical part of the journalistic process and yet the layman has little idea of his function. A tabloid newspaper requires considerable skill by the subs because the copy has to be drastically reduced to fit the column inches. So in order to see what is involved the author has chosen an example from the *Sun* newspaper to illustrate what the job of a sub-editor entails.

Copy from staff reporters or correspondents is usually received over the telephone by copy-takers. The copy then goes via the news desk to the copy-taster on the back bench who sorts the wheat from the chaff. The Night Editor or the Deputy Night Editor then decides where the copy will go in the newspaper (which pages and which columns), and then passes the designed page and copy to the subs' table. On receiving this the Chief Sub gives his sub-editors instructions for each story: the headline type, the type and size for the text, and the column length and width which has been allocated.

Faced with this information the sub starts to 'gut' the original copy by extracting the salient details. This gutting is often drastic and indeed there are many occasions when the article has to be completely re-written (although in such cases the words are taken, where possible, from the original text and from other sources, such as news agency copy). To give an idea of what this involves one sub to whom the author spoke was required to reduce a 1,100 word court report to

220 words.[6] In writing his piece he added two short sentences at the end which meant that the total words were over the 220-figure but the sentences were so constructed that they could be dropped from the copy after type-setting without altering the meaning of the article. This is an essential part of the process because no-one can be exactly certain how long a story will be until it has actually been set in type. Therefore these additional sentences are not intended as an essential part of a report and care needs to be taken by the sub to ensure that their omission will not result in a misleading article.

Once he has finished editing the copy, the sub passes it back to the Chief Sub who checks the wording and headline before forwarding it for type-setting. The Chief Sub is the essential link between what the back bench requires and what the sub actually produces. He also epitomises the detached position of all those in the office team which is designed to produce an objective and balanced report about an event.

Perhaps somewhat surprisingly to the layman, the headlines are not produced by the man responsible for writing the copy; but instead by those on the back bench and by the sub-editors. However, this divorce of responsibility does not lessen the problem of producing headlines which are dictated by the type size and column width. This inevitably creates problems and restricts the scope of the wording which can be used. Writing headlines is a specialist and difficult task, particularly when it has to be done in a limited time. For this reason the back bench may write some headlines and assist subs in writing others. Even their experience cannot prevent the occasional misleading headline but considering the pressure under which they work it is surprising that there are not more gaffes. This pressure is clearly apparent in the typical day of a sub working on the *Sun*. There are about eleven subs on duty on a typical day (a day for them consists of an 8¾ hour shift slotted in during the period 1.30 pm—2.15 am). Before arriving at the office a sub will probably have kept abreast of the news by reading newspapers, listening to radio news bulletins and *World at One*, and watching the television lunch-time news.[7] He is therefore well briefed on the events which have made the news that day before he starts work. During a shift a sub can expect to write any number of articles, and as one of them said: 'this results in periods of intense boredom followed by frantic activity'. When asked why he did it, he replied: 'Once you have experienced it, it's like a drug. I also like the camaraderie and the feeling of pride we take in our professionalism'.[8] It is interesting to

6   Visit to the *Sun* newspaper, 12 December 1978.
7   The author noticed that the habit of relying on other media to keep continually up to date with the latest news was adopted by all journalists involved in the news processing business, be they from newspapers, radio or television.
8   Visit to the *Sun*, 12 December 1978.

36

note that these comments reflect service life which can rapidly switch from the boredom of routine to intense action and where camaraderie and professional pride are highly valued.

The sub-editor is at the very heart of a newspaper's creativity. John Stuart, the Assistant Features Editor of the *Sun* (formerly the Assistant Night Editor) had this to say about the responsibilities and pressures which are imposed on subs:

> Sub-editing is a highly skilled technique . . . . Time, accuracy and polished prose are the essence. The time available to sub-edit, type-mark and headline write any story from one inch up to any length, can be anything from five minutes to an hour. The sub-editor never knows what he is going to be hit with next — murder, Parliamentary debate, air crash, wedding picture caption, complicated Government White Paper report, a coup in Tumbuctoo — he never knows what it will be until it hits him and then he's got to cope with it quickly whilst at the same time ensuring that he produces a fair, balanced and accurate report. He must know law (for the risk of libel, contempt etc) and he must be able to obtain and write in essential omitted facts . . . . If he is lucky he can do the complete job and hand it straight back to the Chief Sub . . . . But there are many times when the pressure of time just will not allow this. On these occasions he must be able to supply his edited copy to the Chief Sub 'on the run' (ie a paragraph at a time) . . . . On such occasions he often has only the chance to give the supplied copy a quick scan before he is committed to scribbling furiously, editing and 'gutting' until he passes the completed copy back to the Chief Sub for vetting.
>
> His finished work comes under the most critical scrutiny . . . type set proof pages are closely vetted line by line by both the paper's resident lawyer and the Assistant Night Editor. In addition, the Editor and his Deputy see page proofs.
>
> The sub-editor is generally a highly dedicated professional technician. He is both an architect (moulding and building the published version of every story) and the paper's last line of defence (helping to save it from the risk of countless legal bombshells inherent in every day's copy flow). The price he pays for it is mental stress and unsocial hours away from his friends and family. But out of it he gets immense job satisfaction.[9]

This description clearly indicates the essential need for coolness

9 Correspondence from John Stuart, 22 September 1979.

under pressure which the job requires and it is hardly surprising that only the dedicated and determined survive for long as subs. They have as much responsibility as the reporter for the words which we read every morning in our newspapers — and yet most of us are scarcely aware of their existence.

Detachment and professionalism

Whilst observing journalists at work the author was struck by the contradictions of the newspaper world. On the one hand there were the pressures of time imposing deadlines which seemed to demand tight control à la the military, and yet the divisions of responsibility appeared less obvious and less defined than one might have presumed. In trying to explain this the Night Editor of *The Daily Telegraph* said: 'the reason that decision making is less defined than you might imagine is because it has probably grown out of experience of the system, team-work, and the relative trust between editors, subs, and various reporters'.[10] Those on the back bench of a daily newspaper have probably been together for years and therefore have developed the kind of mutual understanding which dilutes the demarcation between the various positions of responsibility. However, such a system places considerable reliance on the responsibility of the subs and on experienced correspondents and reporters. The Night Editor simply does not have time to check everything which goes into the news columns and he depends on his back bench colleagues to check the copy submitted by the subs.

Although there is considerable personal influence on copy which is originated by a reporter, and the finished article often differs from the original report, there is little opportunity for the *intentional* management of news due to the deliberate detached filter process to which copy is subjected. The items which are included in a newspaper are affected by the news of the day (which is reflected in the news lists), and by the positioning of advertisements amongst the various pages. These two factors can affect the column length and influence the prominence given to a certain story. Newspapers are captives of the 'news of the day' and therefore the lead stories on page one are actually the best of the available news in the view of that particular newspaper. These determinants are as relevant as any deliberate editorial decision about the different prominence given by various newspapers to the same issue. This is further illustrated by the fact that on the many

10 Interview with the author, 6 November 1978.

days when there are no obvious lead stories, the design of the layout of page one is often the key factor for a tabloid newspaper when considering the candidates for the lead stories.

Sources and the passage of information

Throughout this chapter comparison has been made with the military where appropriate. There is, however, one more characteristic of the news process which also has a particular relevance to the military: the passing of information.

The 'information' in this case is the copy which usually originates with a reporter, is passed by telephone to a copy-taker, then to the copy-taster on the news desk, then to the subs' table where it is gutted (and often rewritten) by a sub, and is finally checked by the chief sub before forwarding for type-setting. The system has at least four links in the chain from reporter to type-setter (or five if the reporter had to rely on an eye-witness account for his original story) and therefore the chances of inaccuracies occurring in the final version which appears in one of the editions of the newspaper are potentially high. Indeed, given the chain reaction and the pressure of time it is surprising that far more inaccuracies do not appear. Incorrect information due to flaws along the communications chain is something with which the military are all too familiar. The less links in the chain, the more accurate the information and anything short of an eye-witness observer briefing a decision maker direct is likely to lead to distortion (this is equally true whether the decision maker is a military commander or a newspaper sub required to produce copy of a limited number of words).

One of the advantages which the media usually has over the military is its number of news sources (as we saw in chapter 2). It is therefore interesting to note what happens when the usual sources are not available. This occurred during the Falklands crisis in April 1982. The Government was taken by surprise by the Argentinian invasion of the Islands and so one of the media's main sources of information proved fruitless. Furthermore, although a number of reporters were either at Port Stanley or Buenos Aires during the invasion there was 'no freedom for the press' as far as filing copy was concerned, especially from Port Stanley. This led to initial reports whose gaps and inaccuracies were not corrected until Rex Hunt, the Governor of the Falkland Islands, and the Royal Marines garrison returned to the UK some four days later. For example, William Langley, the *Daily Mail* reporter in Stanley during the invasion reported:

Shortly after midday I was allowed by the lieutenant 'My name is Francisco, I cannot tell you my other name' — to go under escort to the telephone exchange and call the *Daily Mail*.

But the lieutenant kept his gun firmly in the small of my back and said 'No information.' I was able to report that there had been no shooting in the town and that as far as we knew there were no civilian or Marine casualties.

. . . I gathered that the Royal Marines had all been captured and disarmed and were under guard.[11]

This report gave the impression of token resistance, little or no shooting and no casualties to the British side. This impression was enhanced by the detailed report in *The Sunday Times* the following day entitled 'Three Hours to Surrender'.[12] The report was written in an authoritative manner apparently detailing the course of events and yet, strangely enough, the list of contributors did not include the *Sunday Times* reporter in Port Stanley at the time of the invasion, Simon Winchester. How was the newspaper able to produce such a detailed report of events without his contribution? This, and other aspects of the reporting of the Falklands crisis will be considered in detail in chapter 11 but suffice to say at this stage that this report included some glaring errors which were only subsequently corrected (without including an apology for the earlier mistakes) by the 'Insight' report on 18 April after the Royal Marines garrison had returned to the UK and had been interviewed.

However, the general impression left by the newspaper reports of the invasion was one of little resistance and hardly a shot being fired and yet the Argentines had already admitted that one member of their forces had been killed and two injured during the invasion and their Commander had praised the Royal Marines for their bravery. The truth emerged when the Governor and the Royal Marines garrison returned to the UK on 5 April. It transpired that the Royal Marines had fired over 6,000 rounds of small arms ammunition, killed at least five, wounded 17 and knocked out an armoured personnel carrier with two anti-tank rockets. Furthermore, the destruction of the Royal Marines' camp at Moody Brook, and the garrison's accounts of being on the receiving end of live small arms fire bore witness to the intensity of combat.

For once the British press had experienced the difficulties of having to report a dramatic event 8,000 miles away at the far end of a tenuous communications link with very limited reliable sources (who themselves were restricted in what they could actually report). The media made the same mistakes which some of them had accused the British Army of

11 *Daily Mail*, 3 April 1982.
12 *The Sunday Times*, 4 April 1982.

making in Northern Ireland: they produced inaccurate first statements.

This issue will be discussed further in the chapter on Northern Ireland (chapter 10) and in chapter 11. It is worth recording, at this stage, however, that the comparisons between the military and the media extend to both professions making similar mistakes in like circumstances. This may seem obvious to the academic or the impartial critic, but it has so far escaped the notice of members of the two professions concerned.

The passage of information during the Falklands crisis was affected by a number of factors. Due to the paucity of reliable sources, editors in this country had to rely on a few eye-witness accounts (which did not deal in perspective) and on Argentinian reports padded out by what those on the spot were able to say. All this led to a confused picture in London. To the lack of accurate, reliable information from 'the front' was added the inherent built-in possibility of inaccuracies in the news process. In normal circumstances, if there is a dearth of information, the editorial team can rely on experience and instinct when making their 'subbing' decisions. But in this particular case they had no knowledge of national war reporting on which to draw, nor experience of reporting under the constraints that the military exercised in their information handling activities.

All these factors affected the passage of information and were to lead to increasing frustration between the press and the military. Lack of information is something which journalists cannot abide and a dearth of hard news leads to rumour. In contrast, the military are trained to deal only in fact and, when involved in a conflict situation, they are chary about giving away information for fear that it may lead to loss of life. The totally different reaction of the two professions in similar circumstances was to be the cause of much misunderstanding at the beginning of the crisis.

Further discussion about the problems of reporting the Falklands conflict will be left until chapter 11. But as for the general effect of the news process on the relationship between the military and the media, an appreciation of the fundamentals of the news process and the realities of the passage of information is an essential education for the military. For the press, the Falklands crisis highlighted the inherent inaccuracies of the news process to an extent which had not been previously exposed. Perhaps it is time for the press to review the way copy is processed. Just as the military will have many lessons to learn from this conflict which may be appropriate to a general war, so the press should ponder on whether their traditional methods would stand up to the test of trying to report, say, a European war.

4 Television News: ITN

An average total of approximately 35 million watch the various television news programmes transmitted by the BBC and ITN every day. This is a colossal audience and indicates how many people have come to rely on television news as a main source of information. Yet the overwhelming majority have no idea how television news is produced, do not realise the particular problems which are peculiar to the presentation of news in this medium, nor do they appreciate the pressures under which production staffs, editors and presenters have to work. In order to understand more about the production of television news we shall now take a look at a typical day of a news programme at ITN. After looking at the mechanics of the operation we shall then consider the limiting factors and the characteristics of television news.

The ITN studios are situated in Wells Street, just off Oxford Street in London. The company is comparatively small, employing about 450 people (100 journalists, 250 technicians and 100 administrative staff), and it is headed by the editor of ITN who is also the Chief Executive. The journalists and technicians are split into two shifts and work long hours to enable continuity to be maintained: this means that a story does not have to be 'handed over' in the middle of the day.

Independent Television News produces the national and international news programmes for all 14 commercial television companies in the United Kingdom. During the week ITN provides three news programmes each day: *News at One, News at 5.45* and *News at Ten*. Each programme has its own production team, presenters and individual style shaped to provide the news in the format and length that ITN believes the public want. Therefore *News at One* tends to include 'live' interviews with people in the headlines, the 5.45 programme is designed to provide the main headlines in an easily digestible form for the majority of the population who will just have returned home from work, and *News at Ten* is a longer programme allowing time for an 'in depth' look at the various news items. The newsdesk and foreign desk are responsible for producing the input of the day's news for all three programmes and the only variation concerns *News at One* which has, in addition, its own News Editor and input staff to cope with its earlier time of transmission.

Apart from the production teams for each programme the news room contains the home and foreign news departments, eight specialist reporters, 14 general reporters, a sports editor and a production unit. The role of the production unit is to prepare stories which can be spotted in advance (e.g. White Papers, big Court cases, etc.). This preparation allows for a longer and more polished production than is possible for a straightforward 'news' item. The head of the production unit (assisted by his team of four writers), generates a number of ideas but this is not his prerogative and apart from ideas which emerge from the daily 'look ahead' meetings, any member of the news room is free to contribute.

The presentation and coverage of the news is considered at a series of meetings which are held throughout the day:

10.30 am	Meeting of heads of department, chaired by the Editor of ITN
11.30 am	*News at 5.45* meeting chaired by the producer
3.00 pm	*News at One* meeting (for the following day) chaired by the producer
3.15 pm	*News at Ten* meeting — the producer briefs the chief sub and the newscasters)
4.00 pm	*Look Ahead* meeting chaired by the Editor
5.15 pm	*News at Ten* producer (accompanied by his chief sub, scriptwriters and newscasters) briefs the Editor on the likely running order for the evening's programme
7.00 pm	*News at Ten* meeting chaired by the producer.

The Editor exercises his control over ITN's activities by chairing the 10.30 am and 4 pm meetings, from the *News at Ten* briefing at 5.15 pm, and by being accessible throughout the day; but at the same time the three producers are entirely responsible for their respective programmes.

News at 5.45

In order to see how a production team goes about its work let us take a look at the 5.45 news team on a particular day (21 November 1978). The first event was the 10.30 am meeting which the producer, presenter and chief sub-editor (writing) attended. The meeting was opened by the Editor of ITN and he immediately handed over to the home editor who ran through the home news list. This consisted of the following items:

1	Jeremy Thorpe case:	committal trial at Minehead.
2	Mine disaster:	seven dead and 19 injured in a pit disaster at Doncaster.
3	Hospital:	official inquiry just published about Normansfield Hospital for the Mentally Handicapped, Teddington.
4	Prisons:	the Home Secretary, Mr Merlyn Rees, gives details of the terms for a major inquiry into prison conditions.
5	Aldermaston:	result of the Government inquiry into the contaminated clothing discovered in the laundry of the atomic weapon research station at Aldermaston.
6	Ducks breeding out of season:	A light-hearted piece about ducks breeding out of season because of the mild weather.

Arrangements had been made already to report most of these stories. Desmond Hamill and Carol Barnes were covering the Thorpe case (ITN had already established an outside broadcast unit in a portakabin opposite the Minehead Magistrates Court); Robert Hargreaves, the home affairs correspondent, had just received the report on Normansfield Hospital and was wading through its 750 pages; and the ducks film was already in the cutting room. Other news items on the home front were also being watched in case they became more important during the day (these included unemployment figures and the BBC reaction to LWT's new deal with the Football League).[1]

Next came the sports possibilities. These included a film by Trevor McDonald about Kerry Packer's world series cricket enterprise (this

---

1 On 16 November 1978 London Weekend Television announced that they had just signed a £5 million agreement with the Football League for exclusive rights on league matches for three years.

film was on its way back from Australia but it was unlikely to arrive in time for inclusion in the first two news programmes), coverage of the RAC Rally, and the announcement that Viv Anderson had just been selected for the England football squad (and therefore was likely to be the first black man to be selected for England). The sports editor also mentioned in passing that the All Blacks rugby touring team had a match that day against the Combined Services. The game would be covered by Independent Television cameras anyway but it was evident, even at this early stage, that there would be insufficient time to include the highlights in either of the later news programmes — the game was too low on the priority list.

The final list to be checked through was the foreign news. The leading story concerned the Guyana massacres.[2] ITN had received telex details of three CBS and three ABC tapes on the incident which were on their way to Wells Street and there was promise of a film showing Norman Rees, ITN's North American correspondent, getting reaction from San Francisco (where many of the victims' families lived), which would be available in late afternoon.[3] There was also mention of other films which were available: John Suchet's story from Rhodesia about guerillas sabotaging the cattle dips (this was due at Wells Street that morning); Jon Lander's story from Brussels about the EEC's butter problems; and a CBS film about Vietnamese refugees.

Once the foreign editor had run through her list a brief discussion followed and it was generally agreed that the two lead stories were the Thorpe case and the Guyana massacre. The meeting lasted just twenty minutes.

The next meeting for the 5.45 News team was due at 11.30 am and interest now centred on the CBS and ABC tapes which had already arrived at ITN. It is the chief sub's responsibility to check all films and VTR for all three news programmes.[4] First of all she viewed the ABC tapes (some of which had been used by BBC's *Tonight* programme the

---

2 United States Congressman Leo J. Ryan and four of his party (including two NBC men) were murdered when about to board a light aircraft at Port Kaituma, Guyana having just visited the People's Temple Sect Colony at Jonestown. Shortly after this several hundred of the 1,200 followers of Jim Jones (the founder of the People's Temple) died in a mass suicide ordered by their leader.
3 ITN have a VTR agreement with ABC to have access to each other's material. This provides for economic use of resources and enables one to use the other's film if they are not able to get their own reporter and film crew to cover a foreign story in time (such as the Guyana massacre). BBC has a similar agreement with NBC and both ITN and BBC share CBS' material. The ABC tapes are shipped from the United States each day and reach ITN by 11.30 am. A telex list of the details of each film is received by ITN at 8.30 am and the foreign editor earmarks items of interest.
4 The chief sub (film) is the producer's 'eyes and ears' in the film and VTR cutting rooms. The producer has to divide his time between his desk in the news room and the editing rooms. The chief sub (film) allows him to do this.

previous evening).[5] As a result of *Tonight's* scoop there was nothing left in the remainder of the ABC material which was relevant and new. She was then joined by the producer and viewed the CBS tapes (which had now become significantly important). Neither the producer nor the chief sub (film) was happy with the CBS material so they decided to use nothing from the six tapes but rely instead on still photographs of the massacre.

The producer and chief sub (film) then made their way to the 11.30 am meeting where they were joined by the presenter, the director, chief sub (words), graphics artist, copy taster and the two writers.[6] The producer's 'noon line-up' (or provisional running order) was circulated and then discussed. The producer had chosen the following stories from the home and foreign lists:

1 Packages

Mine disaster:	Keith Hatfield on VTR
Thorpe case:	Desmond Hamill (outside broadcast)
Guyana:	stills/satellite (to be arranged)
Hospital:	Robert Hargreaves film
Refugees:	CBS film backed up by Jon Snow on telephone
Viv Anderson:	Chris Jamieson on VTR

2 Items

Financial Times Index and the £

Prisons

Aldermaston

Sid Vicious:	British punk rock star accused of murdering his girlfriend in New York
President Boumedienne:	President of Algeria ill
ITV/BBC:	possible BBC reaction to London Weekend Television's exclusive deal with the Football League to film next season's football

---

5 ITN had booked satellite time the previous evening between 10.00 pm–10.30 pm with the aim of showing some ABC film on *News at Ten*. Unfortunately the Guyana film did not come up during that half an hour so it could not be used by ITN, but it *did* materialise just after 10.30 pm which enabled *Tonight* to include it in their later scheduled programme.
6 These two writers are joined by a third in the afternoon (who then stays on to write for *News at Ten* as well).

3 Watching (i.e. marginal items for possible inclusion)

RAC rally

Ducks

Cricket: Trevor McDonald's film on Kerry
                                 Packer's world series cricket (if it
                                 arrived in time)

A new item was dramatically added to this list when the meeting was interrupted by a telephone call reporting that it had just been announced that the Road Fund Licence would be abolished over the next five years and replaced by a heavier tax on petrol.

The meeting was conducted in a relaxed atmosphere which allowed everyone in the group to propose an idea or query a detail. This easy style of management ensured that the whole team had a clear idea of the producer's intentions and thus enabled them to contribute more effectively.[7] After ensuring that everyone was quite happy about what they were required to do, the producer ended the meeting at noon. No attempt was made to decide what the running order would actually include at this stage because there were too many imponderables (for instance, when would the Rhodesia film arrive – could we use it? *News at One* were interviewing the Minister of Transport, Mr William Rogers – could we use that? Which new item will develop into the major one? Will anything else break which we shall have to include?).

This uncertainty lies at the very heart of news reporting and it provides the dynamic attraction which is the real drug to those who work at ITN. Reporting the news means reporting real events which have occurred that day however close to the time of transmission they may happen (even during transmission if necessary). Therefore the organisation must be able constantly to update its facts and react to the new stories by selecting the important one and arranging for appropriate coverage. The updating process consists of 'sources' and 'selection'. The sources are provided by reporters and correspondents (updating previous copy or sending in new stories), and by the news agencies with their constant flow of information. The selection is done by the copy-taster.

The copy-taster provides the essential filter of news information enabling the new story to be spotted and the old one to be updated whilst at the same time ensuring that the producer is not overwhelmed by information. A copy-taster requires experience and good judgement.

---

7 *News at Ten* adopt a similar style at their 7.00 pm meeting. The emphasis is on group identity and each individual identifies with the programme at these meetings and team spirit is reinforced every day by these regular daily conferences.

The co-ordinator of this whole process is the chief sub who is the producer's 'eyes and ears'. He and the producer sit beside each other at the news desk and have an ongoing dialogue throughout the day discussing the priority of items, details of stories, and working as a two man unit.

The running order is usually decided at about 3 pm and on this particular day it contained the following items:

1 Pit deaths
2 The Thorpe case
3 Guyana massacre
4 Middle East
5 Car tax
6 Jobless
7 *Financial Times* Index and the £
8 Hospital
9 Prisons
10 Aldermaston
11 Sid Vicious
12 Viv Anderson
13 ITV/BBC football dispute
14 Cricket
15 Ducks

This decision provides a watershed for the production team; now they have got something definite to go on. Script writing becomes of primary importance and the sub-editors, correspondents who are doing 'live' reports from the studio and the presenter (Leonard Parkin) are heavily involved in script writing during the run-up to the programme. All will have been working on scripts since the 11.30 am briefing and during these last few hours the scripts are completed and then passed through the chief sub (who checks them for accuracy, length, writing style, etc.), to the producer for final approval. The 'running order' decision also provides the incentive for tape-editing to be completed, graphics to be finalised, and the impetus for the director to co-ordinate the studio arrangements.

The production of the running order presupposes that the producer has already calculated the timing for each item. In fact the calculations become increasingly more exact as transmission time approaches and the period allotted to each item is restricted by the format adopted by ITN; 'two minutes is a long time for an item in the 5.45 News'.[8]

8 Interview with David Phillips, then Assistant Producer, ITN, 21 November 1978.

Because the production team is used to the format, and also as a result of the high level of professionalism, exact timing does not present much of a problem.

Each news programme has a rehearsal immediately prior to transmission and the *News at 5.45* commence theirs at 5.20 pm. Right up to this moment scripts will have been amended and retyped, and the system is flexible enough to react to a new piece of news up to the moment of transmission and during the programme if necessary. There is no obvious increase in pressure or tension in the newsroom during the period immediately prior to the rehearsal and the actual rehearsal itself is conducted with efficient professionalism.

As we have seen, the presenter has been involved with the development of the programme since the 10.30 Heads of Department meeting and therefore he has been able to contribute ideas right from the start. Furthermore, he will have been involved in script writing throughout the day either as originator, as co-author, or as editor, altering the words to suit his own particular style. He is, therefore, not just the reader of the news but is very much part of the creative team. However it is during the rehearsal that the presenter starts to emerge in his true colours as the anchorman. The programme is actually run by the director from a control room which is physically separated from the studio. Unlike BBC Television News there is no glass partition between control room and studio; the director relies solely on a battery of monitor sets and when necessary he can pass instructions to the presenter who is equipped with an earpiece. The producer sits at the back of the control room from where he can ensure that production decisions are passed on by the director. The chain of command is straightforward and the communications system allows for considerable flexibility in a well organised production team. An example of this teamwork occurred on the day in question. Ever since the news of the pit disaster had been received that morning, the graphics department had been wrestling with the problem of illustrating, by animation, how the disaster had occurred. The animation was used during the rehearsal but the director was still not happy. He discussed it briefly with the producer in the control room at the end of the rehearsal and at 5.41 pm, four minutes before transmission, the producer took the decision to delete the animation. The director immediately informed everyone from his control desk and detailed the resulting script amendments. This was all handled extremely calmly and it was difficult for the layman to appreciate that the programme was due to commence in under four minutes. This illustrates the high degree of professionalism required and the need to react to the unexpected (television newsmen are accustomed to change and are not surprised by last minute alterations to the running order).

The *News at 5.45* for 21 November 1978 was transmitted without mishap. There were no last minute news items, the decision to use still photographs of the victims of the Guyana massacre was fully justified (because the stills complemented the script), and the programme ran exactly to time — to the second!

Limiting factors

Television news is subjected to two major limiting factors: time and the structure of a news programme. The fact that television news works to a series of deadlines dictated by the scheduling of transmissions is an obvious limitation but there are other, more fundamental, restrictions. Both BBC1 and ITN have similar lengths for their news bulletins at lunchtime, early evening and at night. If we stick to our example of *News at 5.45* the full allocation of time is 15 minutes and on 21 November 1978 there were 15 items included in the running order, so the justification for David Phillips' 'two minutes is a long time for an item' is self-evident (even the longer BBC1's 9 o'clock news and ITN's *News at Ten* can allow only 3—4 minutes for a major item). The time limitation imposed by the duration of the programme inherently forces decisions on the varying importance of the news items and therefore the seconds which will be allocated to each topic. This necessarily means that complex issues need to be put over to the public in simple language in under 90 seconds, supplemented by films or graphics as necessary. The art of paraphrasing complicated detail and reproducing the essentials in simple English and brief sentences is one which requires considerable skill and concentration (for instance Robert Hargreaves reduced the 750 page hospital report to 1½ minutes on the 5.45 News and it took him virtually all day to do it). Although this precis discipline is shared by newspaper writers, they are not subjected to the same constraints as television writers who are faced with unique restrictions such as: the time limitation imposed by the running order, the requirement to write a lead-in to a film or to a correspondent's report, or fit a script to a film; and the overriding importance of ensuring that the writer's thoughts are transmitted to the public via the presenter so that the impression is easily comprehended (this is the true art of communicating through the medium of television).[9]

These restrictions lead to a form of 'headline' news because there is seldom time to include anything other than the bare facts. Although it is possible to provide more information in the longer *News at Ten* time is also limited in this programme and it will seldom be possible to develop a report along the lines of a newspaper article. So it can be seen that the restrictions of time affect the style and content of the news to a considerable degree. But perhaps the most significant point about all this is the possibility of distortion due to insufficient time. Insufficient time to find out the facts of an incident; insufficient time to provide a balanced picture; insufficient time in the bulletin to give a rounded account. We shall look at this again when considering the selection of news.

The other major limiting factor for television news is its format. The format changes from time to time (*News at Ten* was launched in July 1967) but the change does not free the news bulletin from its restrictions; it just changes the old for a set of new limitations. Let us look at examples of this. First of all, presentation: a news item can be presented from the studio or from the location of the event. If it is done from the studio, either the newscaster or a specialist correspondent presents the item and this may be supplemented by film, graphics, slides or the printed word. If the report is presented from a location it will normally consist of a filmed report from a correspondent or reporter with a lead-in being provided by the newscaster in the studio. The location report can be ENG film, VTR or transmitted by satellite, but its presentation will still be the same. So there are only a limited number of ways the news can be presented on television and although the BBC and ITN have their different styles and identities the room for manoeuvre is limited.

The format for a television news programme does not just happen, it is carefully conceived. The current style *News at 5.45* was introduced

---

9 During a visit to BBC Television News the author observed a sub-editor working on an item about the European Monetary System which was due to be presented by John Simpson (then the foreign affairs correspondent) on the 9 o'clock news. The sub spent most of the day researching the subject, viewing film, fitting script to the appropriate piece of film, and writing a lead-in about the EMS in which he was required to explain in less than a minute the fact that there was a debate, what the debate was about and why there was so much controversy about it. In the late afternoon John Simpson arrived back from Brussels (where he had been covering the EMS meeting) and together they discussed the details for Simpson's report and the lead-in for his story. A number of ideas were tried and rejected before they were finally happy and they had written what they intended to say; only then was the script submitted to the senior duty editor for approval. The final result was three minutes by John Simpson which consisted of a résumé of the EMS meeting supported by film, followed by carefully considered comment, expressed in layman's language, about the issues involved. This report occupied an experienced sub for almost an entire day. It requires considerable skill to write exactly what you intend to say in straightforward language in a limited number of words.

in August 1976 as the brainchild of Alastair Burnet and David Phillips. The formula they developed was based on their experience and their feel for what was required for an early evening news. They were aware that at that time of the evening the majority of the audience were in the provinces; therefore they sort out news stories from the regions. They were also conscious of news stories that would interest women. Their framework for the ideal programme included the following ingredients:

1   Ideally 8½ minutes of the total 15 minutes should be visual (film, VTR etc.)

2   Straight news reporting by the presenter

3   Always include sport (Britain is a sporting nation)

4   Try to end the news with a light item.

Into this format has to be fitted the news of the day. If there are not sufficient newsworthy items the news bulletin cannot be reduced by the odd minute and equally, the bulletins are only rarely extended to cover a particularly significant event. This results in a familiar pattern of news presentation to which the viewer quickly becomes accustomed. In fact, given the restrictions of time and structure, and the requirement to give a balanced view of an issue, it is interesting to note the differences in style of presentation between BBC and ITN, and within ITN, the marked differences between their three programmes.

The possibility of distortion of news due to the restrictions of time was mentioned earlier. How valid is the criticism? If both BBC and ITN are required to present news impartially, why is it that, to some, the news appears distorted or, to repeat a question asked by an officer at the Staff College, Camberley, during the 1978 Press Day: 'Why is it that almost every time a story appears in the newspapers or on television concerning an incident about which one has personal knowledge, the report often differs in detail from one's own recollections of the events which took place?' This is an oft repeated accusation of the media's news reporting. Let us restrict ourselves to television for the moment and look at the process of the selection of news to see whether we can find an answer to this criticism.

Selection of news

As we have seen, the genesis of the process is the copy provided by the various news agencies. The copy is provided on a 24 hour basis but as far as ITN is concerned their first stage of selection is the production of the home and foreign news lists for the 10.30 am meeting. The Editor is able to influence the initial thoughts for the news programmes at that and subsequent meetings and he is always available to producers during the day if they are in doubt. But even at the 10.30 am meeting his 'selection of news' is being guided by the home and foreign news lists which in turn reflect the news stories which are known about at that time. There is no mystery in the production of these lists; they just consist of the news of the moment.

After the 10.30 am meeting the Editor has little or no influence on the selection of news; this is the responsibility of the programme producers.[10] However, each producer has instant access to the Editor at all times and he may well use this access to consult him about the coverage of a sensitive issue, such as Northern Ireland.[11] This policy of delegating responsibility is also used at the BBC; as Alan Protheroe, then Editor of BBC Television News, put it: 'I intervene very rarely'.[12] It is the producer who is expected to make the decisions about news selection and he is often faced with a dilemma. Let us suppose that a new story has just broken about some scandal involving a public figure. The producer has to double check sources to make sure of the facts, he then has to decide whether he should cover the story, how to present it (legal advice may well be required here) and what order of prominence it should have in the news. Almost invariably these decisions have to be made against the clock with inadequate check on sources. In these circumstances the decision is often taken, after a great deal of discussion with the Editor, not to pursue a certain story for lack of adequate evidence and the item is dropped. Now, by the very nature of things the public do not know when such a decision is taken by the media (for this is equally true of newspapers and radio) and therefore newsmen are unable to defend their cause when accused of irresponsibility and sensational reporting. There is no doubt that these accusations are justified on occasion, but each case should be considered on its merits and general condemnation avoided.

To illustrate this point about responsibility here is just one example taken from television news. One evening at approximately 9.40 pm ITN received a telephone call from the IRA claiming that an Army deserter

10 The Editor of ITN is also the Chief Executive and the responsibilities associated with the position force him to delegate to the programme producers. He is very busy dealing with ITN's Board of Directors, his own management team, the IBA, politicians and lobbyists, as well as attending network policy meetings, giving speeches and involving himself in the day to day running of ITN.
11 The Editor has a 'bleeper' so he can be contacted immediately when he is in the London area.
12 Interview with Alan Protheroe, 6 December 1978.

had defected. They quoted his name and number to add credence to the claim. ITN immediately checked with the Army Press Desk in Lisburn who said they would check and telephone back in five minutes. When the call came through five minutes later Lisburn admitted that a soldier of that name and number was unaccounted for but they did not know any more details at that stage. They promised to give more information as soon as it became available. Faced with these facts and the clock fast approaching 10 o'clock ITN decided not to use the story. This proved to be a wise decision for just after 10 pm Lisburn rang through again to say that the soldier in question was indeed absent without leave but he had been accounted for.[13] Once again the IRA had tried to score a propaganda point by banking on ITN's journalistic instinct to go for a story and the Army's inability to discount the story within twenty minutes. They had overlooked ITN's strict code of responsibility and the mutual trust developed with the Army's press desk in Lisburn.

On this occasion the decision was taken not to include the story. At other times, and in different circumstances, the decision may be the opposite. The pertinent point is that the decisions have to be made regardless of the pressure of time and unverified information. This is a problem with which the military are all too familiar. On more occasions than not an operational commander will have to make a decision against the clock based on inadequate information. For both the military commander and the television editor this can be a heavy responsibility; and for the television men particularly so when one remembers how quickly news becomes stale and the television newsman's automatic reaction to 'go for a story'. Therefore there may be distortion of news on occasions due to a lack of one or more of the factors already mentioned, but this distortion is not deliberate. 'There is simply not the time nor the opportunity to manipulate the news — anyway news items choose themselves as indicated by copy from news agencies, our own resources and stringers.'[14]

One final point about distortion concerns the accuracy of eye-witness accounts. Unless a reporter has received a tip-off, is covering a predictable event (such as the arrival of a VIP at Heathrow Airport), possesses extraordinary anticipation of an event, or has just been plain lucky, he will normally arrive at an incident after it has occurred and therefore will have to rely on eye-witness accounts for his information. One of the failings of human nature is the diversity of views when two or more people are asked to describe an event which they all claim to have seen. Impressions depend on a number of factors such as where the individual was standing, whether he saw the whole incident or part

13 Visit to ITN, November 1978.
14 Interview with David Phillips, then Assistant Editor, ITN, November 1978.

of it, whether he was involved, excitement, and so on. The television journalist, like the policeman, has to use patience and skill to extract the right information but he also has to do it under pressure of time and it may not always be possible to talk to sufficient people to obtain a balanced account of what occurred.

An individual can honestly believe that his account of an event is completely accurate even when it is disproved by other witnesses. Even in an organisation such as the Army which is trained to obtain and pass accurate information, inaccuracies do and will occur so that commanders receive wrong information but act on this intelligence assuming it to be accurate. The media and the military share the common problem of frequently having to rely on second-hand accounts of an event and then act on that information. On occasions both have been guilty of making the wrong decision but at the time they believed their decision to be right, based on the information they had at the time. Like others, journalists do not have the benefit of hindsight before taking a decision.

Characteristics of ITN

The two most vivid impressions of ITN are teamwork and professionalism. The teamwork is apparent in a number of ways; competition is one. There is a healthy respect for the 'opposition' (the BBC) and therefore ITN are always striving to 'get the best story first, with the minimum of facilities'. There is also friendly rivalry between the three separate news programmes within ITN. This emphasis on competition within the organisation helps to raise the overall standard of ITN.

The sense of identity within the newsroom is compulsive and deliberate. Everyone is encouraged to contribute ideas as well as being expected to produce a high standard of work; the daily meetings encourage this identity and help to promote the idea of team membership. The result of the team effort is the programme itself and not unnaturally the contributors crowd into the control room to watch the results of their efforts being projected on the screen. The sense of satisfaction derived from seeing an end product of their labour is something which is experienced by few people in other walks of life.

The presenters are very much part of the team as well. The public see the polished performance of the newscaster on their screens but have little idea of how much they contribute to the formulation of the programme. As often as not they write their own material, work in conjunction with the original writers where appropriate, view VTR, edit and suggest ideas to the producers. We have already seen how Leonard Parkin is involved with the *News at 5.45* and Alastair Burnet pointed out that this is equally true of *News at Ten*. He emphasised the significance of being able to contribute to the construction of the programme and stressed the importance of being part of a team, all of whom knew each other very well.[15] The teamwork at ITN has developed a feeling of elitism and they constantly compare themselves not only with the BBC but also with the three American news organisations ABC, NBC and CBS.

The teamwork also stems from a high degree of professionalism. It is founded on a secure 'command' structure with responsibility and delegation being the important ingredients. Efficiency is paramount, and admiration for and comparison with military organisation and efficiency is not altogether surprising: '. . . the BBC also resembles, in certain respects, the armed services. Indeed, whenever I watch some complicated programme being rehearsed, or going on the air, I am irresistibly reminded of a service situation, with its clear cut network of people, all doing their job in a tightly controlled way'.[16]

Logistic planning is essential and this is based on the 4 pm daily meeting chaired by the Editor when the probable news stories for the following day are discussed. But flexibility is also an essential ingredient so that ITN can react quickly to any news story which breaks and ensure the logistic support is available to enable the report and camera crew to cover the story.

Television news also requires considerable discipline. Discipline is imposed by time, words and technical restrictions. Alan Protheroe explained it this way: 'It's rather like running a specialist battalion — we've got to take those objectives five times a day'.[17]

The discipline imposed by these deadlines demands dedication by everyone, be they journalist, technician or administrator, and yet the overall impression is one of calm efficiency and reliance on the professionalism of each specialist. There was little indication of the tension mentioned by Schlesinger in his book about BBC News, even during the actual transmission.[18]

These characteristics of television news will be familiar to the military reader for the military profession also lays great stress on the importance of teamwork, professionalism, efficiency, logistical planning, flexibility and discipline. Both professions have to make decisions against the clock and the realities imposed by such a situation

15 Interview with Alastair Burnet, 21 November 1978.
16 Sir Michael Swann, then Chairman of the BBC, at a lunchtime lecture at Broadcasting House, 29 October 1974 (*The responsibility of the Governors*, BBC Lunch-time lectures, ninth series, p.7).
17 Interview with the author, 6 December 1978.
18 Philip Schlesinger, *Putting Reality Together*, BBC News, Constable, London 1978, p.63.

inevitably result in common characteristics. Even the reliance on a series of meetings throughout the day as a means of internal communication is a feature common to both professions. These apparent similarities will be pursued in the next chapter to see whether they are equally applicable to radio.

Conclusion

The independence of ITN and BBC Television News is fundamental to democracy in Britain and both organisations have fiercely defended their position on occasions. In an interview with the author, Alan Protheroe stressed the importance of this independence and pointed out that BBC Television News was well aware that it could be used by minority groups to publicise their cause. At the same time television news has a duty to report: 'We must question — that is the role of television news. Remember, don't confuse coverage with attitude'. He went on to talk about the British public, which he believes is well informed, and stated that: 'We do not tell them what to think; we tell them what to think about'.[19] This is a significant point about television news which, in its simplest form, aims to report an event, on occasions analyse it, and leave the viewer to draw his own conclusions.

In this chapter we have looked at the possibility of the distortion of news and considered the factors which affect this and it is clear that there is no intention to distort or to bias. 'Intention' is very important because it influences the whole ethos of news reporting on television. Alastair Burnet put it this way: 'News *does* make mistakes but we are honestly trying to take bias out whereas current affairs are often trying to put bias in'.[20] The intention is clear. 'Honesty' is further supported by the importance that 'accuracy' plays in the portrayal of news. It is fundamental to news reporting.

One is left with an impression of two rival television news organisations which are professional, staffed by dedicated people who are honestly trying to report news as accurately as they are able. Sometimes they get it wrong and sometimes the viewer thinks they get it wrong because of his own prejudices and opinions. It is equally important for the military and the general public to recognise this fact and to look at the coverage of each news item dispassionately, avoiding the temptation to generalise.

19 Interview with Alan Protheroe, 6 December 1978.
20 Interview with Alastair Burnet, 22 November 1978.

5 Radio News and Current Affairs: BBC *Today*

Radio news

No study of the process of news would be complete without considering radio. It has survived the challenge of television in the sixties to emerge in rejuvenated form and confound its critics. During the past decade the expansion of the BBC Radio News service has been quite remarkable. John Wilson, Editor of BBC Radio News and Current Affairs observed: 'BBC Radio News is now responsible for over 100 separate news broadcasts a day; we have become a news factory. We expanded our output four-fold in ten years but the staff has only doubled; until the late sixties there was little more than the main bulletins on the Home Service. In the last few years we have considerably expanded the news on Radios 1 and 2'.[1]

This expansion of the news service provided by the BBC illustrates the particular advantage of radio; people can be doing something else whilst they are listening. This 'secondary activity' has been made practically possible by the arrival of the transistor so that, today, millions of people keep themselves in touch with the day's events by listening to the regular news bulletins whilst shaving, eating, driving, working and relaxing.

The BBC responded to this renewed interest in radio by extending the 6 pm News on Radio 4 from 15 to 30 minutes in July 1977, expan-

---

1 Interview with the author, 22 April 1982.

ding the regular bulletins on Radio 2 in February 1979 and specifically styling the news on Radio 1 for its young audience. The expansion of news programmes has enabled more information to be included in a bulletin which has resulted in a better informed public, but the inherent problem of the inability of the listener to recall what he has just heard has meant the continued use of simple English. The expansion of radio news has been used to good effect to project defence issues to a wider public. A written piece on a military topic which is in the news (such as Trident) will often be repeated in a number of news bulletins on Radio 2, picked up on the 6 pm News on Radio 4 and on Radio 1's *Newsbeat*. Furthermore, the BBC Radio Defence Correspondent, Christopher Lee, is frequently required to do 'live' pieces for the different radio news and current affairs (including the regions) and tailors his material accordingly. To illustrate how defence issues can reach a wide cross-section of the public in one day, Christopher Lee told the author about his broadcasts on a day picked at random: 17 March 1982. On that day he produced three separate pieces on defence associated with Trident; President Brezhnev's offer to freeze SS20 missile development, and a report from the Commons Select Committee. These pieces were in all Radios 1, 2 and 3 news summaries, the 1 o'clock news, Radio 4's 6 o'clock news, the *PM Programme, Newsbeat*, the *Jimmy Young* and *Today* programmes.[2] This ability to repeat news pieces on different programmes, sometimes tailored for a specific audience, has resulted in a much more informed public, especially amongst the younger generation, and supports the claim that BBC radio represents as many different newspapers as there are programmes. A restriction of radio news is that, unlike the newspaper reader, the listener has to receive news in the order and style decided upon by the radio news organisation. With regard to style, this has been offset to some extent by the increased tendency to include 'actuality' reporting (i.e. a radio journalist reports an event from the scene of the incident or a member of the public describes an event or gives his views on a particular issue 'live' on the air). John Wilson considers that: 'actuality is the purest forms of news reporting. It takes the listener to the event itself via the reporter'.[3]

A face lift for *Today*

'Actuality' is used considerably in the BBC Radio 4 programme *Today*. This programme is a good example of the progression of news and

---

2 Interview with Christopher Lee, 19 March 1982.
3 Interview with author, 6 February 1979.

current affairs in BBC Radio and serves to illustrate the philosophy of such a programme. It has the highest audience of any Radio 4 programme (with a peak audience of up to 2 million), it now runs for about two hours (6.30–8.30 am) each week day, and its format is based on the assumption that it is a news programme which is the background to most listeners' mornings and that they probably only listen to it for half an hour at the most (therefore headlines are repeated approximately every 15 minutes). Due to this listening habit the total audience figures reach a maximum of 4–5 million during the two hours. The programme has long had its devotees but a significant decision was taken in 1978 which was to break new ground in the field of news reporting. In April that year Ken Goudie was appointed as Editor of the programme. He had spent 23 years with Radio News and was the first Editor appointed to have control over the programme's current affairs items as well as its news.

Ken Goudie spent the first couple of months after his appointment considering a way to produce a genuine news and current affairs programme without the boundary becoming blurred between the two disciplines, and in July 1978 he launched the new style *Today* programme. His prescription was to be ready to follow a news item with any elaboration which would help the listener to understand its complexity or its importance. This has resulted in news stories being backed up by immediate comment ('live' if possible) from a relevant public figure, provided that this really does throw extra light on to the meaning of the news. In this way the programme has attempted to combine the former separate elements of news and current affairs into a single cohesive whole. This approach appears to have worked because listeners have accepted the credibility which has resulted from the common sense of this new policy.

Night people

As *Today* is arguably the first genuine news and current affairs programme and because it is broadcast first thing in the morning (and thus has to be prepared through the night), it is a particularly interesting programme to observe in the context of the military and the media. The day starts when the day shift commences work at 11 am. This team consists of the Day Editor, two producers and various reporters, and it is their job to plan the following morning's programme in outline and to do as much of the spade work as is feasible. This provides a good 'run-in' to the programme and involves such things as recording interviews already planned in advance, receiving (and editing if necessary) tapes from correspondents abroad, selecting various news items which occur during the day and recording interviews or commentaries about the issues involved.[4] As a result of their day's work the day shift produce 'Prospects' for the programme. This consists of a list of suggested news items together with a summary of the latest development in each item including notes on what has been achieved (e.g. interviews arranged or already taped, commentaries completed, etc.).

'Prospects' are handed over to the night shift just after 9 pm and those attending this meeting include the Editor of the programme, one of the presenters, the Day Editor and his two producers, the Night Editor, the two night producers and a night reporter. This meeting is conducted in a very relaxed manner enabling anyone to make a contribution if they so wish, and it is held at this particular time to enable everyone to catch the headlines of BBC TV 9 o'clock news and also to see *News at Ten*. This essential link with other news media is continued by scanning the national press when the first editions start arriving at about 11 pm for possible stories to follow up, and by constant liaison with Radio News throughout the night (the news room is situated only a few yards along the corridor from the *Today* office).

In order to produce a radio programme lasting approximately two hours, and cope with going on the air at 6.30 in the morning, there is a need to ensure that the concentration required through the night to guarantee thorough preparation is not marred by an imperfect broadcast due to tiredness. The running order has to be produced at approximately 3 am to enable exact timings to be worked out so that there is sufficient time to make any necessary alterations. This is particularly relevant to tape editing and to give some idea of the practicalities involved, it took three hours to reduce a nine-minute taped interview with a spokesman from British Leyland about the Longbridge plant to 2 minutes 58 seconds, without distorting the interview.[5] The production team work throughout the night preparing material for the programme. The two presenters obviously need some sleep to ensure that they are alert when actually broadcasting, but even they are in the

4   The *Today* office receives a number of press handouts, pamphlets and notification of events which are marked in the diary for future action. A number of their 'soft news' items originate from this forward planning, and from a careful study of the press (both national and provincial).

5   Visit to the *Today* programme, 7–8 February 1979. Tape editing is an extremely skilled job. In this particular case the original tape included three attempts before the spokesman produced a satisfactory interview. This is quite usual with interviewees who have little or no experience at being interviewed. By sending the complete tape to the *Today* office the reporter assisted the tape editor because this enabled 'the best piece' to be extracted from each relevant sentence. Some may argue that tape editing is a dangerous practice because of the possibility of distortion, but, assuming the professional integrity of the editor, this method is no more liable to distortion than the sub-editing process of a newspaper. In this particular case the author watched the tape being edited throughout the three hours and the end result was a good, interesting and accurate interview.

office between 4—5 am researching items, writing scripts and noting cues.

The programme itself consists of a mixture of news bulletins or headlines at regular intervals, taped 'pieces' or interviews, and live interview or pieces from the studio. The various items are timed very carefully and yet there is sufficient flexibility to cancel a piece or inject a live interview. On the day the author was with the *Today* programme there were 46 items in the schedule, the 7.45 am news headlines were removed at 20 minutes' notice (because they were a repeat of the 7.30 am headlines and therefore likely to be boring for the listener), and Jim Rosenthal, the BBC Radio sports commentator, as a result of an early morning telephone call came into the studio at 8.15 am to do a live piece about the possible £1 million transfer of the footballer Trevor Francis from Birmingham City to Nottingham Forest.

Impressions

The overall impression which the author obtained from the visit to BBC Radio News and the *Today* programme was one of relaxed professionalism. The relaxed atmosphere enabled everyone to work together when under pressure (particularly pertinent in the newsroom), and also allowed anyone to contribute an idea during the free discussions at formal meetings. This atmosphere also contributed towards teamwork which was a noticeable characteristic of the *Today* staff, and as with all good teams, cheerfulness was much in evidence. Indeed there was regular cheerful banter from the 9 pm meeting right through to the end of the programme the following morning, and this atmosphere was projected from the studio to the listeners during the actual broadcast.

The professionalism was continually in evidence, epitomised by the never-ending attempts to improve the standards of *Today* despite the fact that it already has a large radio audience. Professionalism usually requires dedication and there was considerable evidence of this, particularly with regard to people's attitude to hours of work — they rarely went home immediately their shift ended (for instance, the day producer of *Today* who was still busy in the office two hours after the 'Prospects' meeting). This reluctance to leave the office is also partially due to the need to unwind after long hours of concentrated effort. For example the Editor of BBC Radio 1 and 2 News stayed in the building for two or three hours after he finished his two-day shift because he found he needed to change gear before going home. And a night editor on the *Today* programme remarked: 'When I get home after a stint of night duty I don't even want to look at the news-papers'.[6]

The impressions which have been recorded here will be familiar to the military reader who has experienced long hours on duty, usually at night. The requirement to maintain concentration throughout the night and to be able to make clear decisions when the mind is at its lowest ebb is a peculiarity of military life resulting from the requirement to train for, and participate in, night operations. The professionalism, dedication and teamwork which have already been identified as charac-teristics of newspaper offices and television newsrooms and current affairs programmes were also evident in *Today*, but perhaps the most noticeable impression which one can associate with the military was cheerfulness. The good natured give-and-take and almost light-hearted approach to the serious business in hand reminded the author of count-less similar experiences from night exercises and operations. The resulting similarity in atmosphere created by this good humoured attitude was most striking.

6 Visit to the *Today* programme, 7 February 1979.

6 Common Characteristics of the Military and the Media

An analysis of the characteristics

At the beginning of Part II it was stated that, where appropriate, comparison would be drawn between the apparently very different worlds of journalism and the military. Before visiting the newsrooms and offices of the various media the author considered that the two worlds were indeed very different; but his research has cast a new light on the relationship. In the last three chapters we have looked at the process of news in newspapers, radio and television and certain characteristics have emerged which are common to all three. Let us see how they compare with military characteristics and beliefs.

Perhaps the first word that springs to mind is professionalism. This is clearly apparent in all three media and it is a quality on which the British Armed Forces pride themselves (they are, after all, the only 100 per cent volunteer all-professional forces in Europe). The striving for professional excellence, the insistence on high standards are qualities with which the military can easily identify, and both the military and the media realise that professionalism can only be achieved by dedication and self-discipline. The discipline required by a sub-editor of a newspaper epitomises the requirement for this in newsrooms generally, and the dedication observed at BBC Radio News and Current Affairs was reflected both in television and newspapers.

The next most obvious comparison was the similarities between a news room and a military operations room. Whilst observing ITN's

News at 5.45 the author was particularly struck by this analogy. If one looks on the programme as a military company 'operation', then the producer is the company commander supported by the chief sub-editors, the presenter and the director — the command element of a 'combat team'. Above him are the editor (the commanding officer) and the deputy editor (the battalion second in command). The comparisons are significant especially when one considers man-management. It was most noticeable that the editor was accessible throughout the day but he was careful not to interfere with the programme (reminiscent of the guiding hand of a wise commanding officer).

The 'chain of command' was very evident and the requirement for the producer to give clear and precise directives was the key to producing a good programme. The pressure of time-forced decisions encouraged clear thinking and resulted in scripts which consisted of short sentences written in simple English. The pressure on the team equated to that experienced in a command post exercise. The 'communications' consisted of telephones, copy, televisions, video cassettes and discussions, and the 'team' was surrounded by various means of obtaining, and transmitting, information. 'Delegation' was exercised at all levels and initiative was expected from everyone regardless of their experience. This analogy can also be applied to other media news rooms and current affairs offices. For example, this is particularly applicable to BBC 2's *Newsnight*.[1] The comparison can be extended even further; for instance, the research has revealed the importance of formal meetings as the focal point for the decision making process (indeed ITN has as many meetings as there are 'orders groups' in a battle group preparing for an operation). These meetings may be conducted with more informality than an equivalent military gathering, but there was no doubting the authority of the chairman at the various meetings which the author attended, and the post mortem of the previous day's output which is conducted at their 9.15 am meeting by BBC Radio News compares with the countless debriefs held by the military at all levels.

The modern military commander is utterly dependent upon communications to provide him with information upon which he bases his decisions. These communications are supplemented by personal reports from individuals which enable him to obtain a fuller picture of an incident and provide him with more detailed intelligence. Having made his plan, he then gives the orders to put the operation into motion, either at an orders group, or over the radio. This process is analogous with that of a news editor, or the editor of a current affairs programme.

---

1   Visit by the author to *Newsnight*, 4 March 1982.

News rooms receive a constant flow of information be it from agency copy, telephone calls or on tape. This information is embellished by the more detailed reports provided by reporters or correspondents who either return to the office with their copy, or communicate with the office 'from the field'. Having received the information the editor is constantly required to make decisions against the clock so that the various specialists in his organisation have time to produce the newspaper, the television or the radio programme. The pressure on the decision maker is common to all news media and it is probably the area of closest association with the military. The similarities in organisation may encompass other fields, such as industry, but it is the requirement to make decisions under the pressure of time, often frustrated by inadequate information, which is peculiar to the military and the news media. Both the news editor and the military commander have to stand by the decision they make at the time (nothing is as old as yesterday's news; nobody forgives the unsuccessful commander in combat). In battling with this common problem both of them use similar devices. Responsibility is experienced at an early age and is increased as an individual progresses up the ladder; if he cannot accept or cope with the added responsibility he is moved sideways. Delegation is a characteristic of military command and is also very much in evidence in the news media as is illustrated by these quotes: Sir Larry Lamb, former Editor of the *Sun*, 'I expect the newspaper to operate just as efficiently when I am away';[2] Andrew Hutchinson, Night Editor of *The Daily Telegraph*, 'In reality most of the Managing Editor's responsibility for the news is delegated to the Night Editor'.[3]

In the military, teamwork is an essential ingredient in the continual striving for efficiency. So it is in the news business. Whether it be the teamwork built up through years of experience working with each other in a news room of a newspaper which bears fruit when these individuals eventually end up together on the back bench, or whether it be the type of spirit developed by the *News at 5.45* or the *Today* teams, it is a characteristic of those involved in the news business.

These devices (responsibility, delegation and team spirit) assist the decision making process and together they help to form the atmosphere of an organisation specifically designed to make decisions under pressure, be it a news or military decision. It is therefore hardly surprising to discover that many senior journalists who have experienced the military way of life, or have observed it, admire the efficiency of the military, and identify with it. This is particularly applicable at editorial level as illustrated by David Nicholas, the Editor

2 Interview with the author, 12 December 1978.
3 Interview with the author, 6 November 1978.

66

of ITN, who remarked that many people in the news media business admired the precision and well ordered mind of the military and pointed out that the news media and the military both required 'leadership, determination and judgement — coolness under pressure'.[4]

Conclusion

So in comparing the characteristics of the military and the news media it is evident that a number are common to both and such a list might include:

Professionalism
Initiative
Responsibility
Dedication
Efficiency
Delegation of authority
Teamwork
Self-discipline
Decision making under the pressure of time
Forward planning
Logistics
Flexibility
Unsocial hours

In summary there are probably three areas which indicate the association between these two kinds of professionals. First, both are utterly dependent upon the motivation of the people who work for them. Both professions require considerable self-sacrifice and professionalism from the members of the team and this is directly related to good leadership and management. On his visits to the various newsrooms it was very evident to the author which organisations enjoyed high morale and which were experiencing problems. However much the military and the media become increasingly dependent upon new technology in the future, both will still be reliant upon the goodwill and dedication of individual people.

Second, both the military and the news media are ruled by deadlines. They are probably more time-orientated than most other professions and this dictates the way they do business. Whereas the need for conformity and a control system in the military is accepted and

4   Interview with the author, 21 November 1978.

understood, this is not automatically associated with news rooms. Indeed, during his research into BBC news, Philip Schlesinger commented on the journalists' surprise at the need for this.[5] But the time limitation factor does not allow a news editor the luxury of considering the finer academic points of an issue. It may be argued that the news media in general might benefit from a less 'stopwatch culture' but as things stand at present, deadlines force decisions which means that someone in authority has to make up his mind on an issue very quickly. Sir Larry Lamb expressed it thus: 'Decisions are immediate – we can't run things by committee'.[6]

The third area of association concerns professionalism. Both the military and the media are professions about which little is known by the layman. Apart from anything else it is difficult for members of the public to gain access to either in order to observe them at work. Therefore virtually no one outside these professions has any idea what is involved, and yet from time to time they both come under criticism from the public or from independent observers who are ignorant of the problems involved. This has resulted in both professions placing significant emphasis on self-analysis at various levels within their organisations. The criticism which results from these analytical sessions is balanced by the occasional message of congratulations and the two professions attach considerable kudos to receiving praise from a superior for achieving a high standard of professionalism. The fixation with professionalism within the BBC has been commented on by Tom Burns in his book *The BBC—Public Institution and Private World*.[7] In another article he has also highlighted the isolated position of the producer: 'The isolation is the thing most producers are afraid of. They don't like it, they don't welcome it. That is why they stick constantly to the notion of a team'.[8] He went on to describe the difficulties experienced by a producer in a television gallery trying to get 20 people to do the right thing at a given moment, controlled solely by his voice speaking into a microphone.[9] The isolation of command, the frustrations of exercising control and the importance of teamwork are all symptoms with which the military can easily identify.

5   Philip Schlesinger, *Putting Reality Together*, Constable, London 1978, p.135.
6   Interview with the author, 12 December 1978.
7   Tom Burns, *The BBC—Public Institution and Private World*, Macmillan, London 1977, pp. 122—7.
8   Tom Burns, 'Public Service and Private World' in Jeremy Tunstall's *Media Sociology*, Constable, London 1970, p.152. John Wilson, Deputy Editor of BBC Radio News also highlighted the isolated position of the radio news editor: 'You can often be very lonely as Editor of the Day' (interview with the author, 6 February 1978).
9   Ibid, p.153.

The fact that the journalist and the soldier do not see themselves as kindred spirits, and would probably be surprised to discover that their professions have so much in common, is largely due to the rare occasions when they meet, and the circumstances which surround such a meeting. It is normally associated with some spectacular event which is considered sufficiently newsworthy to attract the attentions of the press. The resulting copy may turn out to be good or bad publicity for the military, but either way it is unlikely to be a dull piece. Therefore there is a tendency for the military to associate the press coverage of military affairs with 'exaggeration', and equally the press tend to associate their visits to the military with 'the spectacular'. Because of limited access, and perhaps lack of interest, very few individuals from either profession have observed the other profession at work for long enough to realise the common characteristics. The significance of this lack of understanding is considered in Part IV.

PART III

PORTRAYAL OF THE MILITARY ON TELEVISION

The military has proved to be an attractive topic for television documentaries and drama. Since watching television is one of the most popular pastimes of modern society, this would appear to be the best medium for keeping the public in touch with the realities of life in today's Armed Forces.

In the following two chapters the author reviews some of the programmes about the military, discusses the relevance of the portrayal of Service life and the military—public relationship, and concludes with the major lessons to be learnt from relevant television documentaries and drama.

7 Television Documentaries: Fact not Fiction

In the past few years there have been a number of television documentaries about institutions to which the general public rarely, if ever, have access. These have included the police, public schools, and the Armed Forces. In the last two years alone there have been *Public School* (1980), *War School* (a *Panorama* four-part documentary about the Army's Staff College, Camberley — 1980), *Fighter Pilot* (1981), and *Police* (1982). It is therefore evident that such documentaries are considered to be worthwhile both by the institution being filmed, and by the BBC. The Forces, in particular, have been the subject of a number of documentaries which have covered the full spectrum of service life: from staff college to fighter pilots, from field marshalls (Desmond Wilcox's interview with Field Marshall Lord Carver in *Top Brass*, 1979) to women in uniform (*Women at Arms*, BBC *Panorama* film, 1979).

In this chapter we shall explore two such documentaries in order to discover more about the relationship between the military and television during the making of these films. This study should provide the answers to a number of questions such as: why are the military considered to be such a suitable topic for TV documentaries? How is the idea for a film conceived? What are the aims of the TV producer? What does such a venture involve both for the TV team and for the military? What is the attitude of the producer or reporter to the military before, during and after filming? What is the result of such a project?

The two documentaries selected for study involved the TV teams spending long periods with the military during filming, thus providing good material for analysis. The films also provide examples of two different types of documentaries: the fifty minute 'special' with commentary and the serialised documentary without commentary. The various aspects of these, and other techniques will be considered in the latter part of the chapter when the discussion will be widened to consider such programmes as *War School, Fighter Pilot* and *Police*. The two documentaries which have been chosen are: *The New Officers* (a *Panorama* special about the training of young officers at Sandhurst) and *Sailor* (the ten-part BBC TV series about life on board *HMS Ark Royal*). These two have been chosen because they represent different television documentary techniques which were employed in the making of two separate films at approximately the same period (1975/76). Subsequent research has shown that the principal lessons which emerged from these two programmes have been substantiated by more recent examples. Therefore *The New Officers* and *Sailor* serve as most suitable vehicles for analysis prior to a general discussion about the problems involved. But first, it is necessary to say a few words of explanation about television documentaries in general.

In the BBC television booklet which provides guidelines for those working in documentary programmes it notes that a documentary is a creative work and points out that this creative responsibility sometimes rests with one individual (the producer), or sometimes it may be shared (i.e. between a producer and a director, or between a producer/director and a writer). The booklet goes on to say that 'when a responsibility is shared, the way it is shared varies from one programme to another . . . But the overall responsibility, combining all aspects of picture and sound, must in the end belong to a final commanding voice, and that is usually the producer'.[1] In practice, much depends upon the relationship between the personalities involved and the format for each documentary stems from that relationship.

The two films which have been selected represent an example of each style of production in that *The New Officers* involved a producer/reporter team, and *Sailor* involved a producer and an executive producer. We shall look at the former through the eyes of the reporter, and at the latter through the eyes of the producer. The BBC booklet also points out that there are many different types of documentary. Again, the two films which have been chosen represent two different formats. In the single programme *The New Officers*, a linking commentary was written and spoken by the reporter and, in addition, he

1   BBC Television Service, *Principles and Practice in Documentary Programmes*, BBC 1972, p.5.

conducted interviews and asked questions on camera. In contrast, no reporter was used for the series *Sailor* but instead the producer employed the 'fly on the wall' technique and allowed the camera to tell the story without a commentary, and the individuals being filmed to speak for themselves.

The New Officers

The original idea to do a television documentary about the training of young officers at the Royal Military Academy (RMA), Sandhurst, came from the then Editor of *Panorama*, Peter Pagnamenta. He had read an article in an American magazine which followed the progress of 'the Class of '75' through the training at West Point, and he thought that a similar approach would result in an interesting documentary about the British equivalent, Sandhurst. He selected David Mills as the producer and Michael Cockerell as the reporter, and the two of them visited Sandhurst in February 1975 after the Ministry of Defence (MOD) and the RMA had agreed to the project.

The genesis of the programme evolved from this visit. Mills and Cockerell knew very little about Sandhurst before they visited the Academy and therefore they listened to the descriptions of the training programme and took in the atmosphere of this unique campus with detached professionalism.[2] Following this visit Mills and Cockerell carried out considerable research about the military and in the process they visited some of the academics who specialise in military studies as well as talking to military officers. As a result of their extensive research the theme of the programme gradually emerged. They decided to look at the relationship between the Army and modern society as seen through the minds of the young officers being trained at Sandhurst. This angle had the added advantage of topicality since the potential influence of the military in British society had been the subject of recent articles in the press.[3]

Filming began at Sandhurst on the basis of good personal relations and the Academy's PRO was appointed as the liaison officer. It had been agreed at the outset that the training programme not only should

2 Cockerell, although new to Sandhurst, was no stranger to the military since he had considerable experience as a war correspondent.
3 There were a number of press articles published in August 1974 which looked at the role of the Army in modern society and considered the feasibility of a military coup in Britain. Amongst these articles were the following: 'Could Britain be heading for a military takeover?', *The Times*, 5 August 1974; 'It would not take a coup to bring British troops on to the streets', *The Times*, 16 August 1974; 'Britain's reluctant Colonels', *The Observer*, 18 August 1974; 'Could we have a military takeover in Britain?', *Daily Express*, 18 August 1974.

not, but could not, be altered to suit the availability of the television team (the syllabus was too intensive to allow such a flexibility). This had a built-in advantage for *Panorama* because it would result in a more natural and realistic film, but it presented a particular problem for the producer and the reporter because they had to select in advance which parts of the syllabus they wanted to film, and so far they had not seen any training at all! Following discussions with the liaison officer and other members of the staff they selected those parts of the training syllabus which they wanted to film during the period April–June 1975. To this timetable was added the interviews with the Commandant, Major General Robert Ford, and with other personalities, such as some of the officer cadets undergoing the training. The intensity of filming depended upon the training programme and varied from two or three sequences being filmed in one day, to a week involving no filming at all.

This suggests that the television team had carefully planned every sequence in advance. This was not the case. The preparation was essential from a logistics point of view, but in effect a documentary film evolves as it progresses and it is powerfully shaped by the sequences which are captured on film. Inevitably some appropriate scenes are not filmed (the opportunity having been missed for some reason), and other shots are considered to be so good that they lead to a new development in the film which had not been thought of in the original concept. Although a good sequence may have been missed on film, however, it need not be lost forever since it can be included in the script during the editorial process. Michael Cockerell pointed out that: 'Current affairs is very much flying by the seat of your pants',[4] and this certainly necessitates flexibility and understanding both from the television team and from the organisation being filmed. The flexibility which is so characteristic of documentary filming may conflict with the military's reliance on a rigid timed programme and it is on these occasions that an understanding of the film-man's approach is particularly valuable: 'Flexibility is so important in documentary filming because we cannot afford to lose what we *know* is a good shot. A good sequence which is happening now, has priority over a future event which *may* be good'.[5] It also needs to be appreciated by the military that most of the film will end on the cutting room floor (12½ hours of the film was edited down to 50 minutes for this particular documentary). Such a ratio of rejection imposes a major responsibility on the producer and reporter to avoid distortion during the editing

4 Interview with the author, 11 December 1978.
5 Michael Cockerell, interview with the author, 5 October 1979.

76

process. It requires considerable skill and integrity to produce a finished product which is a fair reflection of the subject. This is particularly pertinent to interviews.

The evolution of the film was dictated by the television team in a number of ways: by the original idea of looking at the Army and society through the medium of Sandhurst; by the selection of the topics for filming; by the angle of the questions put by Michael Cockerell in the various interviews; and by the linking script dubbed over the finished version. For instance, Michael Cockerell deliberately inserted the following 'voice over' script to dilute the apparently upper-class image created by the filming of the parents of the newly-arrived cadets having tea with the staff:

> Sandhurst still looks like an elegant finishing school for the younger sons of gentlemen, but now instead of a leisurely two year course, officers are turned out in six months flat . . . Most Cadets used to come from public schools and old Army families. Now nearly two-thirds are from State schools.[6]

One of the most usual ways of direct influence is by the questions put by the reporter in a filmed interview. Sometimes they are planned, on other occasions they are spontaneous. Michael Cockerell commented that he will slip in an unexpected question if he thinks it is appropriate: 'it keeps the interview lively — and it can result in a "magic" moment'.[7] This remark illustrates the television journalist's constant striving to produce an interesting programme; if the film is boring, all the effort is pointless because the audience will 'switch off', quite literally. An example of a 'magic' moment occurred in the film which illustrates what Cockerell means by his remark. Early on in the programme he asked an RSM: 'Do you enjoy making it hard and tough for them [the cadets]?' There was a pause, then a broad smile spread across the face of the RSM before he replied: 'Not in the way you ask the question, no!' The smile on the RSM's face transmitted his thoughts to the millions watching the programme far more effectively than words. This was a magic moment created by the unexpected question.

The television journalist's constant search for interesting pictures and dialogue inevitably results in the inclusion of some scenes to which the military may object. This occurred with *The New Officers*. Although the BBC insists on editorial control over documentaries, the MOD had asserted its right at the outset to see a preview of the film before it was transmitted in order to check the factual content and to see whether

6 From *The New Officers*, broadcast on BBC 1, 15 September 1975.
7 Interview with the author, 5 October 1979.

there were any breaches of security. This had been one of the pre-conditions of the BBC being allowed to film at Sandhurst. Accordingly, representatives from both the BBC and the Army met at the BBC studios at Lime Grove to review the film the week before transmission. 'This was the moment of truth because, good as relations were during the making of the film, I got the impression that they still weren't quite sure of us. They seemed to be wary in case we were politically motivated, incompetent or had in some way duped the Army'.[8] A few changes *were* made to the documentary as a result of this meeting which satisfied both parties without encroaching into the editorial control of the BBC.

The film was transmitted as a *Panorama* special on 15 September 1975. It was generally reckoned to be a good documentary[9] which provided a most interesting study of the attitude of young officers to the role of the Army, and at the same time it enabled the public to see how officers of the future were being trained for that role. This extract from a letter by Michael Cockerell to the Director of Public Relations for the Army (DPR(A)) sums up the audience reaction:

Results of the survey by the BBC Audience Research Department:

'. . . the programme had one of the highest audiences for two years and what's called the 'audience appreciation index' was significantly higher than usual.' The following extract comes from a paragraph which was based on a long series of interviews with a representative sample of viewers: 'A glimpse behind the Sandhurst facade to see how an officer is trained in 1975 proved a fascinating and unusual study. Following the recruits' life from the first day, through the difficult training period to the graduation parade, with interviews from both the young men and their senior officers, provided it seems, both an excellent insight into modern methods of the British Army, and also a good idea of the atmosphere of Sandhurst. Hearing what these young men had to say on the role of the Army in modern society was also welcomed, several evidently being relieved to hear that they seemed content to stand aside from all political issues'. The recruits apparently expressed their views clearly, intelligently and 'with conviction', and were found to be most impressive, several reporting viewers indicating that the obvious pride they showed in 'their country' was 'a real tonic': 'I feel proud of our Forces if this is their calibre'.[10]

8 Interview with Michael Cockerell, 11 December 1978.
9 For instance, the programme was well reviewed by *The Daily Telegraph* on 16 September 1975 and Peter Lennon commented in *The Sunday Times* of 21 September 1975 that: 'Michael Cockerell's reporting and Butch Calderwood's camera work made this one of the best Panorama reports for quite a while'.
10 Extract from a letter from Michael Cockerell to DPR(A), 29 October 1975.

If *The New Officers* helped to reassure public faith in the British Army, the subject of the second study not only underlined the special relationship between the British people and the Royal Navy, it helped *HMS Ark Royal* to become the best loved ship since the *Hood*. The wave of nostalgia that followed the BBC series *Sailor*, and the addiction of the public to each episode, was quite unprecedented in BBC documentary history.

Unlike the *Panorama* film on Sandhurst, the idea for a series about an aircraft carrier came not from the editor of a current affairs programme, but from a freelance producer — and it happened quite by chance. At the same time that *Panorama* were completing *The New Officers*, John Purdie was in the process of making a film about the US Ambassador to the United Kingdom. In the summer of 1975 the Ambassador invited Purdie to accompany him on a visit to a NATO exercise in the Mediterranean. During the visit he had the opportunity to go across to the British commando carrier, *HMS Bulwark*. He was immediately impressed by the relaxed, informal attitude on board, which contrasted with the stricter approach on the US ships, and the idea of doing a series about life on board a carrier began to germinate in his mind.

On his return home he went to see the Controller of BBC 1 (Bryan Cowgill) about his idea to do 'a *Warship* for real'.[11] Bryan Cowgill was not quite convinced at first. After all, such a project would have to be a series of several episodes to allow the subject to speak for itself and this would involve the production team spending a long time on board the ship — all of which would involve the BBC in considerable expense. Furthermore carriers had been the subject of documentaries in the past (how could this one be different?) and, even more important, the idea of a serialised documentary had not really been tried before. So there was a natural reticence to embark on a long and costly project about a topic which had already been 'done', using an unfamiliar formula. Nevertheless, he was impressed by Purdie's enthusiasm, by his idea to concentrate on the human aspect of life on board, and by the frank openness of the Royal Navy which had obviously left a deep impression on Purdie as a result of his visit to *Bulwark*. Whether this could be captured on film was another matter; however he decided to back John Purdie's judgement.

That autumn, *HMS Bulwark* returned home and Purdie got permission from MOD to spend a week on board in order to research the

---

11 *Warship* was a BBC drama series based on the life aboard a fictitious frigate, *HMS Hero*.

series. He had already established a good relationship with the Captain and Commander of *Bulwark* and he discussed with them the feasibility of showing all sides of ship life in a television series. Fortified with a number of ideas, and increasingly impressed with the atmosphere on board the ship (especially the camaraderie between the officers and the ratings) he, and his Executive Producer Roger Mills, went to discuss his ideas with the Director of Public Relations for the Royal Navy (DPR(N)), Captain Keith Leppard. He emphasised that he wanted to concentrate on the tradition of the Royal Navy and show that despite the advance of technology the sailor had not really changed much since the days of Drake or Nelson. To do this he would need to have complete access and freedom to film scenes which typified life on board an RN ship. This would include sequences showing, amongst other things, sailors visiting bars and brothels ashore, coming back on board drunk, and being disciplined at the Captain's table. In other words, in order to be authentic the series would have to include 'warts and all'. Purdie convinced Captain Leppard that the risk was worth taking because he felt that the Navy had nothing of which to be ashamed, and by spending three months on board the ship the television team would have sufficient time to present an extremely honest and objective picture of life on an aircraft carrier (in as much as anyone can be totally objective about any subject). Captain Leppard was sympathetic to Purdie's novel approach.[12] However, he took a considerable risk in saying 'yes' because no other establishment organisation had previously agreed to *carte blanche* filming by the BBC. 'This was something of a break-through in television since it enabled me to make the first film which truly reflected life on board an aircraft carrier.'[13]

This decision was the key to the success of the series, but it was followed by a bombshell. *Bulwark* was not available for filming after all. *Hermes* was offered instead but this was declined for, amongst other reasons, its forthcoming programme took her into the North Atlantic and this raised the practical problem of a very few daylight hours in which to film during the winter. The indecision about a suitable ship had now gone on for three months and this was a very frustrating period for Purdie (a freelance producer with no work), and costly for the BBC. The indecision nearly lost the series. Then DPR(N) proposed *Ark Royal*.

John Purdie accepted the offer almost as a last resort since *Ark Royal* had been filmed a number of times in the past. Reluctantly he

12 As a matter of pure coincidence, Captain Leppard had written to the BBC early in 1975 suggesting a documentary on the life on board an aircraft carrier revolving around the professional and social life of the Fleet Air Arm officers of the embarked squadrons.
13 Interview with John Purdie, 5 December 1978.

went down to see the ship in Plymouth at the end of January 1976 at the request of the Captain, Wilfred Graham. The meeting was a success. Purdie and Graham liked each other, and the Captain's confidence was shared by his Commander, David Cowling. On the basis of this initial mutual trust it was agreed that the television team would sail with the ship on 3 February, and stay on board for the visit to Gibraltar, the crossing of the Atlantic to the States, and the visit to Florida. Nothing was discussed in detail at the meeting but both sides understood that the television series would probably consist of a maximum of six half-hour episodes. John Purdie said that the television team would consist of himself and three others (cameraman, sound man, and assistant cameraman).

When the team joined the ship, Graham and Purdie had a meeting at which the ground rules were established. The Captain confirmed that the television team could have the run of the ship; he would let Purdie know if there was anything which they filmed that was likely to be classified, but otherwise there were no restrictions. In return he said that he would not have anything 'staged' for the cameras and they both agreed that no member of the ship's company would be filmed who did not want to be. Although Captain Graham had not realised initially that the film would focus on 'the sailor' it soon became obvious that filming would include 'warts and all'. Within the first 24 hours of *Ark Royal* leaving her home port the television crew had filmed the sailors' last night in the bars of Plymouth, the drunks staggering back on board in the early hours, the drama on the bridge when one of the engines failed as the ship left harbour, and the administering of naval justice following the final night's 'run ashore' in Plymouth. Having agreed to complete access there was nothing the Captain or Commander could do but put their trust in John Purdie's judgement. They both agreed that complete honesty was the best policy especially in matters which could be considered to be typical of naval life as a whole. After all, this was what the series was attempting to capture for the first time. They were confident that in major matters there was nothing to hide. Mutual trust was the key to the whole relationship, and it paid off handsomely for both parties: 'The Royal Navy's co-operation was totally unprecedented in my experience. The Captain, the Commander and I all realised that the Royal Navy had nothing to hide and therefore an open policy was the best solution. I used my own judgement and applied my own censorship on occasions'.[14]

During their three months on board, the television team became very much part of the ship's company.[15] They lived in the wardroom but

14 Interview with John Purdie, 5 December 1978.
15 In an interview with the author on 1 March 1979, Captain Wilfred Graham said: 'they just became part of the ship's company'.

they also spent as much time with the chief petty officers, petty officers and ratings as with the officers and they were soon being welcomed in all messes and messdecks. For his part John Purdie got into the habit of seeing the Captain each evening to give him a progress report of the day's filming; this was a courtesy but was not in any way obligatory. The producer developed the story about life on board by looking for self-contained stories each day. This approach enabled the team to film sequences without interrupting the ship's routine:

> the cameras just filmed life going on — they did not intrude and we soon got used to it. . . . The TV team was almost unobtrusive, all you require is a microphone clipped behind your tie, torch batteries in your pocket, and the camera crew. No arc lights or clapper board; they just film what happens.[16]

The integration of the TV crew into the ship's company and the unobtrusiveness of the camera resulted in some impressive film. The 'rushes' were sent back to the BBC Television Centre periodically for developing where they were then viewed by Roger Mills and Nigel Pope, Organiser Documentary Programmes. They realised that John Purdie had really captured the atmosphere of the ship and consequently kept the Controller and the Head of Documentaries abreast of developments, as well as informing John Purdie about the standard of film during their infrequent telephone calls. It was about half way through their time on board, when the results of the first 'rushes' had been viewed and telephoned to Purdie, that both the television team and the ship's company began to realise that the film was going to be different!

In April, Purdie and his team left the ship in Florida and flew back to the United Kingdom for an immediate start on preparing the first episode. This was a hectic period for Purdie because there was considerable pressure from the Controller to see some evidence of the project which represented a considerable investment in terms of money and programme schedules. The Controller and the Head of Documentaries viewed the first episode at the end of May and they were very impressed. Bryan Cowgill immediately decided that the series should be expanded from six to a maximum of ten episodes and that it should end with *Ark Royal* returning home to Plymouth. He also agreed that it was suitable for the peak viewing time at 9.25 pm after the news.

Having flown back to join the ship to film the homecoming, Purdie then arranged for DPR(N) to see the first episode (which included the last night's 'run ashore' in Plymouth and the sequence on the bridge when the engines failed as the ship left harbour). After viewing the film,

---

16 Interview with Captain Wilfred Graham, 1 March 1979.

Captain Leppard remarked: 'I know we agreed to warts and all — but this is *all* warts!' At a special private viewing at the invitation of Richard Cawston, Head of BBC Documentaries, DPR(N) was concerned that this first episode might create the wrong impression of the Royal Navy at the outset, and he tried to persuade the *Sailor* team to take out some of the warts or to start with another episode. Purdie replied that the series was structured chronologically and pointed out that although a poor impression of the Navy might be created from minor incidents (such as bar scenes and broken down equipment), the Service would gain considerable kudos from the more important occurrences such as the remarkable rescue by helicopter of an American sailor from a nuclear submarine. On balance the film would provide a fair picture of life onboard the *Ark*. The discussions and constant liaison between Keith Leppard and John Purdie during the weeks each episode was being made,[17] was a result of the original agreement between the BBC and the Royal Navy which was similar to that associated with *The New Officers*, namely the BBC agreed to the Royal Navy viewing each episode before transmission in order to check it for any breaches of security, but the BBC insisted, at all times, in retaining editorial control. There *were* disagreements, not only between the BBC and the RN, but also between the hierarchy of the BBC and John Purdie (specifically on the question of the suitability of the 'language' for television). His reply to his critics was: 'we must go into this whole-heartedly, warts and all, otherwise it will be worse than a PR exercise — it will be dishonest'.[18]

Sailor has since become renowned as the first time 'warts and all' television documentary and subsequently other professions which have become the subject of similar documentaries have acknowledged the need for such an approach. Mr Peter Imbert, the Chief Constable of Thames Valley Police, when he agreed to allow the BBC to make the documentary *Police* realised that '. . . during such a long series there were bound to be some warts and blemishes'.[19] But when he made that decision he could not have realised the controversy that was to surround the 'rape' episode (episode 3 was centred around the grilling of a woman by three detectives after she had made a complaint to the police about being raped). Nevertheless in a television discussion programme[20] at the end of the series he said that he was glad that they had let the cameras in and he was delighted in the increased confidence of the public in the police. Just like John Purdie and Captain Keith Leppard before him, he had come to the conclusion that it was the overall

---

17 The BBC were making approximately one episode every two weeks.
18 Interview with John Purdie, 5 December 1978.
19 *The Daily Telegraph*, 4 January 1982.
20 *Police — Impact and Implications*, BBC 1, 22 March 1982.

impression of the series that mattered, not the odd wart. However, it was necessary to show the warts in order to establish credibility.

The first episode of *Sailor* was shown on BBC 1 at 9.25 pm on Thursday, 5 August 1976. It attracted an audience of 5 million which was considered by the BBC to be quite a good viewing figure for a documentary. By the third episode the figure had risen to 6 million and the impact of this prize winning episode about the rescue led to a steady rise in viewing figures each week up to a maximum of 10 million. The public had become addicted to the series. These excellent viewing figures were repeated when the entire series was shown again two years later on Saturday evenings in the *Match of the Day* slot. The most popular episode was part 4 which attracted a viewing figure of 8 million and the second series produced 'exceptional figures for a repeat series'.[21] The details of the viewing figures are shown in table 7.1.

Table 7.1
BBC viewing figures for *Sailor*

Episode	First series (First episode broadcast at 9.25 pm on Thur. 5 August 1976) Viewing figure	Second series (First episode broadcast at 10.50 pm on Sat. 17 June 1978) Viewing figure
1	5 million	5 million
2	4 million	4 million
3*	6 million	6½ million*
4	7 million	8 million
5	7½ million	7 million
6	9 million	4 million
7	9½ million	6 million
8	10 million	6 million
9	9½ million	4½ million
10	9½ million	2½ million†

*Episode 3 was the prize winning episode about the rescue of an American sailor from the nuclear submarine.
†August Bank Holiday weekend.

The series attracted good press reviews right from the start and some of those television critics who had seen previews of future episodes recommended the programme to their readers; others were unconvinced that the series would sustain sufficient interest for ten weeks

21 Interview with Nigel Pope, Organiser Documentary Programmes, 5 December 1978.

and some doubted the wisdom of the Navy providing full co-operation. By the end of the series, however, there was universal praise for the programme:

> *Sailor* last night completed its very successful and often totally engrossing series. . . there can be little of life aboard a large warship which is not now fully familiar to viewers.
>
> (The Daily Telegraph, 8 October 1976)

> It was the original concept, its fulfilment by the crew, and the editing which made *Sailor* so endlessly watchable and in retrospect so valuable . . . we certainly did get a clear notion of what life is like on *Ark Royal*.
>
> (The Financial Times, 13 October 1976)

The success of the series had other spin-offs as well: follow up press articles, continual interest in *Ark Royal* until she eventually returned to Devonport in December 1978 having completed her last voyage, and even the signature tune ('Sailing' by Rod Stewart) reappeared in the pop charts. All this publicity, together with the running of the repeat series by the BBC, kept the Royal Navy in the public eye for a long time. But it was not only the Navy who benefited from the programme; so did the BBC. *Sailor* won three television awards in 1976: the British Academy of Film and Television Arts awards for both the best TV documentary series and for the best single documentary (episode 3), and the Royal Television Society Award for documentaries. Three awards for one programme was a very fine achievement indeed.

Sailor achieved something which is rare in the history of television documentaries: it was well received by everyone; the public, the critics, the Royal Navy and the BBC. It justified the mutual trust that John Purdie and Captain Wilfred Graham established with each other; and the integrity of the producer and the honesty of the Royal Navy stamped their individual marks on each episode. Nevertheless, it was a considerable risk for the Royal Navy to allow the BBC such free access, and everyone involved in this decision must take full credit for it, including the whole Admiralty Board. The series allowed the public to see what life on board an HM Ship was really like, and in the process showed that 'the Navy had a human face'.[22]

---

22 Interview with Captain Wilfred Graham, 1 March 1979.

The lessons

Both *The New Officers* and *Sailor* gave an accurate impression about life in today's Armed Forces and they were successful ventures in that the BBC were satisfied with the viewing figures and the audience reaction, the military were happy with the way they had been portrayed to a mass audience, and the public were educated about the Services. These two productions also share some common factors which indicate the key to their success.

The first point concerns the thorough preparation involved in order to produce a satisfactory film. The film crews spent five months filming at Sandhurst, and over three months at sea on board *Ark Royal*. During this period Cockerell and Purdie got to know their particular subject extremely well, and they became very involved with it. Cockerell remarked that: 'for six months it was my life. I got involved with Sandhurst and the way officers were trained, although I think I retained a professional detachment as a reporter'.[23] As we have already seen, Purdie became accepted as part of the ship's company, but he too retained an essential detachment. They were both personally committed to their programmes and this commitment came across on their respective films. What is also interesting is that both of them had very little specific knowledge of their subjects before they started on their projects and therefore, initially, they represented the average man's view of the Services. However, as they came to know more about the military way of life during the process of making their films, so they developed a definite impression of the military. Cockerell felt that the officer-recruiting emphasis was being shifted away from the public schools and considered that the training was more academic and professional than he had first expected. Purdie quickly developed a very sympathetic attitude towards the Royal Navy and, like Cockerell, he highlighted the courtesy and friendly co-operation of the Forces: 'My strongest feeling was that everyone from the Captain to the lowest rank, was a gentleman in their behaviour towards us'.[24] In both cases, their attitudes were transmitted in their films. The other benefit to derive from their close association with the Forces is that these two communicators now have an intimate knowledge which is shared by very few of their fellow professionals, and by virtually none of the general public. As a consequence John Purdie has often found himself defending the Navy against accusations based on ignorance, and Michael Cockerell (with Francis Gerard) the Army, having made the *Panorama* documentary on The Staff College, Camberley.

23 Interview with the author, 5 October 1979.
24 Interview with the author, 5 December 1978.

Documentaries are essentially about people and in making such a film the importance of establishing good personal relations is vital. This happened in both these cases, and the result was a good working relationship between the television team and the military. On the other hand, if the human chemistry does not work at the beginning then it is probable that there will be discord later on, in which case it is better not to go ahead with the project at all.[25] Once a personal relationship has been established, the next fundamental point is the building of a mutual trust. There will inevitably be some misgivings at first, and there will be disagreements about the finished product, but these two documentaries have amply demonstrated that full co-operation with a television company can result in an excellent programme. Provided the military and television are honest with each other there will be the basis for the trust which is so essential to such a project. For at the end of the day the military *have* to put their faith in the judgement and integrity of the professional communicator. And yet this is really not the risk that it appears to the military because the Services have nothing to be ashamed of. On the contrary, most service-men regard their way of life with approval and pride; and documentaries which have been thoroughly prepared, involving television teams spending long periods with their subject, will inevitably reflect reality. As John Purdie pointed out: 'the Services sell themselves — and anyway, I would have been out on my ear if I had made a biased film'.[26]

In contrast, where mutual trust has not been established, and co-operation has been less than full, this too has been reflected in the film. A case in point is *Women at Arms* (a three part documentary about the role of women in the armed forces of Britain, the United States and Israel which was transmitted in March and April 1979). Although the documentary gave an accurate portrayal of the subject, it lacked the depth of sustained understanding developed in the other two BBC productions. The contrast between the impressions created by the United States and Israeli Forces on one hand and the British Services on the other, was a direct reflection of the amount of co-operation offered by each nation. It was also evident from the film that the WRNS and the WRAF had co-operated more than the WRAC.

The genesis for *The New Officers* and *Sailor* lay in the communi-cators' interest in a way of life about which they and the general public knew very little. The Armed Forces were themselves attracted by the idea of a documentary because it seemed a good way of bridging that same gap of ignorance and educating the public about life in the

25 John Purdie told the author of one ship he visited where the atmosphere was such that he decided not to pursue the matter any further.
26 Interview with the author, 5 December 1978.

modern Forces. These two documentaries, both of which reflected highly on the Services, have demonstrated the immense benefit which can be derived from whole-hearted co-operation with professionals who know their craft. The key personalities in the Services were sufficiently confident in the military way of life that they were prepared to put their trust in the integrity of the producer and the reporter and allow them uninhibited access. The warts and all stories which resulted demonstrated to the public that these films were not just a public relations exercise and therefore they were accepted as being true to life.

The success of these two documentaries has since been exploited by both the military and the BBC. As we have already seen, Michael Cockerell has since made the first documentary about the Staff College, Camberley, which included the first television interview with Major General Sir Frank Kitson.[27] Although the Staff College were initially wary of television cameras being allowed to film this élite course (only the top 25 per cent of Army officers, all in their early thirties, are accepted into Camberley), subsequent reaction from the public and critics have shown that this was a most rewarding enterprise. The programmes were watched by 15 million people, the majority of whom were not only fascinated by being allowed to see behind the scenes of a profession about which they previously knew little, but they were also impressed with the dedication and competence of those officers who contributed to the programme. They were also reassured by the professional way in which the Army prepared its officers for a future war.

This reassurance in the military was subsequently justified when the Forces were called upon to prosecute an extremely difficult military operation over 8,000 miles away in the Falkland Islands. Confidence in the military was extremely important to the success of that operation and television documentaries such as *War School* and *Sailor* were significant in that they had contributed to that public confidence prior to 1982.

War School also helped to destroy the popular myth of the stereotype Army officer. As Richard Last noted in *The Daily Telegraph*:

> *War School* almost effortlessly contradicted this view. The budding staff officers emerged quite clearly not as corporate War House-fodder but individuals — distinct in personality, temperament, outlook and (contrary to popular myth) in class background. Army officers, at any rate, the ones who get to Camberley, don't even cut their hair particularly short any more.[28]

27 Sir Frank Kitson has since been promoted to General.
28 *The Daily Telegraph*, 31 January 1980.

The impression created by *War School* was a direct reflection of the length of time Michael Cockerell and Francis Gerard (the director) spent in filming at Camberley (six months) and also the impact which the Staff College left on them. Michael Cockerell was impressed with what he saw and found the students to be much brighter and more alert than he had originally expected. He also felt that the selection process of army officers, and selection for staff college, produced a type who are different from the rest of society and cultivated that difference: 'the gap between the military and society has apparently narrowed — but not disappeared'.[29]

It has been argued by critics of television documentaries that no documentary can fully portray its subject and that so much depends upon the integrity of the film-maker in what he decides to leave on the cutting-room floor during the editing process. These critics are supported in this view by those members of the profession who are the subject of the documentary, be they soldiers, policemen or school masters. Indeed, a number of military officers complained to the author about the image which was portrayed of Army officers in *War School*, and there was a similar reaction from policemen about *Police*. But the results do not support the criticism and they underline a fundamental fact about such documentaries: they make particularly interesting television because they allow the public to glimpse the life of closed societies. The public are unaware of the intricate details of the relevant profession and are only concerned with the overall impression which they obtain from the film. *Sailor, War School, Fighter Pilot* and *Police* have all been successful documentaries which have educated and entertained the public about the Services and the police. These documentaries have vindicated the authorities who agreed to allow the cameras in and also underlined the integrity of the film-makers. It is extremely difficult for members of a close-knit, élite society to be objective about their profession and therefore to visualise the impact of such a programme on the general public.

This latter point emerged from *Fighter Pilot* (Colin Strong's eight-part BBC television documentary about the training of RAF fighter pilots). He found his film being criticised by RAF officers who remarked that their portrayal on film was not realistic. 'We are not like that really' to which his response was: 'You are the last ones to know what you are really like'.[30] Colin Strong spent three years with the RAF making his film about the young men who were selected on 21 May 1978 at Biggin Hill for fast jet pilot training, in the course of which he shot 600 reels of film. This was a massive undertaking. Even

29 Interview with the author, 16 March 1982.
30 Interview with the author, 22 February 1982.

more daunting was the task of editing these reels to the 16 which he actually required for the eight episodes. (This equates to less than three per cent of the total film which was shot.) Strong was criticised by some (including correspondence in the Royal Air Force *News*) about concentrating on the failures on the course and for lack of balance (in that an insufficient amount of the film was allocated to the flying aspects of training). In his response, the producer pointed out that he did not select the course chosen to be the subject of the film, and once he was committed to it he could not 'adjust' the candidates — 'this would have resulted in a distorted version of events'.[31] He also pointed out that he thought it necessary to bring out the essential human element of the training process.

In this last remark lies the fundamental misunderstanding between the RAF and the producer. At the time that the RAF agreed to co-operate with the BBC over the making of the film they were finding it difficult to attract young men of the right calibre in sufficient numbers to train as pilots. They believed that a series about pilot training would be very good public relations for the RAF and expected that a substantial amount of the film would include flying shots which would provide a good incentive for would-be pilots of the right calibre. But they overlooked the fact that documentaries are fundamentally about people. People are interesting, and a focus on individuals helps to give the film a reference point. *Fighter Pilot* was fundamentally about trainees going through the flying selection process.

This focus on people is an obvious one which has been used by all the documentaries mentioned in this chapter. It is the point which is likely to arouse the most controversy. For example, there was considerable controversy about the episode in *Police* about the man who was the object of a siege operation by armed police who surrounded his cottage in the belief that he was armed with a rifle. However, the human aspect of documentaries is often overlooked by institutions which agree to having their activities filmed in great detail. They should be aware that this is an essential ingredient for such films.

Despite criticism from some circles, *Fighter Pilot* was a successful series. Colin Strong was awarded the 1981 British Academy Awards Certificate for the Best Factual TV Series; it was popular with the public; and there are indications that a higher standard of applicant may be applying to join the RAF as prospective fighter pilots, partly because some have realised from the series that only the best will succeed. Perhaps the most appropriate comment about *Fighter Pilot* came from Air Marshall Sir John Rogers, AOC, RAF Training, who was

---

31 Royal Air Force *News*, 13—26 January 1982.

quoted in the *Observer* as saying: 'A civilian friend told me he thought it did the RAF good, showing that it gets responsible people. It proved that if a low-flying Jaguar nearly takes off your chimney-pot, at least it won't be some school boy at the controls'.[32]

It is evident from the detailed study of *New Officers* and *Sailor* and also from consideration of other documentaries, that such programmes are important in bridging the gap between a particular institution and the public. Be it the Armed Forces, or the police, there is a need for such institutions to be able to have their attitudes and the way they carry out their professional duties explained to the tax-payer. The best medium for conveying this message is television. Such an enterprise cannot be taken at all without the full co-operation of the institution involved and yet they have no right of veto over what the television company chooses to include in the final version of the film. That having been said, in reality, experience has shown that both parties are usually prepared to compromise on areas of potential disagreement in order to achieve a mutually beneficial aim.

There is a clear requirement for the institutions to be fully aware of the realities of making television documentaries such as: the importance of the human interest; the vast amount of film footage which will not be used; the reliance on the integrity of the film-makers; and the realisation that professionals in television documentaries are better judges of what the public want than they are. There is also clear evidence that such documentaries are worth all the considerable effort which such an undertaking requires.

As far as the military is concerned, all the documentaries about the Services have helped to update the public's knowledge about the Armed Forces and, in so doing, have helped to correct some misconceptions and to destroy some myths. As for the BBC, the films were certainly popular and achieved success in the ratings; but the greatest prize was the link established between the military and the British people.

32 *The Observer*, 24 January 1982.

8 Television Drama: Fiction

'If the nation itself is generally bored by defence you cannot blame the television people for not doing anything about it. They have to please their audience . . . I sometimes think that what we need is a Service version of *Z Cars* or *Power Game* . . .'[1] Correlli Barnett spoke these words at a seminar on *Defence and the Mass Media* held at the Royal United Service Institution (RUSI) in 1970. Since then, there have been a number of single plays and drama series on television about the military including *Warship, Spearhead* and *Danger UXB*. The choice of the military as a suitable topic for documentaries has been equalled by the development in drama. In the view of these developments it is now possible to analyse some of these productions in an attempt to discover the relevance of the portrayal of the modern military in television drama.

But first of all we need to get some idea of the impact of TV drama on British society, and consider its influence on our culture. There is a predominant demand for plays and drama in television.[2] In a lecture at Broadcasting House in January 1976 Howard Newby (Managing Director of BBC Radio) remarked 'The BBC is the biggest single market for the writer in Great Britain. In television there are between 70 and

---

1 *Defence and the Mass Media*, report of a seminar held at the RUSI on 13 October 1970, p.3.
2 (a) Dennis McQuail, *Towards a Sociology of Mass Communications*, Cassell & Collier Macmillan, London 1969, p.41; (b) BBC, *The Public and the Programmes*, Audience Research Department BBC, 1959; (c) G. Steiner, *The People Look at Television*, Alfred Knopf, New York 1963.

80 new plays a year. On top of that, something like 200 episodes are specially written drama series and serials . . . in television there are about 20 plays a year by writers who haven't written for television before, and this is not counting the scripts by new writers for series and serials . . . there is nothing like this elsewhere and it is one of the reasons why BBC television and radio drama is exported to all parts of the world'.[3] Drama also predominates on commercial television and during 1976—77 plays, drama and TV movies accounted for 25 per cent of an average week's schedule.[4] Graham Murdoch has noted 'that for large numbers of people, watching television drama has become an habitual experience occupying several hours a day, week in week out'.[5] He goes on to say that television has become increasingly the central means for transmitting traditional forms of drama and introducing new modes to a mass audience.[6] Katz also believes that dramatists may have more influence than was originally thought: '. . . research has tended to look on broadcasting as an agent of information, not entertainment. It may be, as many people are saying nowadays, that the power of television to affect values resides in Light Entertainment and Drama more than in Current Affairs'.[7] Howard Newby certainly believes that dramatists influence our values.[8] If dramatists do have such influence they are unrestrained by the need to respect objectivity, balance and impartiality as are their colleagues in news and current affairs.[9] Sir Michael Swann has highlighted the genuine problem this presents for the BBC when broadcasting modern drama:

Many of the able playwrights of today do not write in sympathy with the assumptions on which society is based; on the contrary, they stray, sometimes a long way, from those assumptions, and any sympathy with them. This is not our fault; and if those who dislike this phenomenon object, and it is perfectly reasonable that they should, then they can readily put the situation to rights, by writing plays that are as good or better.[10]

3 Howard Newby, *Radio, Television and the Arts*, lunch-time lecture at Broadcasting House, 15 January 1976; BBC 1976, p.12.
4 *Television and Radio 1978*, IBA Guide to Independent Television and Independent Local Radio; IBA 1978, p.10. ITV companies produce an average of ten hours of drama from their own studios (IBA 1978) p.45.
5 Graham Murdoch, *Fabricating Fiction: Approaches to the Study of Television Drama Production* (lecture given at the precedings of the Prix Italia Symposium at Bologna in 1976) p.1. Later published in *Organisation and Creativity in Television*, Editizioni RAI, Turin, 1977) pp. 181—98 (English version).
6 Ibid., p.1.
7 Elihu Katz, *Social Research on Broadcasting: Proposals for Further Development*, BBC 1977, p.72.
8 Howard Newby, op.cit., p.11.
9 Graham Murdoch, op.cit., p.6.
10 Sir Michael Swann, *Society in Rough Water*, University of Leicester Convocation Lecture, 6 May 1975; BBC 1975, p.20.

Although the dramatist *does* have considerable freedom in what he writes about modern society (and so he should), both the BBC and ITV retain the right to decide in what form the play should be broadcast. This decision is greatly influenced by the ratings and as a result 'generally speaking, commitment to experiment and the idea of drama engagé is more likely in the context of single play production. This is scarcely surprising . . . serials and series are in the front line of the ratings' battle and consequently there is an understandable reluctance to risk losing or alienating existing audiences by tinkering with the shows' familiar elements'.[11] Ratings also influence the script of various modern day plays and series to the extent that realism may be 'adjusted' to fit a formula which is known to be successful.[12] However, this is usually only an acceptable adjustment under the guise of dramatic licence because 'the more "realistic" a programme is thought to be, the more trusted, enjoyable — and therefore the more popular — it becomes'.[13]

It is evident from all this that drama *can* have an influence on opinions, that realism makes modern plays more credible to the public, that playwrights jealously guard their individualism, and that controversy is much more likely to occur in a single play than in a series. It also follows from the high demand for drama that there is an element of supply and demand, and therefore both BBC and ITV will stay with proven success (hence the endurance of *Coronation Street* and the tendency to commission another series of a popular programme), and they will be constantly on the look out for new ideas which have the potential to develop into a popular series. Ratings are also very important to the TV professionals — the writers, producers and directors — because the building of their reputations depends upon them.

Warship

It was the Royal Navy which first came up with the idea of a Service drama. In the same year that Correlli Barnett made his appeal for the Services' version of *Z Cars* a Lieutenant Commander serving at MOD

---

11 Graham Murdoch, op.cit., p.9.
12 John Elliott, writing about *Mogul*, the BBC TV series about the oil business, noted that to increase audience appeal, the wife of one of the characters 'was incarnated as a slim, sexy blonde . . . the wife in the original format — middle-aged, ordinary and worried by her three children — never appeared on the screen. Realism had taken another knock. It all helped the ratings though'. Quoted in Murdoch, op.cit., p.17.
13 John Fiske and John Hartley, *Reading Television*, Methuen, London 1978, p.160.

saw the possibility of making a television series about the Royal Navy. Ian Mackintosh had already had two fiction books published in 1967 and therefore when he discussed his idea with his Appointer, it was agreed that he would be given the time to write such a series provided the idea was approved.[14] The proposal was submitted in May 1971 and it received support from the Vice-Chief of the Naval Staff (VCNS) and from DPR(N). However, it took a long time to convince both the Royal Navy and the BBC that the project was feasible so it was not until October 1972 that Mackintosh was seconded to the BBC (whilst still a serving naval officer) as writer and script editor for *Warship*.

From the beginning he insisted on documentary accuracy with the BBC and editorial freedom from the Royal Navy by claiming that anything used in the series either had happened, or could have happened. He received very good support from the Navy — a frigate was allocated to represent *HMS Hero*, and aircraft and other naval facilities were made available — but in particular, he appreciated the courage shown by both VCNS and CINCFLEET in supporting his venture by approving the provision of all these facilities and yet allowing him complete editorial control: 'This reflected the arrogance and the courage of the Royal Navy, born from years of independent command at sea without referring decisions upwards, and secure in the belief that the Royal Navy was a good organisation which would sell itself and had nothing to hide'.[15]

Authenticity was the key to the series and Ian Mackintosh personally briefed the actors about life and customs in the Navy so that they would behave appropriately when in uniform. This enabled them to grow into their characterisations and act realistically. They soon became very much part of the Navy when working alongside officers and ratings either at sea or in the dockyard. Authenticity was also important as far as the scripts were concerned. Whilst still insisting on editorial control he sent copies of each script to DPR(N) and the Captain and Liaison Officer of whichever frigate was representing *HMS Hero*. The scripts were naturally circulated to the wardroom, and to the Chiefs and Petty Officers' Mess, and this resulted in a feedback of criticism about anything which was considered to be unauthentic. In this way the Royal Navy played a much larger part in the formulation of the series than they probably realised. This, and Mackintosh's insistence on documentary accuracy, resulted in an accurate drama

14 In the Royal Navy there is an Appointer for each branch of the Service, who is responsible for the career management of the officers in that branch, and for posting them to their various appointments.
15 Ian Mackintosh interview with the author, 7 November 1978.

series about life in the modern Navy. For instance, in one episode which involved a ship's doctor doing an emergency operation at sea, a medical officer not only vetted the script but was made available to advise the actors during the filming of that particular sequence.

The first series commenced in the autumn of 1973 and ran for the normal 13 episodes. It was a success with the public and the viewing figures averaged between 12–14 million. The BBC received a number of letters from the public and the phrases that were typical of many were:

> It's good to see a film about the Royal Navy as opposed to the US Navy.
>
> How good to see clean cut young men with short hair doing a good job.
>
> How refreshing to see people standing up for, and believing in, old fashioned principles.
>
> We can watch this programme with the children.[16]

Warship proved to be so popular with the public that not only was a new series commissioned for 1974, but the programme ran for a further two years. However, the extension of the series created problems because after the first two years it was proving difficult to write good scripts based on the original format. It was at this stage that Joe Waters was brought in as the producer in succession to Anthony Coburn. He had been producing *Dixon* (of Dock Green) for the previous eight years and had successfully changed its image to cope with the competition from *Z Cars* and *Softly Softly*. His appointment was an interesting choice because he did not particularly like the series nor did he know anything about the Navy. Ian Mackintosh was retained as the technical adviser.

Waters joined the series in 1975 and remained as producer of *Warship* until the programme ended in 1977. During these last two series he changed the format and used the Navy more as a backcloth for the development of new characters. He insisted on the usual conditions of editorial control and made it clear that he was not interested in a public relations exercise for the Royal Navy, and stressed that he was primarily an entertainer.[17] He was therefore somewhat surprised to find that far from attempting to interfere with his editorial control all the Royal Navy requested was that they read the scripts. Once he started filming on board ship he was in for some more surprises. Conditioned about the Royal Navy by war films he was amazed at the

16 Ian Mackintosh interview with the author, 7 November 1978.
17 Interview with the author, 7 December 1978.

democratic society of the modern Navy and the easy relationship between officers and men. Although each ship's captain with whom he worked was wary at first, he still received full co-operation from everyone on board the four frigates in which they filmed, and the film crew were overwhelmed by this attitude. For his part, Joe Waters was most impressed by his two years' experience working with the Navy and the discovery of what life was really like on board a frigate inevitably came across in the series. He also paid tribute to the assistance he received: 'The co-operation from the Royal Navy was beyond description – all the way down the line'.[18]

What conclusions can we draw from *Warship*? Well, it was evidently a popular series with the public (which was reflected in the TV ratings), and as a result it ran for four years. It was therefore popular with the BBC because it contained a successful formula which attracted large audiences. It was also popular with the Royal Navy because for four years the public saw a dramatised version of life on board a modern frigate. This kept the Navy in the forefront of the public eye at a time when the general public were extremely ignorant about life in the Service. Both Waters and Mackintosh testified to the fact that a number of letters which they received from the public demonstrated that many people's impressions of the Navy were at least 25 years out of date (fostered on World War II films). Furthermore the letters from ex-RN servicemen criticising small details and complaining that 'it could never happen in the Navy' showed that they themselves were out of touch with the modern Navy (and presumably, they had been giving the wrong impression to their civilian friends over the years).

Therefore, allowing for dramatic licence, the modern Navy was being portrayed for the first time on the television screen for a sustained period. The extraordinary co-operation of the Royal Navy which provided the basis for good personal relations, and the insistence on authenticity, resulted in a realistic portrayal of life on board a frigate. The foresight of the Admirals in 1971 had been fully rewarded.

Spearhead

Although the Royal Navy had provided full co-operation for *Warship*, the series was not well received by everyone in the Navy and a number of minor details were criticised for being unauthentic or inaccurate (the same applied, certainly in the early stages, to the attitude of policemen to *Dixon, Z Cars* and *Softly, Softly*). But whatever the attitude was in

18 Ibid.

the Navy, the other Services were quick to realise that *Warship* had added a new dimension to the whole concept of public relations. It had demonstrated that a drama series could educate a mass audience in their own homes about life in the forces, as well as entertain them, in a way which was not possible in any other medium. It was therefore not surprising that in July 1975 the Army agreed to Southern Television's proposal to make a drama series based on an infantry battalion.

As with *Warship*, the television company received full co-operation from the Army over the making of *Spearhead*. A meeting was held between Southern Television and the Army in January 1976 which the author, Nick McCarty, attended. One week later he spent four days with a battalion in Northern Ireland and he subsequently visited a battalion in BAOR. The Army provided liaison officers throughout the making of the two series during the period 1976–79, members of DPRS were made available for advice as required by Southern, and a number of military facilities were used during filming, including men, equipment and training areas.

Nick McCarty was not particularly enamoured with the Army and his scripts reflected this in their objectivity. The result was the inclusion of a number of issues which could be considered as sensitive such as absenteeism, racialism, the boredom and isolation of life as a soldier's wife in BAOR, thieving in the barrack-room, and realistic portrayal of active service in Ulster. Indeed, the Northern Ireland portrayal was so realistic that Ulster Television decided not to broadcast episode four of the first series (which was about Northern Ireland) because it was due to be screened on 8 August 1978, the anniversary of the introduction of internment. Inevitably there were a number of frank discussions between Brigadier Martin Farndale DPR(A), Nick McCarty and James Omerod (the producer), but both McCarty and Omerod were most impressed by the co-operation they received from Brigadier Farndale and from the general attitude of the military: 'The British Army allowed itself to be looked at in a way that no other establishment organisation would have permitted'. *Spearhead* clearly illustrated the different requirements of the military and the dramatist. The Army wanted itself to be portrayed as a modern, highly trained and efficient organisation. The dramatists wanted to look at the Army in dramatic terms. They wanted to explore what happened to an individual when he put on uniform, they needed to develop the identity of the characters and then use those characters to become the 'carriers' for an idea; and they used a single incident as a vehicle for generalisation. The close co-operation between the Army and the dramatists ensured that the drama was based on realism and this resulted in considerable authenticity, particularly in the second series.

What has been the result of *Spearhead*? It was a popular series with the public and it received much critical acclaim.[19] Indeed at the beginning of the second series the television critic of *The Daily Telegraph* noted:

> On its second tour of duty *Spearhead* could be more than a highly successful drama series. It could represent the frontal assault of a second division ITV Company, Southern seeking promotion in the League . . . On the purely dramatic level *Spearhead* seems to be quite a breakthrough in popular television . . . It has done for the Army what Rumpole is doing for lawyers and *All Creatures* did for vets — giving a favourable fictional image without departing too far from documentary truth. Within the confines of a series format it appears to pack a great deal of authenticity. . .[20]

Despite these encouraging words, however, the third series (which was set in Hong Kong) did not live up to expectations. It is difficult to be specific about the reasons for this and, indeed, the formula which had been so successful in the first two series was used again, but somehow the Hong Kong episodes lacked the dramatic appeal of their predecessors. This difficulty in sustaining the same level of interest in the later series was also a problem with *Warship*. As we have seen already, the BBC introduced a new producer after two years to change the style of the programme to counter the problem associated with the shortage of script material based on the original format. The experience from both these series indicates that there are only a finite number of stories in a given military format. To exceed this number is to risk the possibility of the series losing popularity. There seems to be no reason for the Services to risk this, especially since a good series is most likely to be repeated (for example, *Danger UXB* first shown in 1979 and subsequently repeated in 1982).

Despite this decline in interest in the final series, however, *Spearhead* had entertained the public and at the same time had educated them about life in today's Armed Forces. Whilst offering full co-operation the Army realised that the series would not please everyone, acknowledged that they had no editorial control and fully accepted the need for dramatic licence. At the same time they realised just how ignorant people were about the present day Army and reckoned that *Spearhead* would help to close the gap of understanding. It did.

Like *Warship*, the series received a mixed reaction from servicemen

---

19 *Spearhead* averaged approximately 10 million viewers per episode over the first series.
20 *The Daily Telegraph*, 19 June 1979.

and although it was generally thought to be good, a significant percentage found it to be unrealistic or unrepresentative in parts. It did not become 'compulsive' viewing for most people in the Army. This is probably because any professional who is depicted in a television drama (be he a soldier, sailor, doctor or policeman) looks at the film with a critical eye and questions any detail which is not absolutely accurate, whereas the general public, ignorant of such detail, will only be concerned with the overall effect.[21] The public are also well able to differentiate between authenticity and dramatic licence. For instance in the final episode of the second series set in Northern Ireland, one of the soldiers launched into a tirade against 'the Establishment' after losing one of his best friends in an IRA ambush. *The Daily Telegraph* commented: 'Only when Pte Adams . . . soared from his barrack bunk-bed into a long harangue against politicians, bankers and the rest did it begin to sound less like the thoughts of a private soldier and more like those of a script-writer'.[22] The author viewed this particular episode with a group of soldiers who had served in Northern Ireland. In the discussion which followed they too commented on this uncharacteristic monologue and wondered why it had been included.

The importance of co-operation

Both *Warship* and *Spearhead* have demonstrated that co-operation by the Services can result in an accurate portrayal of military life which is to the mutual benefit of the public and the Forces without detracting from the requirements of the television dramatist. Both these two programmes were series, and as we have already noted, television series are likely to be less controversial than single plays. The experience with plays has been less impressive and has highlighted a basic fault in the public relations organisation's handling of this particular form of drama.

Vanishing Army was a 'Play of the Week' which was written by Robert Holles, produced by Innes Lloyd and broadcast on BBC 2 on 29 November 1978. The play was about an Army NCO who sacrificed his marriage to his career and then lost his leg in a grenade explosion in Northern Ireland. He was invalided out of the Service and the last part

---

21 This observation about the sensitive reaction of a group which is portrayed on television is related to the point raised by Denis McQuail about the need to study the effects of mass communications on minority groups; Denis McQuail, op.cit., pp. 92–3. The author's research has demonstrated that the military are certainly sensitive to, and very critical of, military drama but more research is required to test this theory amongst other minority groups.
22 *The Daily Telegraph*, 31 July 1979 (television critical review).

of the play centred on his failing attempts to adjust to civilian life and built up to a moving climax when he handed back his DCM to the Colonel of the Regiment at the annual regimental reunion. It was a skilfully produced play which was generally well received in the Sergeants' Mess and well reviewed by the critics. Indeed, it was scheduled to be repeated on BBC 1 in August 1979 within a year of the original screening.[23] And yet the Army refused to co-operate in its making.

The script was sent to MOD by the producer as a matter of courtesy because he wanted the use of a military barracks in which to film. He did not anticipate any problems over the script and was therefore surprised by the Army's refusal to co-operate on the grounds that the play gave a bad impression of the Army. This did not deter Innes Lloyd, however, because he used as his technical adviser an ex-RSM who had recently left the Army, and he acquired the use of a disused army barracks from the local authorities for his location shots.

Vanishing Army highlighted a number of points about the military's lack of comprehension about drama. At no stage did anyone from the Army meet the producer. Had they done so they would have been able to judge the professional integrity of Innes Lloyd. Such a meeting would also probably have revealed that it is very difficult to visualise the finished product simply from reading the script. In this particular case a few controversial scenes were eventually dropped completely from the play and skilful casting and acting diluted the effect of other characterisations and scenes which may have appeared offensive when reading the script. For instance the Commanding Officer was described in the script as having 'a rather brusque and impatient manner';[24] in the event he was played as a sympathetic officer with a diplomatic manner who knew his men well and who commanded wisely.

What would the Army have achieved by agreeing to co-operate? They would not have been able to demand changes in the script, but they would have been in a good bargaining position to influence certain alterations in exchange for the loan of a modern barracks for location shots.[25] Furthermore, the provision of an official technical adviser should have ensured that certain inaccuracies were corrected (for instance, the NCO's knowledge of Army regulations was too naive for a sergeant of his experience). An official technical adviser would also have been able to provide guidance to assist the viewer to distinguish

---

23 In the event the repeat was not shown because the scheduled date was just after the Warrenpoint Massacre of 17 soldiers in August 1979.
24 *Vanishing Army* by Richard Hollis (unpublished script), p.75.
25 Interview with Innes Lloyd, 11 December 1978.

between scenes set in 1978 and the flashbacks to 1962. This did not come across clearly in the play and one was left with the impression that the entire drama was set in the seventies. However, professional advice on the appropriate military dress and customs of the time would have helped to make it clear which part of the play was set in 1962.

Vanishing Army was a good television drama about the declining standards of life's values as seen through the eyes of a Senior NCO in the Army. The military would have lost nothing by meeting the producer, offering advice on the script, providing a technical adviser and making available the facilities requested by the BBC. At the same time this would have enabled them to advise on the accurate portrayal of service life. The point about this particular play was that the Northern Ireland scenes were depicted so realistically that one naturally accepted the *whole* of the play as being authentic. The failure to develop any kind of liaison was a mistake since the producer was most particular about authenticity and he would have welcomed advice on this aspect.[26]

The military's failure to understand drama was further demonstrated by a 'Play for Today' which was broadcast on 5 December 1978, a few weeks after *Vanishing Army. Soldiers Talking, Cleanly* by Mike Stott centred on the author's research into the British Army in Germany. It consisted of a series of disjointed interviews with officers, NCOs and soldiers all of whom appeared to be confused about the Army's role in Germany, and about their role in the Army. The subalterns were portrayed as 'chinless wonders' who were usually drunk and obsessed with sex. Interspersed amongst the interviews were some poignant comments about the Army and about NATO, and there were also a few amusing incidents and comments.

The Army was not amused when they read the script and they dissociated themselves from the production completely. But the play would not have been possible at all without assistance from the Army because, in answer to a request from the BBC, PR had not only arranged for Mike Stott to visit BAOR for ten days in 1977, they had also arranged his itinerary; and the script was based on that visit. Stott summed up his experience with simple honesty at the end of the play when the central character (representing the author) stated that the interviews were the result of a series of flukes: '. . . The fluke of which camp the Army sent me to. The fluke of who happened to be there, then. The fluke of which few of the people who were there I happened to meet'.[27] In hindsight the Army must regret not doing their home-

26 Interview with Innes Lloyd, 11 December 1978.
27 Mike Stott, *Soldiers Talking, Cleanly*, Eyre Methuen, London 1978, p.59.

work, finding out more about the author and the play he proposed to write, and arranging his 'flukes' more carefully. But it was not only the Army who were dissatisfied with this production, so were the critics,[28] and apparently so were a number of the public judging by the telephone calls of complaint which were received by the BBC.[29] In this particular case it was not the lack of co-operation by the military that was at fault. It was the lack of comprehension.

Conclusions

As we noted at the beginning of this chapter, dramatists probably have more influence on society's values than had been previously thought, and if this is so, then television certainly provides the outlet for that influence. Not only does drama dominate the ratings and the schedules[30] but a popular drama series attracts much larger audiences than a good documentary series (viz. an average viewing figure of 12–14 million for *Warship* as opposed to a maximum of 10 million for *Sailor*). Furthermore the increasing domination of contemporary drama by television[31] and the development of dramatised documentaries in the 1970s indicates that this influence is likely to grow rather than decline. Drama on British television is of a very high standard indeed (epitomised by such productions as *The Forsythe Saga, Edward and Mrs Simpson* and *Brideshead Revisited*) and infinite care is taken over the authenticity portrayed on the screen. An excellent example of the insistence on authentic detail was John Hawkesworth's production of *Danger UXB*. He had wanted to do a series about the Army's bomb disposal men in World War II ever since 1966 when he read Major Bill Hartley's book about his real-life exploits entitled *The Unexploded Bomb*. He eventually interested Thames TV in his idea and he started work on the series in 1977. He wrote five of the episodes himself, insisted on every historical feature being accurate and received full co-operation from 33 Engineer Regiment (EOD) who not only checked the scripts for accuracy but also lent him equipment from their museum which was unique and unreproducible. Indeed, he admitted that the series would not have been possible without the assistance of the Royal Engineers because of the detailed knowledge required about bombs, fuses, and defusing techniques. The result was a most realistic and highly successful series which both entertained and educated the

28 Television reviews in *The Daily Telegraph*, 6 December 1978, and *The Sunday Telegraph*, 10 December 1978.
29 Visit to Drama Group, BBC, 7 December 1978.
30 Graham Murdoch, op.cit., p.1.
31 Ibid., p.15.

public about the life of a bomb disposal unit in the Second World War. Furthermore, he did not repeat the mistake of *Spearhead* and *Warship* by extending the programme to another series. He was adamant that there were only so many stories upon which to base the various episodes and he refused to consider suggestions of a second series. This was a brave decision when one considers the financial advantages of extending the programme.

As a result of the careful authenticity of series such as this the public generally believe what they see (allowing for dramatic licence). It is therefore very much in the interests of the military to co-operate with productions about contemporary Service life to ensure that the portrayal is accurate and realistic. Failure to provide assistance will not prevent the film being produced, nor will it have any effect on its reception by the public for they will not realise that the military have not co-operated.

Although the military have collaborated to a great extent with some programmes there is still a surprising amount of general ignorance about television drama. There is often a failure to perceive the effects of television on the audience and there is a definite tendency to be too sensitive. It is believed that much of this attitude is due to a lack of real understanding about television drama. For instance, there is no-one currently serving with DPRS who has an intimate knowledge of this subject.

Warship and *Spearhead* have shown that contemporary military life provides a fertile subject for drama which is popular with the public. *Vanishing Army* and *Soldiers Talking, Cleanly* have demonstrated the military's lack of expertise in this field. Dramatists will continue to write about the military and programme-makers will produce plays regardless of whether the Forces co-operate or not. Some are fascinated with the military and many have no first-hand knowledge but have developed preconceived ideas based on biased or out of date notions. The military should acknowledge this and provide the necessary expertise within DPRS with the knowledge of, and interest in, television drama. There is a requirement to build on the reservoir of goodwill already established with some personalities in drama by sending selected individuals to the drama groups of the BBC and ITV companies to learn something about television drama. This knowledge is required both by some of the desk men in DPRS as well as those military officers appointed as liaison officers for drama series. Once again the importance of personal relations emerges as a vital factor. So much can be achieved through imaginative liaison with the televison authorities, and as drama provides an excellent means of keeping the public in touch with the attitudes of the modern servicemen and the issues which face the Armed Forces, so more should be done in the future to meet the undoubted continuing interest in the military as a suitable subject for television drama.

PART IV

THE NEED FOR A CLEARER UNDERSTANDING

The uneasy relationship between the military and the media was highlighted in chapter 1. This relationship has been subjected to particular strain when one profession is required to report on the deeds of the other during conflict. In order to analyse this in depth, the next two chapters consider the conflicts in Vietnam (chapter 9) and Northern Ireland (chapter 10) to see what lessons have emerged which indicate any inherent problems of reporting conflict. These lessons are summarised in chapter 11 which also looks at the lessons to emerge from the Iranian Embassy siege in London in 1980 and the Falklands crisis in 1982 to see whether the thesis is sustained in the light of these two recent events.

The last two chapters in Part IV review the education which the military and the media receive about each other and explore the depth of knowledge which each possesses about the other's profession. In the course of this analysis, chapter 12 discusses the difficulties for the media of reporting the military 'in action' and includes a study of the media coverage of the Vietcong assault on the US Embassy in Saigon in 1968 at the beginning of the Tet Offensive.

9 The Vietnam Lesson

The magnetism of Vietnam

In order to get Vietnam into perspective it is important to remember the scale of the conflict and the rise and fall of American interest in the war. The Vietnamese had been continuously at war from 1941–75. The US military commitment grew from 200 advisers in 1954 to 16,000 troops in 1963, 75,000 in 1965, to a maximum of over half a million men in 1968, and by 1973 the last combat troops had been withdrawn home to the United States; in 1975 the North Vietnamese entered Saigon. The media contingent reflected the US troop involvement and rose from about 20 American and foreign correspondents in 1964 to a maximum of 637 in 1968; and as the American active participation in the war gradually ceased from 1969 onwards, so the reduction in the number of journalists reflected the decline of American interests until there were only 35 correspondents left in 1974.[1] The Joint United States Public Affairs Office (JUSPAO) also grew to meet the increasing media representation and eventually numbered 247 American and 370 Vietnamese — it also provided abundant facilities for the newsman from 'reservations on the daily Air Force C-130 transport flights up country . . . to the paperwork required for MACV/Military Assistant Command Vietnam/, accreditation PX and commissary cards . . . to

---

1 Peter Braestrup, *Big Story*, Westview Piers, Boulder Colorado 1977, pp. 8, 11, and Phillip Knightley, *The First Casualty*, André Deutsch, London 1975, p.402.

periodic screenings of the TV new shows'.[2] The JUSPAO building also contained the military news briefing room for the daily 'Five o'clock Follies'.

Vietnam cost over 46,000 American lives, billions of dollars and was the world's first experience of a 'television war':

> Because of television General Westmoreland fought the most widely visible war in history. Unlike other wars, whose audience was confined to the few camp followers and hardened military wives — who watched for example the fighting from the heights of Balaklava — Westmoreland had a mass audience every night in the intimacy of their homes. It was a war without censorship. Television opened another front, the battle for public opinion in the United States.[3]

The combination of a large scale war and new technology (both in terms of weaponry, television and sophisticated communications) had a considerable impact on the military and the media. From the military point of view the JUSPAO grew into an enormous organisation whose job it was to present the facts to the media: 'they *did* provide good facilities and allowed considerable access . . . but the organisation became "big business" in terms of administration and organisation; there was also a tendency to justify their empire . . . the organisation eventually became so large that it was impossible for them to check all their facts . . . the machine took over'.[4] From the media's point of view the war attracted all kinds of reporters:

> All sorts of correspondents, from all sorts of publications, went to Vietnam. There were specialist writers from technical journals, trainee reporters from college newspapers, counter-insurgency experts from military publishers, religious correspondents, famous authors, small-town editors, old hands from Korea, even older hands from the Second World War and what Henry Kamm of the *New York Times* called 'proto-journalists', men who had never written a professional word or taken a professional photograph in their lives until the war brought them to Saigon. They all wrote stories that were used and presumably read or took photographs that were bought and reproduced.
>   . . . Ambition, principally, had brought them all there. The war was the biggest story in the world at the time . . . and there was no

2 Peter Braestrup, op.cit., p.15.
3 Michael Charlton and Anthony Moncrieff, *Many Reasons Why*, Scolar Press, London 1978, p.147.
4 Julian Pettifer (BBC TV correspondent in Vietnam 1966—75), interview with the author, 12 December 1978.

better place for a young reporter to put a gloss on a new career . . .[5]

One thing in common shared by this odd assortment of correspondents was that most of them had no experience of the military, 'at least [of] the US military apparatus and "language" of the 1960s. Few [of the American newsmen], for example, knew the difference between, say, a mortar and a howitzer, battalions and divisions, logistics and tactics . . . . As one result, many newsmen were ill-equipped to understand, let alone question, official or unofficial explanations of military deployments, problems and progress. They had to learn, in highly unsystematic, patchwork fashion, while on the job. And, as Tet was to show, this was insufficient'.[6] Martin Bell, the experienced BBC television news reporter, who did have previous military knowledge, also stressed his lack of preparation for his first visit to Vietnam in 1967:

> What can you do [before you go]? You read up the cuttings and off you go. But as the cuttings themselves may be written by people who don't know much more about it than you do, especially at that time, it's not a particularly useful introduction . . . over a period of time (I was three months in Vietnam) I could have done a lot more than I did . . . I was too impressed by the hardware of the Americans . . . I was very inexperienced and I don't think I was getting anywhere near the reality of what was going on.[7]

In his admirably researched book about the American news media's coverage of the Tet offensive, Peter Braestrup pointed out that the American newsmen's knowledge was not improved by the length of tours in Vietnam (usually between 12 and 18 months) and he noted that a 'tour in Vietnam was a good merit badge for young reporters out of the city room. It was a boon for young unknowns in TV news . . . . As a CBS network reporter put it, "There was no premium on experience or expertise in our business. The networks see no harm in running a standup piece on the war's progress by a guy who has just come in the country two days earlier". The Tet coverage was to make this plain'.[8]

But amongst the press corps there were some correspondents who were considerably experienced (including a number of former military

5 Phillip Knightley, op.cit., p.402.
6 Peter Braestrup, op.cit., p.14.
7 Interview with the author, 28 August 1979.
8 Peter Braestrup, op.cit., pp. 14–15.

men), who did not rely on the 'Five o'clock Follies' for their information but instead went up-country to see for themselves what was happening. It was these correspondents who very quickly exposed some of the 'facts' produced in Saigon. For instance, many of the journalists were suspicious of the 'body count' figures which were given out at the daily briefings: 'the "body" figures were obviously exaggerated — and proved so in some cases where journalists were able to check'.[9] This was one of the main contributory factors to the credibility gap which grew between the military and the media. This exaggeration over figures contrasts with the strict verification system operated by the RAF during the Battle of Britain in the Second World War. The RAF realised the vital importance of credibility and their insistence on accuracy considerably enhanced their reputation with the press and with the public both at home and abroad.

Although there was no censorship during the Vietnam war 'the military were never sure whether to manage news or not'.[10] Julian Pettifer believes this was the genesis of the credibility gap and Drew Middleton, military correspondent of the *New York Times*, believes that one of the troubles in the war was the lack of censors.[11] The military varied their attitude to the media, tried to measure success in a guerrilla war by reducing everything to measurable terms and resorted to the numbers game (i.e. 'we killed so many — these villages are pro-Government'). The trouble was the numbers were often wrong and proved to be so. This gap of understanding between the military and the media led to an imbalance between the reporting about the progress of the war as viewed from Saigon or Hanoi and this process was assisted by the unrestrained access allowed by the Americans as opposed to the considerable restrictions imposed by the North Vietnamese: 'Western correspondents were allowed into the North only if the North Vietnamese government could see some advantage to itself from the visit'.[12]

The battle for the mind

The imbalance in access, the American attitude to the 'free press' and the complexities of a revolutionary war which defied attempts by commentators to reduce issues to convenient two-minute packages for

9 Julian Pettifer interview with author, 12 December 1978.
10 Ibid.
11 Quoted in Phillip Knightley, op.cit., p.423.
12 Phillip Knightley, op.cit., p.417.

television news summaries, all helped to turn public opinion in America against the war. But probably most significant of all was the failure of many in the media to realise how they were being used by Hanoi to promote the North's propaganda. North Vietnam used the free press of democracy to turn the American people against the war and realised the immense potential of this 'gift' from democracy the moment the Americans entered the war. Dr Richard Clutterbuck related to the author a conversation he had with a USMC officer in 1968. The officer was serving in Vietnam in 1965 when he realised that the local Vietcong commander had been a student of his on a course in the States a few years previously. He arranged with an intermediary to meet the Vietcong leader and during the course of conversation the Vietnamese remarked that the North was bound to win because now that US troops were committed to the war the North Vietnamese would be able to turn American public opinion against their own military. The North would win in the streets of Chicago, Seattle, Dallas and New York.[13] Basic education in the realities of revolutionary warfare, especially about the importance attached to public opinion (the propagandist battle for mind), would have at least made many journalists recognise the professional determination of Hanoi. The most important prize for the North was the erosion of the will of the American people to sustain support for the Administration's military policy in Vietnam.

In this regard, Hanoi received the unwitting support of the media during the Tet offensive in 1968: 'The American media had misled the American people about the Tet offensive and when they realised they had misjudged the situation — that in fact it was an American victory — they didn't have the courage or the integrity to admit it'.[14] Braestrup's extensive research supports this view of General Westmoreland's and suggests a number of reasons for this failure including the appalling lack of preparation amongst the journalists · (including background education about Vietnam, knowledge of the military, inability to speak the language); the inability of the military bureaucracy to realise the importance of providing the media with facilities to follow the military situation; the attitude of some in that bureaucracy who regarded the press as a necessary evil; and the failure of many correspondents to stay out in the field with the troops and experience combat conditions at first hand, despite ease of access to the battle field: 'reporters and photographers were plunged alongside uniformed strangers in a remote, often dangerous locale for a brief time and then whisked away, often with "good film" but without any notion of either why the fight

3 Interview with the author, 16 July 1979.
4 General Westmoreland quoted in *The Guardian*, 4 April 1979.

started or its "before" and "after"'.[15] This ease of access by helicopter meant that those battles within helicopter range were the ones most likely to receive news coverage, so were those battles which had good visual impact on television film. Added to these causes were the usual problems of inaccuracies of the press due to the pressure of time, the editorial effect in America on copy despatched from Vietnam and the microcosmic view of television. Braestrup also pointed out the inability of the media to cope with the scale of the war:

> . . . Tet underscored the peculiarly Vietnam-wide character of the war and the inescapable conclusion, even before Tet made it obvious, is that the US major media, rich as they were in the 1960s, devoted insufficient resources and insufficient critical attention to the conflict. With their narrow technical and man-power limitations, editorial predilections and journalistic biases, the media, as the offensive began, were overwhelmed.[16]

These failings, added to the doubts over official statements, led the media to declare Tet a military defeat for the wrong side. The media then compounded the error (and presented a psychological victory to Hanoi), by challenging the Administration's optimistic view of the previous two years and that in turn led to the subsequent examination of most major statements of fact: '. . . this growing disillusionment of the media must have infected their readers and viewers. The challenge presented to the media was to interpret and put over a high drama of which the public had very little understanding. The media was mistrustful of the official line, unrestrained by censorship and goaded by competition. Inevitably, the reporters of limited experience could only offer a narrow analysis. They believed that the public had no heart for the war so they tried to interpret the war according to what they thought the public felt. But the more they saw of the war, the more pessimistic they became. So their reporters became more critical and cynical which in turn rubbed off on the public and so the cycle began again'.[17]

The effect of media characteristics

Two other factors which had a considerable impact on the impression which the American people had of the war was the media's insatiable

15 Peter Braestrup, op.cit., p.26.
16 Ibid., p.51.
17 Major Patrick Cable-Alexander, *The Media and the American Involvement in Vietnam* (unpublished, 1976), pp. 26—7.

appetite for sensationalism, and the selection of news. The sensationalism took many forms and included both the written word and the visual impact. For instance, American reporters wrote about the first marines who landed at Da Nang in 1965 as: 'storming ashore, whereas they had walked up the beach unopposed. Almost any action produced emotive comparisons – "the biggest since Inchon", "the second biggest since Normandy" '.[18] But the most lasting memories were those left by television: the picture of the US marine setting light to the thatched roof of a Vietnamese house with a zippo lighter; the summary execution of a Vietcong suspect in Saigon by Police Director Loan during Tet; the little girl, running naked down the road at Tram Bang, screaming in pain severely burned by napalm. Julian Pettifer recalls that after he had sent back several films from Vietnam in the early days of the war he received a telegram from his editor which congratulated him and then added: 'All we want now is a picture of you in extreme danger'. Not only did this annoy Pettifer but what added to his annoyance was the realisation that 'all the public remember of my Vietnam coverage is me crouching behind a wall in the middle of a battle during the Tet offensive'.[19]

Although television has no method of recall (unless one uses a video-set recorder), the brain possesses the capability of recalling such sensational moments as those just described and these images become symbolic references of the war. The problem is that the camera can only capture what actually happens within its arc at a specific moment. It cannot relate that picture to the broad panorama which is visible to the naked eye of the observer on the spot, nor can it tell you the circumstances of the picture – that is up to the reporter. But if the reporter fails to do this, for whatever reason, then the impression with which the viewer is left is the dramatic effect of the picture. For instance, the girl who was burned by napalm had in fact been placed in a pagoda for safety, but she sneaked out with several other children to watch the battle. As Sir Robert Thompson pointed out: 'It was a picture which shocked the world. But during all these battles in Hau Nghia province, out of 350,000 people only thirteen civilians were killed in the whole invasion period [1972]'.[20] This microcosm effect of television led to the re-examination of the attitudes of a number of television editors and commentators in the United States and has since resulted in concern being voiced about the effect of television on

18 Phillip Knightley, op.cit., p.385.
19 Interview with author, 12 December 1978.
20 Sir Robert Thompson, *Peace is Not at Hand*, Chatto and Windus, London 1974, p.108.

the public:

> Television has a built-in bias towards depicting any conflict in terms of the visible brutality. You can say, of course, that that is what war is — brutality, conflict, starvation and combat — all I am saying is that there are other issues which cause these things to come about, and television does not always deal with them adequately . . . . One wonders if in future a democracy which has unhibited television coverage in every home will ever be able to fight a war, however just . . . . The full brutality of the combat will be there in close-up and colour and blood looks very red on the colour television screen.[21]

> If there are one people in the world who are never, but absolutely never, going to understand the war in Vietnam it is the Americans who watched it on television. The war was meaningless to them; they don't know what happened at any single stage of that war and they never will and they are a lost generation as far as that is concerned and this is what worried me about television. The war was lost on the television screen of the United States.[22]

The impact of the media, especially television is also greatly influenced by the selection of news. This is dependent upon a combination of factors: whether reporters are actually at an event to cover it, how they report it and what happens to that report during the editorial process in the news room. Sir Robert Thompson related an incident about the battle of An Loc during the North Vietnamese offensive in 1972 when the defenders won a symbolic battle eventually repulsing an attack by three North Vietnam regular army divisions and in the process knocking out 39 tanks in the town. Although the main battle was over, the town was still being subjected to sporadic artillery fire when Thompson visited An Loc a few weeks later. He described his short visit to President Thieu the next day and the President immediately arranged to visit the besieged town. 'The strictest security was observed and no announcement was made of his impending arrival. When he jumped first out of the helicopter the Province Chief, who was there to meet the party, broke down and wept. The troops in the surrounding bunkers, on seeing the President, rushed forward, lifted him up and carried him into the town. There was no press correspondent to see or report it.'[23] The fact that the press were not at a

---

21 Robin Day quoted in *Defence and the Mass Media*, Report of a Seminar held at the Royal United Service Institution on 13 October 1970, p.6.
22 Sir Robert Thompson, quoted in *Television and Conflict*, Institute for the Study of Conflict Special Report, November 1978, p.10.
23 Sir Robert Thompson, *Peace is Not at Hand*, p.107.

particular event to report it had a significant effect on the impression of the war which was conveyed to the public. The omissions were as relevant as the sensational inclusions and, as Sir Robert Thompson's story illustrates, quite often the press were not informed of an event for security reasons.

Events which were reported often bore little resemblance to reality. Richard Clutterbuck visited Vietnam whilst serving with the British Army in Singapore just before the Tet offensive in 1967. He discovered that there was far less tension in the villages than he had experienced in Malaya during the emergency and in particular he noticed that there was considerable evidence of constructive efforts which had not been reported by the media (such as the development of the agricultural policy and the effects of 'miracle' rice). On his return to Singapore, Clutterbuck telephoned a friend who was the Far East correspondent of a London daily newspaper and told him that his reports did not reflect a balanced picture of the situation in Vietnam: 'you have just picked out the spectacular but uninhabited mountain tops appearing through the cloud in a satellite picture and ignored the mass of land under the cloud where people actually lived'. The correspondent invited him to come and see him and they were joined by two American reporters who had also covered Vietnam. During the ensuing conversation the journalists agreed with Clutterbuck's analogy and produced as the reason the thesis of a circular economic argument: newspapers' survival depends on the number of copies they sell — headlines sell newspapers (i.e. 'sensations') — dull stories result in a loss of circulation — reporters only survive if they provide the stories which the newspapers want — therefore the public actually decide what stories reporters despatch. As one of the reporters remarked: 'If you saw two papers on the news-stand, one with the picture of a burnt baby screaming under the headline "American troops napalm village" and another with a picture of happy peasants in a padi field sub-titled "New strain of miracle rice doubles the harvest" — which would you buy?'[24]

This theory is plausible and it is circular. It has become clear since the end of the war that the combination of the competitiveness of American newspapers, the media's desire for sensationalism, whether an event was covered or not, the way the report was angled and what news editors did with that report, all contributed to the image of the war which the newsmen presented to the American people. The stories that were 'spiked' and the film that was left on the cutting room floor were equally important. Indeed there has been as much concern expressed for the omissions as for the inclusions and this highlights the

24 Interview with the author, 23 February 1979.

considerable responsibility which is placed on the shoulders of the editorial staffs. As Clutterbuck and Braestrup have uncovered, the Vietnam war revealed that far too many in the news media had not realised the immense complexities of the conflict and therefore, on occasions, they were guilty of misinforming the public.

The realities of war reporting

Added to the complexities of this particular war were the realities of life as a war correspondent which are common to all wars. These characteristics are seldom explained by correspondents during a war and usually only emerge in books written by some of those reporters once the war has ended. Unimpaired by deadlines, and aided by the passage of time in which to reflect, some reporters have written most impressive accounts of the Vietnam war which have related to the realities of the conflict and have also tried to explain them. The reflective views expressed in books such as *A Rumour of War* by Philip Caputo and *Dispatches* by Michael Herr give a far more realistic view of the conflict than most reports dispatched during the war.

Those people who have seen action seldom talk about the realities of war to those who have not been involved, but it is as important for a young journalist to realise what he is likely to be subjected to whilst reporting a war as it is for the young soldier about to go into action for the first time. Reporters do get involved:

> No matter how detached and impartial you may believe yourself to be, I defy anyone to sit through a heavy mortar or artillery barrage, or spend an hour cowering under sniper-fire in a ditch and not feel a sense of identity with and therefore a certain support for your fellow-sufferers. Coupled with this there tends to be fear of and dislike for the opposing side. And with this increased sense of involvement there may also be a certain amount of distortion caused by the violence becoming personalised. There is a tendency to equate the events in your own tiny sector (possibly a company front), with the overall situation. I readily confess to suffering from such 'tactical myopia': if someone is shooting at me it is an event which acquires a greater significance than does the fiercest firefight at which I am a spectator.[25]

Reporting wars is a dangerous occupation: 45 war correspondents were

25 Christopher Wain, 'Television Reporting of Military Operations — A Personal View', RUSI *Journal*, March 1974, p.72.

killed in Vietnam and a further 18 were listed as missing.[26] 'I remember when I was mortared because I was wearing a white shirt — I was terrified . . . . On two occasions I have been in situations where I thought we were going to be over-run and I realised how vulnerable I was as a defence correspondent.'[27]

Another reality of war reporting is censorship. Even in wars without official censorship (such as Vietnam) a certain amount of self-censorship is exercised by war correspondents. Julian Pettifer recalled that: 'You have to censor films from the horror and language of war. It's a crude, nasty business'. He did quite a bit of editing of film in Vietnam to protect the public from some of the horror of the war.[28] Christopher Wain, in defence of television's apparent inability to re-present the realities of combat on the screen, said: 'It is true that some of the most distressing aspects of warfare are not shown on television screens — but that is thanks to self-censorship, not because authentic film is non-existent. Robert MacNeil — a BBC *Panorama* reporter — has described in his excellent work "The People Machine" how he sat in a New York cutting-room watching NBC film from Saigon being edited. It showed (in sound and colour) a young marine undergoing an emergency battlefield operation without anaesthetic. MacNeil said the film was horrific: had it been shown in its entirety it would have caused a public outcry. In the event the worst scenes were edited out and the sound muted — largely to spare the feelings of those with husbands and sons in Vietnam. It was censorship for the most laudable of reasons reasons — but what the editor was really doing was to make accept-able something which in reality was quite unacceptable'.[29] Michael Charlton also responded to the question of 'self censorship' but linked it to the degree of experience of the reporter and suggested as a reason for some irresponsible reporting: 'A striving for effect. When you are young you are keen to exploit the opportunity to establish your name. As you become older and grow in experience there comes also a greater sense of responsibility. One trouble is that for television reporting there is seldom the equivalent of the "spike" on which the written press can impale the more imperfect or dubious offerings. Film costs a great deal of money, is often from a single only source, and it is therefore more likely that it must and will be used'.[30] The importance of experience amongst both reporters and editorial staff is clear.

26 Phillip Knightley, op.cit., p.405.
27 Christopher Wain, Defence Correspondent for BBC Television, interview with the author, 16 March 1979.
28 Interview with the author, 12 December 1978.
29 Christopher Wain, RUSI 1974, pp. 70—1.
30 Interview with the author, 6 December 1978.

Experience is also important when one considers how vulnerable a journalist is to propaganda. We have already seen examples of how the American press were used by both sides but a specific example brings home the dilemma which faces a correspondent in such a circumstance. In an interview with the author, Julian Pettifer expressed his concern for being used for propaganda purposes and mentioned an occasion when he was reporting the guerrilla infiltration into Thailand during the Vietnamese war. He was given a tour of the 'operational area' by the Thai Army but suspected that the whole incident was being managed by the authorities because nothing seemed authentic — the villages did not appear to be genuine and the 'defectors' produced by the army were unconvincing. Pettifer was so suspicious that he did not use this report at all (he believed the real aim of the exercise was to obtain more aid from the United States).[31] This incident highlights the importance of experience, so as to spot the tell-tale signs which indicate the real 'truth' and the moral courage required by a reporter to refuse to use a report when considerable money, time and effort has already been expended in its making.

Perhaps the most relevant reality for war correspondents is the luck of being at the right place at the right time — but you have to work for your luck. Julian Pettifer was the only British television correspondent in Saigon during the Tet offensive. He just happened to be there at a time when others had taken some leave but he also had a tip off from a CIA agent that something might be brewing; and once the fighting started he was unable to get out of the city to other trouble spots so he was forced to concentrate on the fierce street fighting going on around his hotel. There were a number of reporters killed during the battle and perhaps the reason Pettifer survived to issue his report was because he had cultivated the friendship of the CIA agent who personally guided him round the streets and kept him out of too much trouble.[32]

The realities of reporting a war are only really learned by experience and yet there does not appear to be the systematic attempt to pass on the lessons to the next generation of reporters with the result that similar mistakes are likely to occur in the future. This is the relevance of the Vietnam war. In particular, the use of television highlighted the most common fault of all; generalising from the particular:

> For the first time the horrors of war were brought into the sitting room and it has been tritely said that the British would have lost

31 Interview with the author, 12 December 1978.
32 Ibid.

the Boer war on television. I have discussed the problems and shortcomings of television with many people. The camera has a more limited view even than the cameraman and argues always from the particular to the general. If on television one child is shown to be scarred by napalm then every child has been scarred by napalm. If one house is destroyed then all houses are destroyed. If a police chief shoots one prisoner then all prisoners are shot. The proof of one — the camera does not lie — is proof for all. Moreover the director and crew naturally want the more spectacular shots and in war the most spectacular picture is that of destruction. The camera must go where that sort of action is. All activity of a less spectacular nature, even though constructive and more important, is neglected. This inevitably leads to distortion and lack of balance. It even becomes false when small rent-a-crowd rioters arrange a rendezvous and wait for the cameras to arrive before starting. After one such 'riot' in Saigon in support of Air Vice-Marshall Ky's Presidential candidacy, in which about 200 people were involved, a former member of the British Labour Government who was there to cover the election asked: 'What are the other two million people in Saigon doing?' The camera did not answer that.

The point is that every allegation ever made about South Vietnam can probably be proved at least in one instance. It could be equally proved about the other side if access could have been gained to the material or event. There is no issue in this world in which we are dealing with the darkest black on one side and the purest white on the other. What is necessary is to differentiate between the lighter and darker shades of grey.[33]

In the same passage Sir Robert Thompson also quotes Dr Henry Kissinger's perceptive remark: 'The dilemma is that almost any statement about Vietnam is likely to be true; unfortunately, truth does not guarantee relevance'.[34]

The lessons

In the context of the relationship between the military and the media, the main lessons from Vietnam are the inexperience of reporters at the beginning of a major conflict, the realities of propaganda (especially its impact on public opinion), sensationalism (either through eye-catching

---

33 Sir Robert Thompson, *Peace is Not at Hand*, Chatto & Windus, London 1974.
34 Ibid., p.39. The quote from Dr Kissinger originally appeared in an article in *Foreign News*, January 1969.

newspaper headlines or the visual impact of television), selection of news, the realities of war reporting and generalising from the particular. As we shall see in the next chapter about Northern Ireland, many of these lessons had to be re-learnt when the British Army was deployed to Ulster despite the overlap of these two campaigns. Little or no attempt had been made to prepare reporters for the realities of the conflict and the military were equally caught off-balance.

The message from the Vietnam war was quite clear: both the military and the media needed to be educated about the realities of reporting conflict. There is little evidence to suggest that this message has been fully hoisted home.

10 The Northern Ireland Experience

The longer you look at Northern Ireland the more complex it becomes. Outsiders frequently miss the complexities of the situation.

Edward Curran, Deputy Editor, *Belfast Telegraph*

The complicated situation of Ulster is still not understood by the majority of people in the remainder of the United Kingdom despite the multitude of words and commentaries which have been produced on the subject. And yet, the media are not entirely to blame for this failure. The historical aspect (so vital to Irishmen), the geographical proximity to Eire and England, bigotry, charm and fanatical hatred, have all combined to confuse those reporters interested in objectivity; and for those journalists *not* interested in objective reporting there has always been someone ready to tell them what they wanted to hear to reinforce their own prejudices.[1] Ulster abounds with bias of every shade, and with the outlets to publicise those opinions.

In this chapter the author has attempted to weave his way through the bigotry, the prejudices and the hatred of the last ten years in order to discover which trends have emanated from this decade that are relevant to the relationship between the military and the media. The soldiers who have served in the Province and those journalists who have also 'served' in Ulster, or who live there, will appreciate how difficult

---

1 As an indication of the depth of hatred and bigotry that exists in Northern Ireland, an Army officer, who had his family with him on an 18 month tour of duty in the Province, told the author that within three weeks of first attending a Protestant school in Belfast, his six year old son came home one day and announced that 'all Catholics should be shot'. Subsequently the small boy became confused when his parents pointed out that one of his grandmothers was a Catholic. Interview with author, 6 September 1979 (name withheld).

a task this has been. At the outset it is important to stress that the scene *has* changed in Northern Ireland and it continues to evolve; there is therefore the danger of generalising from the particular and arriving at an outdated conclusion. Nevertheless certain lessons have emerged in the past 13 years which have stood the test of time and withstood the realities of Northern Ireland.

Propaganda

Both the military and the media have shared a significant experience in Ulster; they have both been subjected to the venom of the extremists, exposed to 'the fury of both sides',[2] and been condemned by the antagonists. Neither the public nor the academic critic has experienced this hatred and it is therefore a factor of life in Ulster which has been overlooked by the academic theorists. This hatred towards the soldier or the reporter was only an extension of the hatred either side had for the other; and from this hatred grew bigotry which in turn provided fallow ground for propaganda: 'As natural propagandists these people were wonderful, as many journalists, observers and politicians new to Ulster were to discover'.[3] For over a decade that natural ability has been put to most effective use, particularly by the Provisional IRA. In his thesis entitled *Revolutionary Propaganda and Possible Counter-measures*, Maurice Tugwell has included a chapter on the propaganda of the Provisional IRA which is well documented and shows that propaganda has always been a key factor in the Provisionals' strategy. He provides a number of examples to show that their tactics included discrediting the more effective Security Forces' tactics or units (such as plain clothes operations and the Special Air Service), undermining the people's faith in the part-time Ulster Defence Regiment (UDR), briefing 'eye witnesses' at incidents,[4] and timing events so as to obtain maxi-

---

2 Interview with a BBC reporter, 6 December 1978.
3 Maurice Tugwell, *Revolutionary Propaganda and Possible Counter-measures*, Defence Fellowship thesis 1976–77, unpublished, p.233.
4 Tugwell detailed the automatic action taken whenever the Security Forces shot an insurgent:

> The Provisionals drilled the Catholics to cover up whenever Security Forces shot an insurgent. Almost invariable such an event set this procedure in motion. The man's weapon was spirited away. The victim was taken where he could be cleaned up of any forensic or other evidence indicating the use of a firearm. 'Eye witnesses' were briefed and presented to news reporters. Their evidence hardly ever varied: the civilian had been unarmed, innocent of any offence, and the soldier's shot had been unwarranted. In short, the Army had committed murder. This, it was hoped, would discredit the Army and deter soldiers from opening fire on terrorists in future.

Maurice Tugwell, op.cit., pp. 236–7.

mum publicity often at the expense of the Security Forces.[5]

The vulnerability of broadcasting, especially television, to this sustained and sophisticated propaganda has since been acknowledged by Lord Annan in his report on the future of broadcasting ('terrorism feeds on publicity')[6] and it was also mentioned by Brian Crozier in the introductory summary of the special report produced by the Institute for the Study of Conflict following a Conference on Television and Conflict in April 1978:

> It is a well-known phenomenon that the objects of terrorism include the dramatisation of a cause. Terrorists want publicity. They want to shock public opinion, they want to be noticed. It is therefore a primary objective of terrorists that they should gain access to television screens. An enormous captive audience is at their mercy . . . . Any 'brutality' by the Royal Ulster Constabulary or the British Army was usually recorded on television — indeed the television crews were often waiting following a tip-off from the IRA. But there is not, to my knowledge, a television record of the knee-capping of IRA 'traitors', or of the application of tar and feather to individuals of whom the IRA disapproved.[7]

This comment is supported by the facts from Ulster: in July 1974 'an analysis of sixty bomb explosions showed that over 80% were timed to obtain maximum coverage on television news;'[8] on 26 January 1978 the IRA produced an M60 machine gun for the television cameras in Londonderry on the anniversary of Bloody Sunday; on 26 August 1979 (a Bank Holiday), the IRA assassinated Earl Mountbatten of Burma whilst he was in his motor boat a few hundred yards off-shore in Donegal Bay (the bomb blast also killed the Dowager Lady Brabourne, Lord Mountbatten's 14 year old grandson and a young Irish boatman), and they also murdered 18 soldiers in a well planned ambush at Warrenpoint, Northern Ireland; and on 17 October 1981 Lieutenant General Sir Steuart Pringle, Commandant General of the Royal Marines, was blown up in his car outside his home in West Dulwich, London, by

5 'The Provisionals were alert to the benefits to be gained by acts timed to upstage any security force word or action that smacked of self-congratulation . . . . four months later, when the GOC was speaking to the press at his headquarters, twelve bombs were let off in nearby Belfast. Of this exercise Maria McGuire [a defector from the Provisionals] wrote: "We drove him off the front pages of the Belfast Evening Telegraph with a dozen bomb explosions in Belfast, demonstrating very clearly just who was winning in the Six Counties".' Maurice Tugwell, op.cit., p.242 (McGuire quote from Maria McGuire *To Take Arms*, Quartet Books, London 1973, p.75).
6 Lord Annan, *Report of the Committee on the Future of Broadcasting*, HMSO, London 1977, p.270.
7 *Television and Conflict*, Institute for the Study of Conflict, 1978, p.4.
8 Major I.D. Evans, 'Public Relations Practice Within the Army', NDC Latimer, unpublished 1976, p.7.

an IRA booby-trap bomb. Propaganda, and its dependence on publicity, is a fundamental factor in Ulster which affects both the military and the media alike, and it stretches far beyond the geographical boundaries of Northern Ireland. The military were reasonably prepared for this eventuality but initially many unsuspecting journalists who were new to conflict were totally unprepared for the ensuing manipulation by clever propagandists.[9] Propaganda has continued to haunt the relationship between the military and the media in Ulster.

Propaganda, however, can be a two-edged weapon. Only six days after the bomb attack, as a result of which he had lost part of his right leg, Lieutenant General Sir Steuart Pringle held a press conference in King's College Hospital. He had already won the 'battle for the headlines' as a result of his extraordinary bravery during the 40 minute ordeal on 17 October 1982 whilst rescue workers cut him free from the wreckage of his car, and his subsequent frank and very human press interviews on 23 October won unashamed admiration from both the press and the public. The General was naturally aware of the propaganda value of holding a press conference so soon after the bombing incident,[10] but it went beyond that. As the *Sunday Express* noted:

> Of course, his decision to meet the Press will not have been without an element of calculation. He will have wished to signal to his men that their commander was still at their head . . . but his gesture had an impact that even he will not have calculated. For surely, nothing was more warming than the way he was so obviously moved by the goodness and heroism of ordinary folk. It was one of his own neighbours . . . who comforted him as rescuers worked to free him from the tangled remains of his car.
>
> When his would-be murderers strapped the bomb to his car, could they have possibly imagined that the outcome of their barbarity would be a source of inspiration rather than despair?[11]

Even the IRA hunger strikes and self-inflicted deaths of republican prisoners in the Maze Prison during the summer of 1981, although

---

9   Tugwell comments:

> Reporters are accustomed to confused and contradictory versions of any incident. It is one of their skills to sort out truth from error. Few newsmen could bring themselves to believe that every civilian was lying. In consequence the Army's case, often resting on a single witness, was routinely called into question. Only after many months in Northern Ireland did one experienced reporter (Tony Geraghty of *The Sunday Times*) conclude: 'I speak as someone of Irish extraction on both sides, yet even I am surprised on occasions at the instant and expert mendacity to which journalists, and no doubt other interested parties such as the police and security forces, are treated in episodes of this sort'.

Maurice Tugwell, op.cit., p.237.
10 Interview with the author, 6 April 1982.
11 *Sunday Express*, 24 October 1981.

initially achieving propaganda gains, soon lost credibility and finally collapsed in the face of the British Government's determination. This had a far-reaching effect particularly in America because the initial success of the money collecting activities of Noraid in the United States during the hunger strike was to be short-lived, and by early 1982 one of the directors of Noraid was facing conspiracy charges brought by the FBI for shipping weapons to the IRA. Events like this have not gone unnoticed in the States and their newsworthiness can lead to subsequent reflective and balanced articles about Ulster which can have a considerable impact on American public opinion.[12] And then there was the incident with the British coaster which was sunk by the IRA off the Irish coast on 23 February 1982. Prior to evacuating the crew, the IRA took photographs (which were subsequently issued by them) of the ship's Captain and his crew being held at gun-point. Unfortunately, the IRA had ordered the crew to shout 'Up the Provos!' just before the picture was taken. The British crew's sense of humour got the better of them — they all burst out laughing!

It is important to recognise the radical change in attitude which was required of the British Army from the start of operations in August 1969. This will be discussed in detail in chapter 13 but suffice it to say at this stage that it had to adjust rapidly to an unaccustomed position in the limelight. Added to the attention of the media was the onerous burden of adjusting to the new role of providing aid to the civil power within the United Kingdom. The extraordinary delicate judgement required by every soldier serving in Northern Ireland meant that any individual might have to make a decision of political significance at a moment's notice. This is as true today as it was at the beginning of the campaign and the burden is not necessarily lightened by experience, nor by the change of policy which has placed the Army in a far more supportive role to the police. Therefore in 1969 the British Army found itself in a new role carrying out an extremely difficult job and being reported on by the media which it did not understand. Naturally enough, it was suspicious of the press. This suspicion grew as the newsmen produced evidence of the Army's worst fears: incidents were exaggerated,[13] a number of journalists had no knowledge of the military, many were ignorant about the Irish problem, and the reported

---

12 Such an article was David Reed's 'Northern Ireland's Agony Without End' published in the US edition of *Reader's Digest*, January 1982.
13 After one incident in 1969 the author had to telephone the duty officer at the Unit's base in Devon to warn him that the press and TV reports had over-dramatised the violence. The duty officer then contacted the families to reassure them. This was a lengthy but essential process and illustrates the strain unwittingly imposed on the families by the dramatic nature of the news media.

facts of an incident often did not tally with the details remembered by the soldiers involved in that incident. The suspicion was 'confirmed' as a number of officers found that they had been misquoted, or that the sense of their argument had been altered on recorded television programmes as a result of editing.[14] The situation was further aggravated by the partisan local newspapers which the soldiers read during the long tedious hours between patrols, and by the occasional anti-Army comment in the national newspapers or on television. Just as many journalists did not understand the propaganda factor, so the majority of soldiers did not understand the 'facts of life' about the media. The Army paid the price for its low regard for the Public Relations Service and for its neglect of education about the media.

Although the Army rapidly recovered from the low ebb in public relations terms, it has never fully recovered from this initial suspicion of the news media. Unable to voice its opinion, severely restricted in military options, the military have been further frustrated by the publicity given to terrorists including interviews with members of the IRA. Already fighting with one hand tied behind their backs, the apparent desertion of the media from its support for the forces of law and order was the last straw. This frustration, aggravated by the intermittent tactical propaganda successes achieved by the IRA, has led to some errors of judgement. This came to a head in 1976 when the front page of *The Times* contained an article by Robert Fisk entitled 'Army regards press as destructive in Ulster, papers show' which gave examples of disinformation and planting of false information by the Army.[15] During the same period it was revealed that the Army had been forging press cards.[16] These rare lapses in integrity over a 13 year period have left a permanent mark on the memories of the journalists involved.[17] Many of these errors could have been avoided if the Army had not temporarily lost its faith in relying on honesty and facts to counter IRA propaganda. Tugwell has stressed the need for honesty in combating terrorist propaganda:

The information staffs should not be drawn into speculation when briefing the media, nor should they attempt to 'slant' the facts in

14 *Defence and the Mass Media*, Report of a Seminar held at the RUSI on 13 October 1970, p.11.
15 *The Times*, 24 February 1976. In a letter to *The Times* on 27 February 1976 Lieutenant Colonel W.H. Shillitoe, the author of one of the 'papers' revealed by Robert Fisk, took the newspaper to task, accused it of misrepresentation, exaggeration and claimed the article provided a confirmation of the criticisms he made of the press in his papers (which were, he claimed, the fragment of a book he hoped to write on the interaction between the Army and the press in Northern Ireland).
16 The faking of press cards was discontinued as soon as it came to the notice of higher authorities at Headquarters Northern Ireland.
17 Visit to BBC Radio News, 7 February 1979.

an effort to affect the interpretative process. They must provide information that is disagreeable to authority just as freely as that which is welcome. Just as the public and media are entitled to a totally different standard of behaviour by the security forces from that expected from insurgents, so they are entitled to complete honesty from information staffs.[18]

This point has been fully recognised today by the security forces in Northern Ireland and accountability is stressed at all levels. Furthermore, the Army has acknowledged the part which the local newspapers can play: 'the local press can help explain your actions'.[19] There have indeed been incidents when the local media have blatantly misused facts provided by the authorities to support a particular slanted article but too often this has been used as an excuse to condemn all the local press.

The occasional failure by the security forces to recognise that truth was the best weapon against the IRA propaganda has puzzled a number of journalists. A senior newsman in Belfast remarked: 'When truth is the best bet — why not use it? In 90 per cent of incidents, all the Army has to do is tell the truth'.[20] The evidence produced in this and the previous chapter suggests that the main reasons for this were ignorance and suspicion of the media; and yet the Army has a good public image with the British public largely as a result of favourable reports about its activities conveyed by the media. Indeed some critics have suggested that the media are heavily biased on the side of the security forces.[21]

The realities of reporting in Northern Ireland

Perhaps the best way to understand the journalistic difficulties of reporting in Northern Ireland is to hear what the media have to say about the realities which faced them. In an article in *The Listener*, Jeremy Paxman listed amongst his reasons for the reporting failure in Ulster: the inadequate explanation of the background to the present violence at the beginning, logistics (especially the limited number of reporters who know about Ulster and are prepared to work in a 'danger zone') and perspectives, 'what seems a reasonable story to someone sitting in NW1 or W12 may be nonsense to the people on the ground'.[22]

18 Maurice Tugwell, op.cit., p.330. Since this was written, the requirement for information staffs not to be drawn into speculation has become policy.
19 Interview with Brigadier Colin Shortis, Commander 8 Brigade, 28 March 1979.
20 Visit to Northern Ireland, March 1979.
21 *The British Media and Ireland*, Campaign for Free Speech on Ireland, 1979.
22 Jeremy Paxman, 'Reporting Failure in Ulster', *The Listener*, 5 October 1978, p.429.

He also pointed out that whereas in 1977 the media were accused of aggravating the violence and were under a series of attacks from the government and 'establishment' political groups, 18 months later the attack came from those 'who believed that government has no further need to criticise, since it now controls the broadcasters. If the television journalists themselves are not held on a leash, their editors and employers certainly are'.[23] The multiplicity of criticism from both ends of the spectrum has become a reality of life for the media and as the varying arguments have tended to cancel each other out over the years, so the media has relied more on its own experience than evidence produced by the critics. The hatred of the extremists towards the press is a reality which has already been referred to. An illustration of what this meant in effect concerns a woman reporter from *The Boston Times* who was introduced to a local inhabitant in the shopping centre in Andersonstown by a member of 45 Commando Royal Marines in 1977. Having been introduced, the shopper replied, 'I don't care where she's from — she's with you'.[24] This hatred could be quickly converted to violence when dealing with extremists and some journalists have taken considerable personal risks in their attempts to get a story. Simon Winchester, then of the *Guardian*, related in his book *In Holy Terror*, that during an interview he had with members of the Provisionals in 1971 the proceedings came to an abrupt and premature halt when as a result of a telephone call from Sean MacStiofain (the Chief of Staff in Dublin) the IRA suspected that he might be spying for the British.[25] Such incidents can affect the integrity of journalists and it is interesting to note that this dramatic event was not referred to in the subsequent *Guardian* article which instead took as its theme a confident Provisional IRA faced by ineffective security forces led by over-confident senior military officers.[26] Indeed, Winchester reflected about this omission in his book and particularly about the inefficiency of the intelligence-gathering of the IRA in mistaking him for an Army agent: 'Perhaps I should have appended it to my story. The IRA was in a "confident mood" as the paper's headline read — but by all accounts the mood was not reinforced with the knowledge needed for its proper application'.[27] The dangers involved in investigating the terrorists as opposed to the softer option of investigating the authorities has been a reality of reporting in Ulster which has received scant publicity, and is something

23 Ibid., p.429.
24 Interview with Major Brian Woodham RM, former Second in Command 45 Commando RM, 29 May 1979.
25 Simon Winchester, *In Holy Terror*, Faber and Faber, London 1974, pp. 182—4.
26 *The Guardian*, 20 December 1971.
27 (a) Simon Winchester, op.cit., p.184; (b) See also Tugwell, op.cit., pp. 252—4.

which the IRA have used to their advantage.

Inevitably the implied threat is not restricted to the journalist but also includes witnesses. Martin Bell of BBC Television News told the author of an incident concerning the origins of the Peace Movement in 1976. The movement grew out of a tragic accident in which three small children were knocked down and killed by a car containing IRA gunmen which was being pursued by the Army. Martin Bell arrived after the bodies had been removed from the scene of the accident and he found an eight year old boy who had seen it all happen:

> I put him on camera and he gave me a coherent account of what had happened. Believable as it only can be coming from the 'mouths of babes' — no-one could have told him what to say — he just said it, and this I subsequently learned caused an awful lot of offence to the IRA because it precluded them from making their own version . . . . One then has to ask oneself is this fellow going to be victimised, and I figured that even the IRA wouldn't have it in for an eight year old kid.[28]

Martin Bell went on to point out that a journalist is obliged to report an incident regardless of whether he was at the event: 'You can't fail to report just because you were not there at the time. You always rush out as quickly as you can but you are very seldom on the scene'. If a reporter *does* arrive at an incident soon enough, however, he can often forestall attempts to manufacture 'the facts':

> I remember one case particularly, in the Ardoyne, where some youth had been killed and it had been fairly clear that he had been carrying a gun because, as soon as one got there with one's camera, there was deep hostility from the local people. Whereas, if in fact he had been an innocent bystander then they would have said, 'come on in and see what these bastards have done to us'. But no, I was chased out at gunpoint by the IRA. They had not had time to manufacture a fancy story.[29]

The realities of reporting in Northern Ireland are such that it is often extremely difficult to establish the true facts of an incident. The very real threat from the Provisional IRA to journalists and witnesses alike; the obligation to report an incident which obliges the reporter to take heed of 'eye-witness' accounts without being able fully to check them out; the constant requirement to meet deadlines (which frustrate the reporter, and at the same time aid the skilful propagandist) — all these

28 Interview with the author, 28 August 1979.
29 Ibid.

realities can foil attempts to uncover sufficient facts of a disputed incident in time to provide an objective report for the relevant deadline. It is the familiar problem of being required to make a decision against the clock, thwarted by insufficient or unverified information. In such circumstances the reporter can find himself dancing to the terrorists' tune, and on occasions it requires personal courage by a journalist to include *all* the facts in his article.

The broadcasters' principle of impartiality

Impartiality is a difficult principle to follow amidst the entrenched attitudes of Ulster and it has therefore faced the broadcasters with a particular dilemma right from the beginning. On 23 November 1971 the Governor of the BBC, Lord Hill, wrote to the Home Secretary, Mr Reginald Maudling, following a period of considerable governmental pressure on the BBC:

> We see it as our over-riding responsibility to report the scene as it is, in all its tragedy, to all the people of the United Kingdom. We do not side with the Catholics or the Protestants. The BBC and its staff abhor the terrorism of the IRA and report their campaign of murder with revulsion . . .
>
> In short, as between the government and the opposition, as between the two communities in Northern Ireland, the BBC has a duty to be impartial no less than the rest of the United Kingdom. But as between the British Army and the gunmen the BBC is not and cannot be impartial.[30]

This principle created tension internally within the BBC which resulted in some accusations of censorship by the management, whilst Hill defended his action by stating that it was necessary in order for the BBC to retain its independence.[31] Meanwhile similar protests about censorship were voiced by reporters and producers following the banning of the *World in Action* film *South of the Border* by the ITA in November 1971. What in fact was happening both within the BBC and ITA was an adjustment by broadcasting to the realities of observing the principles of impartiality and objectivity whilst reporting Northern Ireland:

30 Lord Hill, *Behind the Screen*, Sidgwick and Jackson, London 1974, p.209.
31 (a) Lord Hill, op.cit., pp. 210—11; (b) Philip Schlesinger, *Putting Reality Together,* Constable, London 1978, pp. 212—13.

The tension emerging between the broadcasters and their employers was a tension between an old feeling about broadcasting and a new one, between the view that broadcasting should invariably create and transmit a simulated, balanced model of the prevailing political scene and the view that broadcasting should now exist as a reporting tool pure and simple. The doctrine of impartiality had forced on broadcasting organisations a social role that now made them extremely vulnerable. Some objectivity did not flow naturally out of the material being presented, it had to be imposed by hierarchy.[32]

The conflicting difficulties of fulfilling their obligations to impartiality, and the requirement to inform the public whilst not providing a platform for terrorist publicity, have plagued the broadcasters throughout the campaign. The Annan Report noted these difficulties. On the section on Ulster it stated:

Northern Ireland is a special case . . . The BBC told us that they could not be impartial about people dedicated to using violent methods to break up the unity of the state. The views of illegal organisations like the IRA should be broadcast only 'when it is of value to the people that they should be heard and not when it is in the IRA's interest to be heard' . . . . In considering what should be broadcast the BBC intensified the reference-up system; and they told us that they gave particular consideration to the effect of BBC broadcasts on the Army in Northern Ireland. The IBA told us that they had to consider under the IBA Act whether a programme was likely to encourage or incite to crime or lead to disorder, and they also took into account what the public believed might be the affect of such a programme.[33]

In considering the terrorists' desire for publicity and the use of broadcasting for that purpose, the report said:

Terrorism feeds off publicity: publicity is its main hope of intimidating government and the public; publicity gives it a further chance for recruitment. The acts terrorists commit are each minor incidents in their general campaign to attract attention to their cause. No democracy can tolerate terrorism because it is a denial of the democratic assumption that injustice can, in time, be put right through discussion, peaceful persuasion and compromise. By killing and destroying, the terrorists are bound to extort pub-

32 Anthony Smith, *The Politics of Information*, Macmillan, London 1978, p.124.
33 Lord Annan, op.cit., p.269.

licity — and hence one of their ends — because such news will be reported. But there is no reason to abet them by giving additional publicity. This is not a problem on which an unequivocal ruling or recommendation can usefully be made because it can be assessed only within the situation obtaining at the time the decision is to be taken. We recognise the particular reasons why the Government of the Irish Republic decided to proscribe broadcast interviews with members of illegal organisations, but within the different political and broadcasting structures in the United Kingdom we think that the decision whether to permit such appearances must remain with the broadcasting organisations, and should not rest on the fiat of a British Government. We would expect these difficult decisions to be taken at the highest levels in the BBC and in the IBA. We also think it important that programmes should not be made which might be shown in some parts of the United Kingdom but which could not be broadcast in Northern Ireland because of the effect they might have on the situation there.[34]

In the first ten years the BBC has held just four interviews with terrorist spokesmen from Ulster and controversy has surrounded each broadcast. Following the interview with the spokesman from the Irish National Liberation Army (INLA) on the BBC television programme *Tonight* on 5 July 1979, Sir Ian Trethowan, the then Director General of the BBC, justified the interview on the grounds that the BBC, like the press, had a job to inform the public about the nature of terrorism in Ulster although this may 'sometimes mean distress and shock to some members of the public', and pointed out that because of the impact of a filmed interview on television these were only undertaken very infrequently and only after very careful deliberation at the highest level within the BBC.[35] Commenting after a previous television interview with an IRA spokesman, Merlyn Rees, the then Secretary of State for Northern Ireland, remarked: 'If it makes people realise all over the UK that I am dealing with people who are out to shoot, kill and maim for political reasons . . . they will understand the nature of the problem, it won't have done any harm'.[36] There are others who argue that such interviews play right into the hands of the terrorists who use the freedom of the press as a weapon against democracy: 'No country in the world permits an armed bank robber to justify and rationalise his

34 Ibid., p.270.
35 Ian Trethowan's letter to the Editor of *The Daily Telegraph*, 14 July 1979.
36 Richard Francis, *Broadcasting to a Community in Conflict — The Experience in Northern Ireland*, lecture given at the Royal Institute of International Affairs, Chatham House, 22 February 1977, BBC, p.13.

crime on television, yet terrorists and "freedom fighters" obtain frequent access to the screen'.[37]

The IRA do gain immense publicity from broadcasting and on occasions they have manipulated television most skilfully; the broadcasters do have an obligation to impartiality but at the same time it is essential that they maintain their independence from governmental control. Both the BBC and the IBA have been criticised by the Right for helping to undermine government policy, and by the Left for being in the hands of the government of the day. Representatives from both ends of the political spectrum have often appeared to be more concerned with accusing the broadcaster of not sufficiently representing their own views on Ulster than with the immense difficulties of reporting on events in the Province. The broadcasters have faced up to the problems with integrity and have gradually developed practical solutions to the immense difficulties as they have gained experience. Whilst still BBC Controller, Northern Ireland, Richard Francis gave a lecture to the Royal Institute of International Affairs about the problems of broadcasting in Northern Ireland which clearly explained the dilemmas and the problems. It concluded with these words:

> So the experience of broadcasting in Northern Ireland, for all the threats to society and to human life, suggests that the practice of free speech within a well-tested framework of responsibility is the best, if not the easiest, way to cover extraordinary circumstances. I believe we have a contribution to make to the maintenance of democracy, both by providing a forum where harsh differences of opinion can be aired and by reporting and courageously investigating the unpalatable truths which underlie the problems in our midst. I am sure that if and when the communities of Northern Ireland reconcile their conflicts it will be by understanding them rather than by ignoring them, and I would like to think that amongst those who will have contributed most to that understanding the broadcasters, and the BBC in particular, will have played their part.[38]

The broadcasters have tried to find practical answers to realistic problems. They have not always received the credit due to them for these efforts. Nor has sufficient notice been paid to the phenomenon of the development of television side by side with the growth of terrorism in Ulster. This has become an inherent characteristic of low-level conflict and the 'box' has had to learn to cope with the terrorists' ceaseless attempts to manipulate its use.

37 *Television and Conflict*, op.cit., p.12.
38 Richard Francis, op.cit., p.16.

Accuracy, selectivity and interpretation

Both the press and broadcasting have been accused of inaccuracies in their reporting of Northern Ireland. These accusations can be supported by factual analysis in certain instances but from this has often developed a general condemnation of the mass media as a whole. What is often forgotten is the news media's honest attempts to try and report accurately. The news process described in Part II of this book has shown that many things can affect the passage of copy from incident to publication and these factors are even more potent in a situation like Ireland. Annan noted that inevitably there will be mistakes when 'reporters and cameramen have to make difficult split-second judgements on the ground',[39] and human error at all levels is a continual problem in any conflict situation. But that does not mean that the inaccuracies are deliberate. However 'selectivity' is a different matter. Selection of certain facts from those available, and omission of others, can lead to distortion in news items or can be used to reinforce a prejudiced viewpoint in an article. Furthermore the 'selective' nature of television can contribute to a distorted picture of an incident or misrepresentation of issues (*viz.* Vietnam). The Independent Television Companies Association (ITCA) has acknowledged this problem in connection with Ulster: 'a brief, isolated incident of violence does not necessarily tell the whole story'.[40] 'Interpretation' is another problem. Tugwell provides an illustration of this by an example of a remark by a senior Army spokesman that the gunfights which followed internment in 1971, together with the arrests, had seriously weakened the IBA: 'Technically, he was correct. However the news media interpreted the statement as being an official claim that the Provisionals were nearly beaten, which their continued acts of violence showed was certainly not the case. This caused the same sort of friction between media and military that had existed in Vietnam prior to the Tet offensive, a resentment at what newsmen considered to be official attempts to paint a rosier picture than circumstances justified'.[41]

This comment illustrates one of the inherent problems of reporting Ulster. There are others which need to be recognised both by the military and the media: the media have been guilty of inaccuracies, exaggeration and distortion, but countless incidents have been reported accurately and factually; television does have a dramatic impact; head-

---

39 Lord Annan, op.cit., p.270.
40 ITCA, *Evidence to the Annan Committee* (ITCA 1975), p.55. The ITCA used this problem as one of their reasons for recommending more time to be allocated to television news programmes.
41 Maurice Tugwell, op.cit., p.242.

lines are dramatic; strong military action will tend to antagonise local public opinion; military frustrations, and the newsman's job to inform the public, is an area of friction which is a direct result of terrorism — and it will be influenced by irresponsible journalism, and exploited by the terrorists. All these symptoms are products of the Ulster conflict. They are characteristics which have emerged during the last 13 years; they are the realities of life which need to be recognised by every soldier and journalist in Ulster. They are unlikely to change and therefore both should acknowledge these facts of life and try to work out a practical solution to the mutual benefit of both.

The first statement

These characteristics are exemplified in the problem of 'the first statement'. When an incident occurs there is a direct conflict between the requirements of the military and the media. The media have deadlines to meet and therefore put pressure on the military to issue a statement about the incident. On the other hand, the security forces need time to evaluate the facts of the case before they can issue a statement which is factually correct. In a number of incidents the Provisionals, unhindered by legal restraints or strict regard for the truth, have nipped in with the first statement. This is crucial because, as one journalist put it to the author on a visit to Ulster: 'the impact of the first account of an incident is likely to have a lasting impression even if it is subsequently proved to be utterly untrue'. Because of the media's insatiable appetite for news which must be 'up to the minute' the first statement is a valuable weapon in the propagandist's armour; he uses this fundamental characteristic of the news media to publicise his version first and thus forces the other side to react to his initiative.[42] Maria McGuire, the defector from the Provisionals wrote:

> There was a further press conference due on 20 December [1971] — this time it was the turn of the Commander of the British troops in the six counties, Major General Sir Harry Tuzo, to give his assessment of the campaign against us. And so, on 19 December, we held our own press conference in Dublin, in

---

42 Jacques Ellul, *Propaganda: The Formation of Men's Attitudes* translated from the French by Konrad Kellen and Jean Lerner, Alfred Knopf, New York 1966, pp. 46—71: 'Propaganda is based on current news . . . This situation makes the "current-affairs man" a ready target for propaganda. He is unstable because he runs after what happened today; he relates to the event, and therefore cannot resist any impulse coming from that event. Because he is immersed in current affairs, this man has a psychological weakness that puts him at the mercy of the propagandist'.

which we said that our organisation had not been seriously affected by internment, our supplies of arms and ammunition were still intact, and that the British Army was powerless to prevent our operations. Naturally these claims were put to Tuzo the next day — our tactic of compelling other people to react to us, and not the other way round.[43]

Another incident occurred in 1977 which illustrates the effectiveness of this tactic. At 1.10 am on 4 August a patrol from 45 Commando Royal Marines was on the waste ground about 80 metres south of the Andersonstown social club building.[44] A single shot was fired very close to them (in the darkness they thought it was fired at them). The Marines cocked their weapons and fired one shot at where they thought the gunman was positioned which was in a garden about 50 metres south west of the club building. This shot was fired about 15 seconds after the first one. The patrol then immediately followed-up into the area where the gunman was thought to be, but they found no gunman and no empty cartridge case. There was another patrol about 250 metres away which also heard the shots. They moved rapidly into the area of the incident and found Jack McCarten, the 55 year old manager of the social club, beside his car in the forecourt of the club dying of a gunshot wound in the back.

Shortly after this incident the Provisional Sein Fein issued a statement saying:

> At approximately 1.30 this morning the British Army shot dead the Manager of the Andersonstown Social Club, Mr Jack McCarten, as he was leaving the Club. The British Army has since issued a statement that Mr McCarten was shot dead in cross-fire. This is a deliberate lie. Sein Fein views Mr McCarten's death as a premeditated act of murder carried out by the British Army.

This statement directly challenged the announcement put out by the security forces which was neither positive enough nor very clear. Sein Fein had taken the initiative and forced the opposition to react to them. The security forces took up the challenge and that night a member of the patrol was interviewed on both BBC television and Ulster Television. His matter of fact account of what had happened contrasted with the emotional language of the Sein Fein announcement and convinced most impartial viewers which side was telling the truth.

---

43 McGuire, op.cit., p.75.
44 45 Commando RM were stationed in Andersonstown, a predominantly Catholic area in the centre of West Belfast. The details of this incident have been obtained by talking to members of the Commando, and from newspaper articles.

However some of the local press continued the controversy and speculated about the event. Attempts were made to discredit the Marines and this campaign was helped by the fact that, because of the inevitable delays due to forensic procedures, the police were unable to confirm immediately that the remains of the bullet extracted from McCarten's body were *not* part of a 7.62 mm round. Doubts were ended when the bullet fired by the patrol was extracted from a large horse-chestnut tree and forensically matched to the marine's weapon. The security forces were prepared to cut down the tree in order to extract the bullet to prove their innocence, but in the event it was possible to cut out a segment from the tree with the bullet head imbedded in it.

All this took time and it was some 72 hours after the incident before the police were able to prove conclusively that it had been the Provisional Sein Fein who were lying, not the Marines. Predictably the press coverage of this event three days later did not match the headlines on 4 and 5 August despite the lengths to which the security forces went to establish the facts. Although in this case the security forces had issued the first statement it was not sufficiently positive and Provisional Sein Fein immediately seized the initiative and challenged the credibility of the Royal Marines. This forced the security forces to dance to the opposition's tune and the ensuing counterclaims were publicised by the media because this was considered newsworthy.

The failure of the news media to show as much interest in the recovery of the bullet from the tree and the subsequent forensic proof underlines the fundamental problems associated with such events: (1) that newsmen are prisoners of current events − a weakness which is exploited by the skilful propagandist − hence the impact of the initial 'story'; (2) the frequent failure of the media to provide balancing comment after the event has ceased to be news; and (3) the dilemma for the security forces who so often have to wait for the legal proof to underseal their credibility. This restriction is fully exploited by the terrorists and their fellow travellers but is too rarely appreciated by newsmen from the mainland, or members of the international press, who have little or no knowledge of the local conditions. In this particular case the law of libel and the rules of *sub judice* prevented publication of information which would have enabled objective journalists to set the incident in context. As far as this particular incident is concerned the questions still remain; if the security forces did not shoot Jack McCarten, who did, for what reason, and why at that particular time when there were patrols in the area?

The Dunloy incident

The restrictions imposed by the rules of *sub judice* and the difficulties associated with the issue of the first statement are well illustrated by the Dunloy incident. On 11 July 1978 a two-man SAS patrol shot dead John Boyle, a 16 year old boy, who picked up an Armalite rifle from an arms cache in a graveyard adjoining a farm in Dunloy which the soldiers had been observing. These simple facts hide the tragedy of the incident because the stake-out was set up as a result of the Boyle family discovering the cache and reporting it to the police. The police did warn the family to stay away from the area because of the Army stake-out but the warning was not given to the family until an hour after John Boyle had gone back to the graveyard to see whether the cache was still there. The innocent teenager was shot dead by the soldiers, who were no more than 10 yards from him, because he picked up the Armalite rifle and 'pointed it at them'. In these circumstances they did not issue a warning because their immediate judgement was that it would have been foolhardy if, as they assumed, he was a terrorist.

The shooting occurred in the middle of the morning. At 1 pm Headquarters Northern Ireland (HQNI) issued this statement: 'At approximately 1022 hours this morning near Dunloy, a uniformed military patrol challenged three men, one man was shot; two men are assisting police enquiries. Weapons and explosives have been recovered'. At 5.40 pm they issued a second statement:

> We are now able to give the full facts of the incident at Dunloy this morning. At 1022 hours this morning a two man patrol operating in the area of an old graveyard in Dunloy heard a tractor approaching the graveyard. It stopped and shortly afterwards a man ran into the graveyard, went to a gravestone and reached under it. At this point the man saw the two soldiers; he straightened up pointing an Armalite rifle in their direction. The soldiers fired five rounds at the armed man who was killed. The Armalite was subsequently found with its magazine fitted and a round in the breech ready to fire. In addition a blast incendiary bomb, a revolver, a mask, a combat jacket and a beret were found under the gravestone.
>
> A man leaving the scene on the tractor was arrested by the Army, and a third man who arrived shortly afterwards in a car was detained. Both were handed over to the police. . . . In our first report we said, a challenge was given; on detailed investigation we find this was not so. It was impracticable for the soldiers to issue a warning before firing as the man was ten yards from them pointing a rifle at them.

The significant variation in the two statements, plus the fact that the RUC stated that they were satisfied that the three men were not connected with terrorism,[45] brought a predictable storm of criticism from the press: 'Ulster United in Outrage' (*The Guardian*), 'Paisley Calls Army "dishonest" About Death' (*The Daily Telegraph*), 'Boy, 16, is Shot Dead in Army Blunder' (*Irish Independent*). The different statements, and the fact that an apparently innocent boy had been killed without warning, cast considerable doubt on the credibility of the Army and resulted in speculation about what had actually happened.[46] The Secretary of State for Northern Ireland, Roy Mason, sent a personal message of sympathy to the Boyle family and promised a full investigation by the RUC.[47] This put the matter *sub judice* and as the two soldiers were subsequently charged with the murder of John Boyle, the Army were unable to answer any of the allegations until the soldiers were cleared of the charge in July 1979, some twelve months later. After the acquittal the GOC NI, Lieutenant General Sir Timothy Creasey, issued the following statement:

I have never doubted that the two NCOs who were on an operation properly mounted at the request of the Royal Ulster Constabulary, acted in good faith.

The dilemma that these two NCOs faced making their split second decision is one that can face any soldier in the Province at any time. They know that their actions can be subjected to the full scrutiny of the law.

The British Army is deployed in strength in those areas of the Province where the danger is greatest, their living conditions are often cramped and less than comfortable, and their working hours are very long.

The major part of their operations is out of sight until the focus of public attention is directed at their actions, but they have learned to live with the constraints made by the rules of *sub judice* which have to be accepted, often in the face of wild allegations.

The Army will continue to carry out their task to defeat terrorism in the Province in support of the civilian power, willingly, cheerfully and with good nature and tolerance.[48]

This carefully worded statement by General Creasey not only demonstrated his support for the two soldiers but also explained the

---

45 The RUC issued their statement at 5.50 pm, 11 July 1978.;
46 For instance, *The Sunday Times*, 16 July 1978 and 13 August 1978.
47 All unnatural deaths in Northern Ireland are fully investigated by the RUC.
48 *Visor* (edition 274), 6 July 1979. Part of this statement was also reported in *The Daily Telegraph*, 5 July 1979.

difficult circumstances under which the British Army operated. It provided the balance to the unsubstantiated allegations and speculation which had been made in a number of newspapers immediately after the event. Regretfully, and typically, his statement was not quoted in its entirety in all newspapers.

This incident brings out a number of relevant points. As luck would have it, the very day it occurred a new Chief Information Officer arrived at HQNI. He was therefore unable to provide practical advice about the first statement which nevertheless was issued in good faith on the basis of the facts as they were known at the time. The reason that the details which emerged later differed from the original version was due to the poor communications between the scene of the stakeout and Lisburn. It was not until the incident had been fully investigated on the ground, that the facts became clear. However, in providing a comprehensive factual account in their second statement the Army failed to say why the initial statement was inaccurate (i.e. insufficient knowledge of the facts due to poor communications). It was this failure in explanation which caused the Army's credibility to be doubted.

The Dunloy incident has provided a number of lessons from which both the military and the media can learn. Because of the confusion which inevitably surrounds such an incident the military should only issue the briefest of statements immediately after the event containing no details. This can be equated to the operational 'Contact Report' procedure in which the Army is well versed. There is then likely to be a long delay before any subsequent statement can be made, whilst the incident is fully investigated. This will be a period of frustration for newsmen but it is important that the media appreciate that the security forces will need time to establish the facts; pressuring the Press Desk at Lisburn because of deadlines will not produce 'the facts' any quicker. In return for this co-operation the media have a right to expect complete honesty from the Army. Such a course of action would also help to minimise manipulation of both the security forces and the media by IRA propaganda.

The importance of the 'first statement' has become even more enhanced since the change in policy of the Army's attitude towards providing assistance for the media's every request. This change of policy occurred soon after Lieutenant General Sir Richard Lawson had taken over as GOC in January 1980. The genesis of the idea lay in the IRA's proven determination to match the security forces for the battle of the headlines. It was reasoned that if the military presence were to be reduced on the ground, then this should be reflected by public relations policy as well. A less aggressive military appearance in the streets and fewer banner headlines in the newspapers should have an effect on the long-suffering war-weary population – and help to undermine the support and sympathy for the IRA. This would gradually get the Province back to a more normal way of life. The public relations policy adopted was such that although journalists were not hindered in their efforts to acquire information about the Army's activities, neither were they offered any positive assistance. This naturally drew a reaction from some journalists,[49] but on the whole the reasoning behind the decision was accepted.

It is difficult to assess the success of this policy, but there is one recent significant example of the consequences of forcing terrorist organisations into a media cul-de-sac. On 24 March 1982 Sir John Hermon, the Chief Constable of the RUC, declared that: 'terrorists in the Province were reeling from the blows inflicted upon them by informers whose evidence had led to the charging of almost 200 terrorists who were mainly members of the IRA and the Irish Liberation Army. . . . The terrorists are becoming desperate'.[50] This was reported in the following morning's newspapers. That evening the radio and television news bulletins and evening newspapers contained headlines about an IRA ambush on an Army patrol in Belfast which resulted in three soldiers being killed and nine civilians injured. It transpired that the ambush had been set up on the night of 24 March when five gunmen seized a terraced house overlooking the planned killing ground. That was the day when the Chief Constable had given his interview. The three soldiers, all members of the Royal Green Jackets, were the first regular troops to be killed in the Province for six months.

This illustrates once again the terrorists' need for publicity and serves to underline the importance of the marriage between operational and public relations policies. But whether the security forces are pursuing a high or low profile policy, the accuracy of the first statement is crucially important and therefore it is vital that the Army provides assistance to the media, including access, when an incident occurs.

Credibility

The whole crux of the relationship between the military and the media is credibility – and so much depends upon the first statement: 'You

---

49 Peter Gill, documentary producer with Thames Television wrote a letter to *The Times* in December 1980 in which he pointed out that in the course of that year he had received markedly more assistance from the Pakistan Army on their North West Frontier with Afghanistan and with the Iraqi Army in their war with Iran than from the British Army in Northern Ireland.
50 *The Times*, 25 March 1982.

lose everything if your first statement is wrong. Credibility rises if you admit your mistakes'.[51] Ulster has shown that credibility depends upon the truth, and the higher the credibility the more sympathetic will be the coverage in the national press and the more objective provincial newspapers in Northern Ireland, and the more likelihood of continued public support. Ulster has also shown that the majority of British newsmen have tried to report events objectively and accurately.

The military have had British public support throughout the campaign because of sympathetic coverage by the media; because the military have been seen to be carrying out their task more humanely than most other armies might in similar circumstances; and because of the general condemnation of terrorism (undersealed by the bi-partisan political policy towards Ulster). The Army does have a good public image today, largely as a result of Ulster, but it is not always evident that the Army itself is aware of this. The Army has tended to be oversensitive when it has been criticised by the media, and failed to realise that in the majority of cases it has been the soundness of the Army's image which has been the very rock on which wild allegations have foundered. This faith in itself is vital for the Army because Ulster has demonstrated time and again that it may well have to concede propaganda victory to the IRA in the short term in order to win in the long term. On occasions the Army has lacked the necessary patience and foresight to appreciate this. This failure has partially been due to ignorance of the media's role in society which had led to suspicion of journalists and some restriction in access. And yet, when access has been granted, and soldier and reporter have actually met on the ground, there has usually been common understanding and the resulting article has invariably been sympathetic towards the Army.[52] Experience has also shown that in some circumstances both the military and the media benefit from immediate access being provided at both the Press Desk and on the ground when an incident occurs. The media prefer first hand accounts and this enables the military to provide its account of the incident immediately.

Although the military has received sympathetic coverage from the majority of the British press, this is not necessarily the case with foreign press coverage. The IRA have always been aware of the importance of public sympathy for the cause abroad, especially in the United States, and they have found fertile ground amongst some of the American

---

51 Interview with Robin Walsh, News Editor BBC TV Belfast, 30 March 1979.
52 For example, *The Observer* article of 4 March 1979 by Tom Davies about the stress to which troops serving in Ulster are subjected. This article resulted from the death of Trooper Maggs (see p.196).

media. The following example illustrates how the basic facts of an incident can be twisted to provide damaging propaganda and throws an interesting light on the press.

It concerns the report by an American journalist, Michael Daly, who wrote a dramatic article for the *New York Daily News* about the apparent lack of control of an Army patrol when dealing with a mob of youths throwing petrol bombs the day Bobby Sands died. One of the youths was shot by the patrol. The *Daily Mail* read Daly's article and were so incensed with its portrayal of the apparent callousness of a young British soldier shooting down an unarmed '15 year old' youth, that they checked out the story with the Press Desk at Lisburn. If this article was correct it demonstrated a disgraceful lack of control by a British Army Unit. However, the telephone call revealed that there were a number of inaccuracies in Daly's story and after checking the facts with the Army, they published an article on 8 May 1981 which included the full Daly account followed by their own piece which exposed a long list of inaccuracies. The basic facts of the incident as reported in the *Daily Mail* were as follows:

> On the day of Bobby Sands' death an Army patrol came under continuous attack by youths throwing petrol bombs. Soon, the soldiers were surrounded by flames, and the mob, ignoring the plastic bullets, were closing in all the time.
>
> Eventually, the young officer in charge of the unit took the view that his men were in mortal danger. After shouting warnings, which were ignored, he ordered the use of real bullets. Two of his men fired one round each.
>
> One of the mob, a youth named Anthony McCartan fell with a gunshot wound in his right leg.[53]

Around the basis of this incident Daly had written an angry and emotional article about the pressure of the British Army in Ulster designed to appeal to the large Irish readership of the *New York Daily News*. The only problem was, his piece was proved to be blatantly dishonest. The *Daily Mail*'s exposure revealed that: the named British soldier, who was the central figure of Daly's account, did not exist; no journalist accompanied the patrol (Daly implied that he did); and a reported conversation between an officer and the soldier overheard by Daly, never took place. Furthermore, even the basic facts were wrong: the youth who was shot by the patrol was Anthony McCartan (not Johnny McCartin); he was 18 years old (not 15); and Bobby Sands prison number was 950/77 (not 1066).

53 The *Daily Mail*, 8 May 1981.

In the preamble, the *Daily Mail* voiced its concern about the blatant anti-British propaganda which had appeared in many published articles about Northern Ireland in the United States for a number of years but which had reached 'a crescendo of dishonesty' during the weeks leading up to Bobby Sands' death. It also pointed out that Daly's 'report' was pure invention and a malevolent piece of propaganda.

On reading the *Daily Mail* article, the *New York Daily News* telephoned Lisburn to check out the accuracy of Daly's article. Lisburn refuted a number of facts in the article. Daly was immediately flown back to New York, questioned for a number of hours by his newspaper executives, and then placed on temporary suspension whilst his reporting was investigated. The *Daily Mail* received justifiable praise for their exposure of Daly by Mr Humphrey Atkins, the Secretary of State:

> The *Daily Mail* has done a very valuable journalistic service showing the lengths to which some elements of the overseas Press have been sensationalising the present situation in Northern Ireland. There is an intensive propaganda campaign being waged by the Provisional IRA and its supporters, particularly in America.[54]

What made this incident even more poignant was the fact that Michael Daly had just been awarded the Columbia University School of Journalism Mike Berger Award!

For the PR organisation at HQ Northern Ireland this was an important incident. A blatantly fictitious American article which could be used for propaganda purposes had been exposed by a British newspaper, with their assistance. As a result, the credibility of the Army in Ulster had been enhanced.

The lessons

Northern Ireland has provided salutary lessons for soldier and journalist alike. The soldier's tactics have been considerably influenced by the effect on public opinion, and the problem of countering PIRA's skilful propaganda has not always been solved. The journalist has been surprised by the intensity of bigotry, by the propaganda, and by the difficulty of achieving accuracy. Perhaps the greatest area of misunderstanding has been the failure of the military to recognise the media's duty to report events and its right to comment. The reporting of a

---

54 The *Daily Mail*, 9 May 1981.

terrorist act does not mean that it is condoned: 'remember, don't confuse coverage with attitude. It is the duty of news agencies to report events . . . we must question — that is the role of TV news'.[55] Similarly, 'just because people are opposed to terrorism it doesn't mean that the media cannot criticise the security forces'.[56] Considerable progress has been made in the relationship between the military and the media in Northern Ireland since 1969 but one is still left with the impression that neither has really understood the other's problems or appreciated the impact of the conflict on that relationship.

Following the publication of the 'Army documents' criticising the press in February 1976[57] *The Times* editorial of 27 February 1976 remarked that such criticism was not surprising since:

> . . . the security authorities and the press have essentially different tasks in circumstances that have no precedent within the United Kingdom in recent times. In conditions of near civil war the army are engaged in a conflict that is both military and psychological. Because they are fighting urban terrorists who are pursuing their political ends without scruple or regard for the democratic wishes of the people in either part of Ireland, and in the process have put civilized life in jeopardy in Northern Ireland and elsewhere in the United Kingdom, there is an unqualified national interest in the army's success in this struggle. Yet that success cannot be obtained without the sustained support of public opinion. So the security authorities are engaged in a propaganda war which it is in the national interest that they should win.
>
> The press, however, while sharing in the general national interest, have different responsibilities. A newspaper that is realistic will accept that the army must wage a propaganda war, but a newspaper that retains its principles will have no part itself in the conduct of that war. Its task is to see that its readers are informed as fully and clearly as possible. That includes not merely the events on the ground but the nature of the conflict, political attitudes on both sides, the relationship of the IRA to the local community and the changing strength of the organization itself. The more complete and accurate the picture, the more adequately the task is performed.
>
> Sometimes that will suit the security authorities, sometimes not.[58]

---

55 Interview with Alan Protheroe, then Editor BBC TV News, 7 December 1978.
56 Interview with a senior journalist during author's visit to Belfast in March 1979.
57 See p.128.
58 *The Times*, 27 February 1976.

The article went on to note the failings of both sides: the use of false press cards by soldiers, the security authorities' dismay when journalists refuse to accept official statements at face value, the uncritical treatment by the media of IRA statements, 'the perennial danger of the journalist getting too close to his sources of information so that he comes to regard them as his clients rather than his contacts', and sometimes the personal bias of a journalist against the forces of authority. Added to this is the 'temptation, to which television is particularly subject because of the very nature of the medium, to concentrate on the dramatic episode rather than presenting the picture in context'.[59]

This frank article outlined the natural tension that is inherent between the roles of the soldier and the journalist, and which has been highlighted by Northern Ireland. The experience of the last 13 years will have been wasted if the military and the media do not develop a much closer understanding of each other's role in a conflict situation.

59 Ibid.

11 The Inherent Problems of Reporting Conflict

Lessons from Vietnam and Ulster

What are the lessons to emerge from the reporting of conflict? There are a number of inherent problems which are directly related to a state of conflict. First of all, the media can be 'used' for propaganda purposes: 'the television camera is like a weapon lying in the street. Either side can pick it up and use it'.[1] Second, the practical problems for the broadcasters of achieving 'impartiality' and 'objectivity' are immense and require considerable integrity on the part of the individual making the decision about a specific incident; and the problems are not necessarily made easier by experience since each incident has its own peculiar factors. Third, there is the problem of distortion by the media as a result of giving an overall impression from the sensationalism of one particular event. This is particularly pertinent to television which is primarily a visual medium and therefore its objectivity can be unwittingly affected by picture selection and editorialisation. Fourth, the difficulties of obtaining and reporting accurate information about an incident due to the characteristically confused situation surrounding an event, and the pressure of making decisions against the clock. The simple statement that the 'first casualty of war is truth'[2] begs a

---

1 Richard Clutterbuck, *Living with Terrorism*, Faber & Faber, London 1975, p.147.
2 The original statement: 'The first casualty when war comes is truth' is attributed to Senator Hiram Johnson, 1917, quoted at the beginning of Phillip Knightley's book, *The First Casualty*, André Deutsch, London 1975.

question to which there are many answers resulting from a multitude of complex reasons. Fifth, there is an automatic bias built in to reports by the news media which is directly related to access. Newsmen can only report what they can see or (as is more usually the case), what the witnesses to whom they talk claim they saw. And sixth, the effect that a reporter's first experience of combat can have on his copy:

> The initial emotional shock when you first experience the sustained horror of combat can result in over-writing and misleading reports. The only parallel I can think of is that of Bomber Command in the last war when people generally lived a peaceful and civilised existence, and then were exposed to shock and horror for a few hours before returning to a civilised environment.[3]

Studies of the reporting of conflict in such places as Vietnam and Ulster have shown that these characteristics have become an inherent problem for journalists. However, the fact that they are inherent, that they are one of the 'side-effects' of conflict, has not been fully acknowledged by either the military or the media. This has led to suspicion and mistrust and there is no clear indication that either side really understands the other's problems despite the considerable number of years soldiers and reporters have worked beside each other during military operations.

There is a definite requirement for the media to explain its role in society to a largely ignorant public (and this includes the military). By publicly explaining the ethics of journalism the media can educate the public about its difficulties and at the same time demonstrate how the journalists themselves see their responsibilities. The most appropriate medium for doing this is television (because it reaches a mass audience), and there are indications that Granada Television had found the right format in its six-part series *State of the Nation*. This series was broadcast in June and July 1979. It was about journalistic ethics and its formula allowed for a number of professional communicators to be subjected to probing questions from experienced American lawyers about a fictitious but topical scenario. The series was entertaining and very educational because it allowed the public to see how the media viewed their responsibilities in given circumstances. The topicality of the chosen subjects for discussion was illustrated by the last programme about terrorism; this was recorded ten days before the BBC's *Tonight* interview with the INLA (see p.134), and one of the participants in the programme was Richard Francis, then Director, News and Current Affairs, BBC.[4]

---

3 Christopher Wain, interview with the author, 16 November 1979.
4 The transcript of each programme in this series has been published in a book by Brian Lapping, *The Bounds of Freedom*, Constable, London 1980.

The explanation of the role of journalism will enable the soldier to put the journalist's job into perspective for he needs to be aware of the problem with which the reporter or editor is faced in a conflict situation. He also needs to acknowledge that in a democracy with a free press there will inevitably be the occasional conflict of interest. The pressing need for the two to understand each other's problem is emphasised by the logical alternative to a free press: censorship. Since censorship would be counter-productive in any scenario short of total war there is a requirement for mutual understanding for the need for responsible journalism on the one hand, and the need for access and honesty on the other.

In order to emphasise the continuing relevance of these lessons the remainder of the chapter is concerned with two events which were widely covered by the media: the siege of the Iranian Embassy in London in 1980 and the Falklands crisis in 1982. Both these events not only reinforced the lessons already discussed in this chapter but also introduced others which add to the problems associated with reporting conflict.

The Iranian Embassy siege

For six days in 1980 half a dozen terrorists held 21 hostages at the Iranian Embassy in Princes Gate, London. The siege ended dramatically at 7.23 pm on 5 May when the SAS launched a two-pronged assault on the Embassy. They completed the job in just eleven minutes. If that was not enough, the attack was carried out in front of the world's press including live television coverage.

This was really not surprising since, given the general terrorists' appetite for publicity, London was an obvious choice for the six terrorists from the Iraqi-backed Arab minority of Khuzestan to publicise their cause. Not only was London reputed to possess the best media coverage in the world but also it had one of the largest concentrations of Arabic journalists. There is no doubt that the terrorists achieved their aim (very few people were even aware of the existence of an Arab minority in Iran before the Embassy siege).

The relevant events of the siege to the theme of this book are as follows.[5] The Metropolitan Police organisation for handling the press was set up immediately they were alerted to the seizure of the embassy. Their procedures were developed by Sir Robert Mark, practised at the

---

[5] This account of the siege is derived from Richard Clutterbuck's book, *The Media and Political Violence*, Macmillan, London 1981, pp. 134–41.

Balcombe Street siege, and therefore were well developed. Specific positions were allocated for television cameras and journalists were restricted to certain controlled areas. The police gave periodic briefings to the press some of which were off the record requesting that certain events should not be reported, or places filmed. On some occasions the police requested the media to report or broadcast certain information in the hope that the kidnappers would hear it, and thus be affected psychologically by it. Although the BBC pointed out that they could not broadcast directed messages, in the event they did because of their newsworthiness.

The majority of journalists behaved most responsibly being fully aware that lives were at stake and also being conscious that they had more to gain from preserving police goodwill. An example of noticeable co-operation was the BBC's agreement to allow Tony Crabb, the line manager of Sim Harris (one of the BBC men trapped in the Embassy as a hostage) to be available to assist the police negotiations. There were, however, others who ignored the police request to stay within the cordoned off area and at least one national newspaper slipped a man through the cordon (disguised as a hall porter). There was also the now well known saga of ITN's positioning of a cameraman at the rear of the Embassy.

The Metropolitan Police sent a memorandum to news organisations seeking 'co-operation in refraining from publishing or broadcasting details of the deployment of personnel in the immediate vicinity of the Embassy or the use of specialist equipment'.[6] In his letter to *The Times*,[7] David Nicholas refuted the passage in Dr Richard Clutterbuck's book *The Media and Political Violence* which claimed that ITN had smuggled a camera into a flat overlooking the back of the Embassy 'in defiance of the police request'.[8] He said that the police made no such request. He went on to point out that there was no way that the pictures taken by the rear-view camera could have got on to television screens accidentally because 'the technical linking arrangements would have required no fewer than three editorial decisions before the signal from the rear-view camera could be plugged through to transmission'.[9]

This is, of course, quite true, but it leads us to the centre of the relationship between the media and the relevant department responsible for providing press facilities (in this case the police) at the scene of a 'conflict incident'. Whereas there is no question about the honest

---

6 Extract from letter to *The Times* by David Nicholas (Editor of ITN), *The Times*, 17 July 1981.
7 Ibid.
8 Richard Clutterbuck, op.cit., p.138.
9 *The Times*, 17 July 1981.

intention of responsible editors in the media the problem occurs when they are unaware of the significance of the material they have obtained. This is particularly pertinent to radio and television broadcasts which can be transmitted 'live' on an editorial decision. In this particular case, whether the police specifically banned reporters from the back of the Embassy is immaterial since they had definitely requested that no details of the deployment of personnel, or the use of specialist equipment be reported or broadcast. The fact that the SAS 'abseil' assault was transmitted four minutes after the attack had taken place does not absolve ITN from their agreement to comply with the Metropolitan Police's memorandum since there was no time limit on that request. The fact remains that the highly successful abseil technique cannot be used again in a similar situation because it received world-wide publicity by courtesy of ITN cameras and subsequent press photographs. Without this disclosure this technique could have been an option for the future since the one remaining terrorist was probably unaware of how the SAS actually achieved their unorthodox entrance.

The successful operation also thrust the publicity-shy SAS Regiment on to the world stage. From that moment on the regiment appreciated that they were going to attract headline news whatever they did and that this was a fact of life with which they would have to live in future.

It is this realisation which lies at the heart of military—media relationships associated with a conflict incident. Any such event is bound to attract intense media interest and activity. They will want information; they will want access — and they will broadcast and publish regardless whether they receive co-operation or not. However, they will be able to produce more detailed and authentic reports with the co-operation of the authorities. This was recognised by Sir Robert Mark when, as Commissioner of the Metropolitan Police, he also realised that the more the press were taken into his confidence the more co-operative they were likely to be. He used this approach to achieve considerable restraint from Fleet Street at the Spaghetti House and Balcombe Street sieges in 1975.

However, this relationship was not achieved overnight. Indeed, Sir Robert sowed the seeds for the relationship in 1972 soon after he became the Commissioner for the Metropolitan Police. He invited the editors of Fleet Street to Scotland Yard and announced a new era of co-operation. The editors were sceptical, but were prepared to give him a chance. They subsequently found him to be as good as his word. This approach would appear to be readily adaptable to the military—media relationship. An early rapport should be established between the editors and the appropriate personalities in the media. Once the principle has been established the rapport should be passed on to the subsequent military officers in the relevant appointments. It is essential that this rapport should be continuous and not based on personality, but be tied to the appointment. This is important since the average of two-year military appointments disrupts the smooth flow of good relations and is one of the major stumbling blocks in the development of good relationships over a long period. The fundamental issues to be resolved at such meetings are the media's requirement to publish and the military's desire for non-disclosure of certain information on the grounds of security. The litmus test for withholding information should be: will the disclosure of specific information (including photographs or film) be likely to put lives at risk and thus jeopardise the operation? It is important that the media are aware of this potential hazard at the outset of any rapport which is established. Only by continual contact being maintained between the relevant parties will the establishment of the essential trust, which is so necessary in a crisis, be established.

The establishment of this trust early on is vital. By the very nature of things, conflict incidents usually occur very quickly and without warning. It is far too late then to try and establish a rapport between an unknown military liaison officer and editors, or between a public relations officer (PRO) and reporters. In incidents such as Princes Gate, there will be a requirement for the military liaison officer to take the editors into his confidence and rely on them to brief their own journalists. The liaison officer should tell the editors as much as he is able within the bounds of security and be in a position to offer facilities. At the same time, he should explain what information, if disclosed, might jeopardise the operation and point out that, although the media's desire for news is well understood, they may well be restricted to certain areas in order to guarantee the security of the operation. Such a procedure can only be established on the basis of mutual trust and it must involve all the press and broadcasting organisations (there must be no hint of special treatment or 'exclusives').

In return for this co-operation the media have a right to expect honesty from the military. Past history has shown that the media are quite prepared to accept a logical reason for not disclosing certain information — but they will not forgive deception. Nor should they. Furthermore, it will undoubtedly undo all the good that might have been achieved through the painstaking establishment of goodwill.

An indication of the possible common ground for establishing the procedure outlined above was illustrated by Alan Protheroe when he appeared in the BBC television programme *The Editors* on 16 June soon after the Embassy siege. He said that the job of the media is 'quite simply, to disclose, though not necessarily to disclose immediately'. It is this sort of common sense approach which should enable both the military and the media to find an acceptable compromise between the opposing requirements of the two professions. This can only be achieved, however, if a good rapport is established right at the outset, and certainly well before the two sides meet over a crisis incident.

The Falklands crisis

Perhaps the best British example of the inherent problems of a conflict situation was the start of the Falkland Islands crisis. There was initial confusion about what was actually happening followed by a rapid chain of events which included a quick and impressive mobilisation of the Royal Navy's Task Force (which included 3 Commando Brigade Royal Marines and considerable support from the Army). There was then a long period of speculation which reflected every twist and turn on the diplomatic front whilst the Task Force sailed to the South Atlantic. The tempo then picked up again when British forces recaptured South Georgia and intensified when the Argentinian cruiser *General Belgrano* was disabled and the British destroyer *HMS Sheffield* was disabled and subsequently sunk.

The phases in the crisis were distinctive and the saturation media coverage ensured that the British public, and subsequently a much wider audience, were able to follow the events in detail. This study is largely concerned with the events at the beginning of the crisis because the tenure of media coverage throughout the subsequent period largely reflected the decisions which were taken, or not taken, at the outset.

It is important to realise that at the beginning of 1982 nobody anticipated that Argentina and Britain would be in a state of armed conflict in April over the dispute about the Falkland Islands. Regardless of whether the British Government could have, or should have, known earlier about the intention of the Argentinians to invade the Falklands on 2 April the realisation that this was going to happen only dawned on people at a very late hour. As a result, there were only four British reporters at Port Stanley when the invasion took place and since the resistance only lasted a short while there was no time to get off their despatches before the Argentinians seized control of the town and restricted the journalists' access to telephones. Those that were eventually allowed to telephone through reports were naturally restricted in what they could actually say. In contrast, the Argentinians had reporters with the invasion force and soon afterwards were transmitting pictures from the state-controlled television stations.

The rapid turn of events, the geographical isolation of the islands, limited communication facilities and restrictions on the contents of the journalists' reports all combined to produce a vague and inaccurate picture of what had actually happened during the invasion. This was further complicated by British coverage of the Argentinian media reporting. Ignorant of the full meaning of state-controlled television, the British public initially tended to accept the Argentinian version at face value. This ignorance was assisted by the British television organisations' practice of reporting Argentinian coverage without commenting on its bias. Their propaganda was dramatically exposed some three and a half weeks later when the British recaptured South Georgia (the Argentinian press had still not reported the surrender of their own forces 24 hours after their capitulation). But like all good propaganda, the misinformation was hidden amidst some hard facts, especially at the beginning of the crisis, and the Argentinian version was often more accurate about that information which it suited their purpose to report.

The net result was a confused and misleading impression of the Battle of Port Stanley. We have already seen in chapter 3 how the facts of the battle were initially inaccurately reported, giving a false picture of the resistance until this was subsequently corrected when the Governor and the two Royal Marines commanders gave a press conference some four days later. But by then the damage had been done. By a strange quirk of fate, the media had been guilty of the very crime of which they had accused the Army over the Dunloy incident in Northern Ireland. They had issued an inaccurate first statement.

This mistake was to be repeated again on 5 April when newspaper reports indicated that the 22 Royal Marines on South Georgia had killed only three Argentinians before being overwhelmed (they did however admit that a helicopter had been shot down and a corvette damaged by an anti-tank rocket). All this information, however, came via Argentinian Government sources and yet there was little or no attempt in the British press reports to indicate the source of this information. As with the Battle of Port Stanley, the full facts about the Battle of Grytviken emerged when the Royal Marines commander in South Georgia, Lieutenant Keith Mills, was repatriated to Britain on 20 April. There had been a fierce two hour battle during which he estimated that his force had killed between 10–15 Argentinians and wounded at least 20 others. He also reported that they had shot down two helicopters (a Puma and an Alouette) and was told by an Argentinian officer after his capture that had one more rocket hit the corvette she probably would have sunk.

This detailed information could not have been obtained until reporters had an opportunity to hear from the man on the spot at first hand. So why were the media so determined to report the information they received initially from the Argentinian Government sources as fact, as opposed to 'alleged fact'? It is probable that the significance of this was overlooked in the pressure of getting the information from the end of a long and tenuous communications line whilst trying to meet deadlines. Nevertheless, this led to the British (and world public) receiving an initial false impression of both battles. Battles are always confused and therefore particular care needs to be taken over the reporting of facts. Just as the military need time to get at the facts of an incident (be it Northern Ireland or the Falklands), so the media need to give themselves time to check out the sources of their information. If they cannot do this before a deadline expires, then the onus is on them to report 'alleged facts' until such time as these have been verified. The credibility of the first statement is just as important for the media as it is for the military.

The speed of the development of the crisis led to another interesting development in the military—media relationship. It was decided at the outset that no censorship should be imposed and the editors had agreed with the Ministry of Defence to act responsibly as far as national security was concerned and to consult MOD or the D-Notice Committee if in doubt. Reporters and correspondents were allocated to ships of the Task Force during the hectic 72 hours it took to mobilise the force and they then reported its departure for the South Atlantic on 5 April, their accounts being dovetailed into the massive land-based media coverage of the departure of the Fleet on a bright and sunny Spring day. To those who watched the spectacle on television there was almost an aura of crusade about the departure of this large naval and amphibious force, and the air of expectancy, patriotism and apprehension came across most vividly. Just as the American public had become hooked on the television coverage of the Vietnam war, so had the British on the television coverage at the beginning of the Falklands crisis.

But there were significant differences between the two. As we have seen, access in Vietnam was relatively easy, therefore television coverage was extensive, and furthermore it was possible for a reporter to 'drop in' to a particular area by helicopter for a few hours and then return to Saigon that evening. This was not true of the Falklands. Access was extremely difficult and limited (for instance, it was only possible to accommodate a limited number of journalists on the ships of the Task Force). Furthermore, for operational and technical reasons it was not possible to transmit television pictures direct from the ships (film had to be transported back to the UK by a returning ship or aircraft) and radio and newspaper reports were also restricted by the security implications of the communications. This particularly affected television coverage of the Task Force activities which was severely limited. However both BBC and ITN compensated for this in the first three weeks of the crisis by including television coverage from Argentina, Uruguay and Chile. This resulted in a daily diet of television news on the conflict to which the public became addicted, and this addiction was catered for by the introduction of *Falklands Extra* to

ITN's *News at Ten*, by BBC's *Newsnight's* nightly coverage of the issues involved, and by constant analysis by television documentary programmes such as *Panorama* and *Weekend World*.

There was no freedom of movement for journalists as there had been in Vietnam. Those reporters who had been assigned to the Task Force were stuck with it. It became quickly apparent from their despatches that they soon identified with the sailors, soldiers and marines on board. In circumstances such as these it was considered that censorship was not necessary since the reporters knew that they were sharing the risks alongside the Armed Forces and therefore their own safety was equally involved. Nevertheless, keen as the public were to be informed about events, there was genuine concern for the security of those embarked on the ships and many queried the need for some of the detailed information which was reported and the speculation as to the various options open to the British force. The general feeling was: if the Services have a job to do, let them get on with it unhampered by saturation media coverage. This view is naturally relevant to one's perspective. The general public's view of the possible turn of events, based on widespread media coverage and comment, including world reaction, was different from those embarked on board the ships. As a general point, in the final analysis all will depend on the responsible attitude of the editors and reporters, and upon their judgement of what will be acceptable to the public. In the event, little information of operational significance was given away initially by the media. Furthermore, the impression of the cheerfulness, professionalism and confidence of the Task Force, as portrayed by the despatches from the embarked journalists, was most marked and the transmission of this impression was important to the resolve of the British public and therefore its continued support for the Government's action. On balance, therefore, the initial policy of relying on the responsibility of the editors not to undermine the operational security appeared to be justified.

Subsequent events, however, caused this policy to be questioned. As the Task Force sailed further into the South Atlantic and more ships, aircraft, men and equipment were mobilised to reinforce it, so more information was published by the media. Indeed, so much information was given to the public that one did not have to be a trained intelligence officer to work out the possible military options. There was increasing concern in military circles about the effect that this might have on the safety of the Task Force. This concern was proved to be right once the two antagonists joined battle in the waters around the Falkland Islands, at the beginning of May. The first major conflict occurred during the period 1–4 May in the course of which the British sunk the Argentinian cruiser *General Belgrano* and a patrol boat; shot down two Mirage fighters and a Canberra bomber; bombed the airfields at Stanley and Goose Green; and severely damaged another patrol boat. In retaliation, the Argentinians attacked *HMS Sheffield* with an Exocet missile fired from a Super Etandard aircraft and shot down a Sea Harrier over Goose Green.

The loss of the *Sheffield* was a serious blow to the country and it brought home the harsh realities of war to the British public. It was something which had been anticipated by defence correspondents who had experience of previous campaigns ('wait until the coffins come home' was how one of them put it), but it was a shock to press men (including editors) new to battle, as it was to the public. In the aftermath, the inevitable accusations were made: certain elements of the media were accused of being unpatriotic; the BBC were accused of pandering to Argentinian propaganda; the tabloid newspapers were accused of promoting too much blood lust and jingoism, whilst the Ministry of Defence was accused of not providing sufficient information on time. It was almost like a re-run of the beginning of Vietnam and Northern Ireland — the same mistakes being made all over again; the same clichés were being trotted out.

What are the major lessons to emerge from the early days of the crisis? From the military's point of view it became obvious very early on that insufficient attention had been paid to the PR aspects of the operation. This was due to a combination of factors: there was no Chief of Public Relations (CPR) at the beginning of the crisis (the previous occupant had retired in December 1981 and had not been replaced by the beginning of April 1982); a new Director of Public Relations (Navy) had only just taken over; the RN public relations organisation had no previous experience of handling such a crisis; and no experienced professional PR advice was available to the Chiefs of Staff. As a result, the vital importance of sustaining public support was not recognised at the outset and therefore MOD was not able to counter Argentinian propaganda or even provide basic information and pictures to enable the British and world press to counter this for them. This lack of foresight and logistics planning was to rebound only weeks later as the credibility gap grew. Despite the experience of Northern Ireland, MOD made the same mistake again about issuing an initial statement about an incident which was too categorical, only to have to correct it subsequently. For instance, on 9 May the Defence Ministry spokesman announced that an Argentinian spy ship, the *Narwhal*, had been fired on by a Sea Harrier and subsequently boarded by the Royal Navy, but there had been 'no, repeat no, casualties'. The Argentinians said there were casualties. The following day the MOD spokesman admitted that his first information was incorrect; subsequent reports revealed that there had been 14 casualties as a result of the attack.

Another problem was the invasion of privacy. There was considerable concern and outrage amongst the military about the harassment of Task Force wives by the press, particularly after the losses sustained amongst the members of the crew of *HMS Sheffield*. This is a particularly ghoulish facet of some departments of the press which has been commented on earlier in this book, and it is aided and abetted by those members of the public who agree to be interviewed in their moment of anguish. But the agreement of a very few members of the public to be interviewed conveniently hides the considerable stress to which the other families are subjected. At 7.45 on the morning after the *Sheffield* was hit a man in a smart suit approached the house of a wife whose husband was on one of the ships in the Task Force. Fearing the worst, she opened the door only to be met by a reporter who wanted to know whether she was Mrs So-and-so whose husband was on the *Sheffield*. An hour later two more men approached the house. They also turned out to be reporters. Not surprisingly the woman broke down and spent the next few days recovering with friends. This was not an isolated example and it was to be repeated time and again in the following weeks. Invasion of privacy is one of the worst aspects of media activities and experience from the Falklands crisis suggests that there is a requirement for a Code of Conduct to be drawn up between the military and the media in order to protect servicemen's families against undue harassment in circumstances such as these.

Relatives of those serving in the Task Force were also subjected to undue stress when Mr John Nott, the Secretary of State for Defence, disclosed 'bad news' on ITN on the evening of 25 May 1982 'about a big attack on British ships but failed to name them'.[10] The ships were subsequently named at noon the following day as *HMS Coventry* and the *Atlantic Conveyor* but by then the vast majority of the Task Force relatives had spent a needless twelve hours of worry. Mr Nott admitted in the Commons on 26 May that his decision to delay naming the ships might have been the wrong judgement and this episode is yet another example of the need to take into consideration in future the feelings of relatives of those involved in a conflict due to the impact of the mass media.

The last two examples indicate the conflicting requirements of the military and the media. Indeed, the most important lesson of all to emerge from the Falklands crisis was the need for a mutually agreed set of guidelines on which to base military–media relations in any future conflict situation. The 'open cheque' approach established at the beginning of the crisis raised one important issue from which the Ministry of

10 *The Times*, 27 May 1982.

Defence never fully recovered: just as the Americans were never quite sure whether or not to manage news during the Vietnam war, neither were the Ministry of Defence during the Falklands dispute. Julian Pettifer believed that this led to the credibility gap during the Vietnam war (see chapter 9) and there were indications of the same thing happening in the Falklands crisis. For instance, from 7 April 1982, the day the naval blockade of the Falkland Islands was announced, it was presumed that one of the nuclear-powered submarines enforcing the blockade would be *HMS Superb* and this was duly reported in most of the newspapers and broadcasts the following day. The media were therefore surprised and somewhat embarrassed when *Superb* was discovered, on 21 April, to have been in her base on the Clyde for the past five days, and had never been deployed to the South Atlantic to enforce the blockade. Although MOD pointed out that it was not their policy to give the locations of HM ships either in peacetime or war, nevertheless the media were surprised that nobody had put them straight 'off the record'.

The failure to brief the media off the record led to all sorts of difficulties. Unable to check on a number of facts and lacking any form of 'in confidence' briefing the media reported all they saw and heard. Worse still, they speculated. The result was a mass of information about ships' movements, composition of the force, weapon capabilities and continual comment about the various options open to the Task Force. There was even an interview with a Harrier pilot who had just flown a combat mission which included his comments about the best tactics to adopt against Argentinian fighter aircraft. All this provided an alarming amount of intelligence, totally unclassified, which could be used by the Argentinians (and presumably was). The publication of some of this information endangered the Task Force and certainly made it more difficult to carry out operational missions. It would have been relatively simple to have prevented the disclosure of such information if guidelines had been agreed in the calmness of the years of peace before the crisis when there was no major conflict involving British forces. But this assumes that the public relations aspect of the conflict was considered to be as important as operations and logistics. Sadly this was not the case. In contrast to the most impressive logistical organisation of the Task Force there were no PR contingency plans 'on the shelf' thus underlining the low priority allocated to PR from within MOD.

Even without the advantage of previously agreed guidelines, MOD could still have retrieved the situation if they had adopted a positive attitude to military—media relations at the beginning of April. However, the ignorance of the importance which the media attaches to 'in confidence' briefings meant that the military were generally suspicious of the press and therefore were not prepared to adopt this approach.

Particularly relevant is the fact that the Royal Navy had not been faced with such an operation since the Second World War and, in a climate of ignorance, they failed to draw upon the lessons learned by the Army in Ulster.

This ignorance and suspicion quickly led to a breakdown in the previous good relations between the defence correspondents and PR officers in MOD. Editors were not taken fully into confidence about the difficulties of covering a maritime operation mounted over 8,000 miles. As a result, the media either did not understand the problems involved or else they were unwilling to accept the unique position in which they found themselves — there would be no access without authority. Furthermore, the lack of flexibility and common sense about the releasing of information meant that the co-operation of the editors was soon lost. The failure to provide background briefs and give off the record information at the beginning of the conflict meant that informed PROs were unable to ensure that correspondents and reporters fully understood events which they were required to report. Such information would have enabled the British press to counter Argentinian propaganda and the evident authority of the reports would have influenced reporters from other countries who were not privy to these briefings. As it was, the British media, especially the defence correspondents, soon made it obvious that they were not being briefed in confidence, and this was reflected by the Western press, especially by the Americans.

The failure to appreciate the importance of public relations led to a problem that was unique in this technological age: the technical problems associated with the transmission of television pictures and photographs due to the distances involved. The fact that some of the press did not appreciate the difficulties involved was summed up by one editor who, on hearing that South Georgia had been recaptured, told one of his reporters to 'get down there within 24 hours and come back with a story!' The delay in obtaining pictures was most frustrating for the media.[11] (In exasperation, David Chipp, the Press Association Editor-in-Chief remarked that 'the speed of transmission of pictures is 20 knots an hour'.)[12] It also meant that the British Government lost a good opportunity of countering Argentinian propaganda by releasing pictures of the damage caused to the Port Stanley runway and its immediate vicinity by bombing, and of the recapture of South Georgia (the first pictures of the latter were not released until 19 May — three and a half weeks after the event).

11 For fuller discussion about the frustration see Alan Protheroe's article in *The Listener* 3 June 1982 (pp. 2–3).
12 *Observer*, 9 May 1982.

Even more frustrating were the technical problems which prevented the transmission of television pictures once the ships were south of Ascension. It was not possible to transmit ENG pictures via satellite due to interference from the sophisticated electronics of the naval ships, and the other alternative (use of the satellite facilities at Ascension) was not available for operational reasons. Despatch of the old-fashioned television film was restricted to '20 knots an hour'. Some military officers thought that the lack of television pictures was no bad thing because it might have affected operational security. This showed a complete ignorance of the news process, editorial responsibility, and demonstrated a failure to appreciate the self-censorship imposed by British reporters in Vietnam. In contrast to the possibilities of inaccuracies which can occur in the passage of newspaper copy due to the number of links in the chain (see chapter 3), television and radio reports direct from a ship are not subjected to any such problems. Indeed, Brian Hanrahan's television broadcast after the first Sea Harrier attack on Port Stanley ('I counted them all out and I counted them all back') was the most effective counter to the Argentinian claim of shooting down British aircraft during the attack — and all the more authentic because it was from an independent eye-witness. However, as useful as such reports were, the delay in transmission due to the requirement for embarked reporters to transfer to another ship and then wait for a set transmission time to send their reports resulted in some of these being received out of sequence with reports from other sources (especially from Argentina). This led to inevitable confusion about the real facts of a particular event and to the questioning of the credibility of some British reports.

An early appreciation of the logistics problems involved, coupled with an energetic determination to solve them by the provision of suitable equipment embarked on board HM Ships before they sailed from the UK to ensure that television pictures could be transmitted by satellite, would have solved the technical problems. The decision about whether or not to broadcast the pictures would then have been taken at editorial level in London, with appropriate advice from MOD about anything which might have jeopardised operations. But all this assumed that MOD appreciated the vital role which the media had to play during the conflict. As we have seen earlier, this was not the case. There were no PR 'contingency plans' for such a situation and, on the other hand, the system was not sufficiently flexible to produce a good enough solution from a 'standing start'. Once again, PR suffered from being the poor relation of the staff system, especially within MOD. The military did not pay sufficient attention to the importance of PR policy at the beginning of the crisis and they paid the penalty. As the days grew into weeks so the cracks appeared in the military—media relationship and the credibility gap grew wider. This was to have a significant impact on public opinion.

No democratic nation can wage war without the full support of its population. This support will largely depend upon the lead taken by the government, sustained confidence in the military leaders, the interpretation of events by the media — and upon credibility. All these factors assume the ability of the press to have access to information on which to base news reports and comment. On the other hand, although the freedom of the press is very important there will be occasions in a conflict situation, just as there will in a siege scenario, when to reveal certain information, either wittingly or not, may jeopardise the whole operation. As Sir Frank Cooper, the Permanent Under Secretary of State at the Ministry of Defence said in his evidence to the House of Commons Defence Select Committee following the Falklands war, key facts were withheld from the media, particularly on the eve of the landing at San Carlos Bay. 'When I saw the press on the evening before the landing I did not tell them the whole truth, I make no bones about that whatever'.[13]

The time has come to put an end to the 'we'll muddle through' attitude and there is a clear requirement for the Ministry of Defence and the media to establish agreed guidelines for typical conflict situation scenarios. This will require careful thought and continuous dialogue if the right guidelines are to be produced. The appointed committee would need to consider such things as: the need for off the record briefings; the special position of defence correspondents; the requirement to provide adequate facilities to cater for the varying needs of the British media; the need to provide facilities for the world's press; the position of television as a war reporting medium; the enhanced position of radio as a war reporting medium; and the security aspects of still photographs (one picture of a Rapier anti-aircraft missile located on the Falklands was better than any which could have been obtained by Argentinian low-level air photo reconnaissance).

This list is far from complete and there will be many other aspects which will need to be considered by the committee (including how any agreed Code of Practice with the British media can be extended to include the foreign press). What is important is that such a study should be done now, before the next crisis occurs. Not to do so will result in a repeat of the mistakes made at the beginning of the Falkland crisis; and Northern Ireland; and Vietnam.

13 *The Times*, 22 July 1982. At the time of writing the conflicting requirements of the military and the media as they applied to the Falklands crisis are still under discussion by the House of Commons Defence Select Committee.

Conclusions

The American media made some bad mistakes in Vietnam, and the British media went through a number of crises adjusting to their role in Ulster. British journalists gradually learned from their experience and there are now a number of newsmen who have a deep knowledge of the British Army in Northern Ireland. However, even experience in Ulster did not mean that a journalist would understand how the Army operated in BAOR, or that he would know anything at all about the Royal Navy, the Royal Marines or the Royal Air Force. The subsequent reporting in the Falklands crisis proved this point. The relevant lessons to emerge from the four conflicts studied in this chapter have already been discussed at length. What has not been mentioned so far is the relevance of improving the mutual knowledge of the military and the media professions at the outset, through education.

There is a self-evident need for the military to learn about the media's position in society as part of their general education quite apart from the media's relevance to their profession associated with the press requirement to report the actions of the military. But perhaps the requirement for the media to be educated about the military is less obvious. However, it would seem prudent for all trainee journalists in Britain to be taught something about the function and organisation of the military as part of their general education. After all, it is their job to inform the public, and a basic education about the military would help them to carry out this function more easily and efficiently. The relevance of this proposal is indicated by the fact that a sizeable percentage of the working population is directly associated with defence (either as service personnel, civil servants or civilians employed at MOD establishments), and a significant proportion of daily international and national news is concerned with defence matters.[14] The importance of this proposal is illustrated by the studies of Vietnam, Ulster and the Falklands which have revealed that neither the American nor the British peoples have really understood the issues involved, nor appreciated the military's difficulties. The lesson from the recent past is clear: conflict attracts a large number of non-specialist journalists on whom the general public depend for information, and they are more than likely to be misinformed about any future conflict unless more is done to prepare young journalists for such an eventuality. The education of the military and the media about each other's profession is discussed in the following two chapters.

14 During the author's visit to BBC Radio News on 6 February 1979 he saw an example of how much military related topics are included in daily news; in just two hours the news agency copy received in the news room included 10 items which were about the military or defence issues.

12 The Media's Knowledge of the Military

In the last chapter we considered the inherent problems associated with the reporting of conflict and during the course of this analysis it became apparent that there has been a great deal of conflict in recent years with varying degrees of intensity, which required to be reported. This leads us on to the general question of the media's knowledge of the military and the relevance of that knowledge. In this chapter we shall evaluate how much journalists know about the military, we shall analyse their education on this subject, and will then consider whether there is a requirement to improve this education and, if so, how this could be achieved. One may well question the need for journalists to be educated about the military. After all, isn't that why Defence Correspondents are employed? Such an attitude, however, overlooks the fact that the reporting of armed conflict is now almost an everyday occurrence and the coverage of such conflicts is usually done by general reporters because editors prefer to keep their Defence Correspondents at home to provide the expert analysis. This point was very much borne out by the Falklands war. It follows from this that a basic knowledge about the military is an important part of the education of *every* journalist.

The first point to recognise is that the only journalists with any experience of military life are those who served in the last war, those who were once regulars or National Servicemen, or past and present members of the Reserves. The second point concerns the enormous changes which have taken place within the Armed Forces since the ending of National Service in the early 1960s. These changes have touched most aspects of Service life from technical developments to social innovations and yet to the casual observer there has been little apparent alteration in the Service way of life. This impression, aided by the facade of the traditions of military life, has deceived many of those who once served in uniform to think that life in the Services is still very much 'as it was in their day'. Even though their knowledge of the Armed Forces is dated, however, the vast majority of editors and senior journalists understand the military and have a high regard for the Services. What about their successors? As National Service ended in 1962 the majority of people who did conscription are now over 40 years old. This means that the next generation of editors of national and provincial newspapers, and the overwhelming number of practising journalists, have had no military experience at all. As far as television is concerned some of the key editorial posts in current affairs have already been filled by young men in their early thirties (for example, in 1978 the Editor of the BBC television programme *Tonight* was 32, and the Editor of the BBC television's *Nationwide* was 31).

Inevitably the gap of understanding due to lack of personal experience will get wider each year. Ignorance of the Armed Forces already exists amongst people of influence in the media and amongst those who will provide the next generation of editors. This lack of knowledge has been compensated for, to a certain extent, by those journalists who have reported Northern Ireland during the past decade (for instance since 1971 BBC Radio News has regularly sent reporters back to Ulster on a roster system for a week every six to eight weeks whenever possible).[1] Useful as this experience is in enabling a journalist to gain a better understanding about the military, however, his knowledge of the Army is restricted to what he learns about its operating procedure in an internal security role in Ulster — it does not necessarily enable him to comprehend how the Army operates in BAOR, nor does this experience educate him about the other two Services. Furthermore, only a proportion of reporters are assigned to Ulster and virtually none of the sub-editors in the press or broadcasting are sent there. The lack of comprehension about the military was exposed by a number of inaccuracies in press reports and articles at the beginning of the Falklands crisis.

We have a situation today where the majority of young journalists have had no experience of military life and are unlikely to come in

1 The BBC Radio News regular roster system was stopped in the summer of 1979 following the appointment of a Regional Correspondent based in Belfast. However, it is still intended to keep reporters in touch with developments in Northern Ireland by sending them over there periodically.

contact with the military unless the Armed Forces are 'in the news'. Amongst Western European nations this situation is unique to Britain because in other countries the overwhelming majority of journalists will have been conscripted and therefore have acquired a fundamental knowledge of the military. This lack of military experience in British journalism contrasts vividly with the Fifties when there were many ex-servicemen working in the press. Bill Moore, now the Senior Public Relations Officer of the Army Headquarters, South West District (formerly a sub-editor on *The Mirror*, and Deputy Editor of *The People*) illustrated this in an interview with the author:

> In 1953 on the subs table at *The Mirror* nearly every person was an ex-serviceman and these included an ex-fighter pilot, an ex-commando and a former gunner officer. In addition the Night Editor was ex-Intelligence Corps, the Production Editor had been a Mosquito pilot, and Hugh Cudlip had been a colonel.[2]

The training of journalists

Has anything been done to fill this gap of understanding by educating young journalists about the military? In order to answer this question we need to look at the training of journalists. This is supervised on a nationwide basis by the National Council for the Training of Journalists (NCTJ). Under the supervision of this body an average of approximately 600 trainee journalists per annum attend those colleges of education which run courses in journalism. A further 150 undergo in-company training schemes supervised by the NCTJ.

Of the total of nine colleges in Great Britain and Ireland which run courses in journalism, only three actually arrange for the trainees to visit military units as a means of improving their understanding of the military (these are the colleges at Harlow, Highbury and Sheffield). Since 1972, trainee journalists from the Harlow College have visited Army units in the Colchester area as part of their course. The visits last for one day and the young journalists are requested to complete a questionnaire about their impressions of a typical officer and soldier *before* the visit, and at the end of the day they are invited to answer the same questions again. The programme also includes a journalistic exercise which requires them to write a feature article about the visit. The originator of this scheme, Frank Warner, is now a Senior Lecturer in Journalism at Highbury College, Cosham, and he has taken the idea

2   Interview with the author, 14 March 1979.

with him to his new appointment which has resulted in a similar link being established between Highbury College and the Army units in the Tidworth area. The value of these visits emerges from the questionnaires which reveal that the vast majority had not visited a military establishment before and that their initial impressions of officers and soldiers are confused and often outdated. By the end of the day the young journalists have a much clearer picture of the military and the majority come away with a favourable impression of the servicemen whom they have met. There is little doubt that both the media and the military benefit considerably from the improved mutual understanding which results from this exercise.

Both parties also benefit from the Editors Abroad Scheme which is sponsored by the Facilities branch of DPRS and enables provincial press representatives to spend a few days with an Army unit serving abroad (the other two Services run similar schemes). Such a visit was arranged by Headquarters Eastern District when they invited 14 journalists to observe an exercise involving 7 Field Force in October 1978. Only 50 per cent of the journalists had visited the Army before, so this was an education for the remainder as well as providing all the reporters with an interesting topic for a feature article. Another new venture introduced by the Army was the invitation to a quarter of the local radio station managers in this country to visit HQ UKLF and the School of Artillery, Larkhill, in April 1979. This scheme acknowledged the increasing importance of local radio and was also a contributory move towards the education of the media since many of the managers were in their late twenties and therefore had little or no contact with the military before this visit. The Editors Abroad Scheme has also been extended to senior editors who, for the past four years, have been invited to visit BAOR and Berlin where they have the opportunity to talk to appropriate senior military officers from the C-in-C downwards. The latest visit was in May 1982.

Such visits are valuable and worth all the effort involved in arranging them but they are limited to certain areas and very much depend upon the initiative of key individuals in the press and in public relations. When one considers that there are approximately 35,000 journalists in the country, the visits arranged by the Harlow, Highbury and Sheffield Colleges, the Editors Abroad Scheme (which provides facilities for approximately 400 journalists a year), and the visits to home establishments (such as the local radio visit to UKLF), only cater for a small percentage.

In contrast to the vast numbers involved in the press, there are very few new journalists who enter broadcasting each year. BBC News and Current Affairs now take 12 new trainees per annum; ITN take just two. The BBC scheme is a joint television and radio venture which prepares successful applicants both for news and current affairs. Most of those accepted for this training are graduates and the competition is extremely high (for instance, there were 1,000 applicants for the 12 places in 1982). The training scheme has been going for approximately 12 years and the course now lasts a maximum of two years. This consists of an initial seven months' basic instruction on such topics as production and tape-editing, lectures on equipment and studios, lectures on relevant legal aspects, and a concentrated news writing and T-line course (newspaper shorthand). This is followed by attachments to various departments in news and current affairs in both radio and television. ITN's course for its two graduates was started in 1960 and lasts for two years. Both organisations rely to a great extent on 'on-job' training and expect their bright young trainees to learn as they go along.

Although the numbers recruited into broadcasting journalism are small, the audiences they reach out to are enormous and therefore there is an obligation for them to realise the importance of their positions as 'transmitters of news' for the public. The Annan Report voiced its concern about the standard of training in this area in these words:

> We hold in the highest regard the admirable standards and professionalism of the handful of leaders in the field of public affairs. They need to be emulated by less experienced journalists and production staff. Those working in news and public affairs need to be trained so as to be better informed, if necessary by becoming specialists in a certain area.[3]

The BBC scheme does include the occasional lecture from a guest speaker and Service officers have been invited to talk to the trainees.[4] Furthermore all those who go to BBC Belfast receive a military information briefing. There is also the odd lecture given by a reporter who has had experience of reporting wars (such as Martin Bell). But one is still left with the impression that some of the young researchers working on current affairs programmes and sub-editors working in news rooms have little basic understanding of the military. There is some evidence to suggest that the broadcasters are making the same mistake as the military: concentrating on the more interesting aspect of the problems of reporting conflict without teaching the basic fundamentals. The research undertaken for this book indicates that trainee broad-

---

3 Lord Annan, Report of the Committee on the Future of Broadcasting, HMSO, London 1977, p.290.
4 The author was invited to give a talk to BBC trainees in December 1979.

casting journalists would benefit from being better informed about the military.[5]

Varying knowledge about the military

It is evident from this survey of the training of journalists that very little formal education about the military is included in the various courses. We shall see in the next chapter that the military colleges have been forced to justify the inclusion of any 'marginal' subjects in their curricula, and by the same token, colleges specialising in journalism will need to be convinced that education about the military is a necessary part of a journalist's general training. So let us see what are the effects of the current lack of knowledge amongst media personnel. Perhaps the most striking impression is the considerable variation of knowledge amongst journalists: from a defence correspondent at one end of the spectrum to a general reporter with no previous contact with the military, at the other.

The defence correspondent fulfils a valuable function both for the military and the public. He keeps the public abreast of developments in the military by his coverage of the technological, operational, training and recruiting aspects of Service life, and by explaining the intricacies of defence policy (for example the implications of the Trident decision); and he provides for the military an independent voice which can, on occasions, comment on areas of concern such as pay and conditions of service, or the need for the introduction of some new equipment. The specialist knowledge acquired by the defence correspondent enables him to become both a guardian of the taxpayer's and the serviceman's interests. This important dual role can only really be sustained by specialist journalism.

As with all correspondents, there is considerable journalistic scope within the confines of the specialist field as is illustrated by the Terms of Reference for the BBC TV Defence Correspondent, Christopher Wain:

> To report and interpret for the general news audience defence subjects of all kinds; from developments in land/sea/air hardware through defence organisation and actual military operations to the wider field of national and international defence systems and their strategic, political and economic implications. The Defence Correspondent's contributions will therefore reflect, in addition to

5 Personal observation by the author from visits to newsrooms and current affairs offices undertaken 1978–79.

day-by-day events, long-term aspects of defence theory and practice and their impact on international relations.

Defence is an interesting field in which to specialise and therefore it attracts journalists with varying degrees of previous military knowledge. Some have experienced military life before, but many have not (and this is likely to be the trend in the future). In an interview with the author, Henry Stanhope, the Defence Correspondent of *The Times*, explained how he got the job and talked about its attractions:

> I joined *The Times* as a general reporter in 1967 . . . and then the vacancy of Defence Correspondent came up (in 1970) when Charles Douglas-Home, who was my predecessor, was promoted to the Features Editor. I applied for the job as Defence Correspondent and was lucky enough to get it.
>
> *Author:* Did you have any interest or background in defence before that?
>
> *Stanhope:* Not really. I had an interest in defence but more on the foreign affairs side. In fact, I think as the years have developed my interests have gone more to the defence than the foreign affairs, the political side. I have become more interested in the nuts and bolts of defence.
>
> *Author:* Why is it a good area for a reporter to go into?
>
> *Stanhope:* Well materially it is good because it is not a job in which you are kept at your desk from 9 until 5 (or from 11 until 7, if you like). It is a job with a lot of foreign travel and when you do get stories they can be quite good ones. The Services are also quite pleasant to deal with. In my time I have dealt with various sectors of society like doctors when I was a science correspondent, and actors when I was an art correspondent, but on the whole the Services and Whitehall are probably the nicest, easiest to get on with . . . Intellectually it is an interesting field – for instance, the strategic complexities of the military balance in themselves are worthy of intellectual study. So there is enough to bite on if you want to get involved in the more obtuse academic side of defence. Also there are some quite good action stories on the straight news coverage side – so you get a wide variety. Because you are not occupied on a full diary day after day you have quite a degree of freedom to develop your own interests and stories.[6]

6   Interview with the author, 10 October 1978.

172

Whether a defence correspondent has possessed any previous military knowledge or not, he quickly acquires an extensive understanding about defence as a result of research into this specialist field, from his visits to Service establishments and units, and through the contacts he develops with politicians associated with defence, and with various personalities within the Defence Public Relations Staff (DPRS). These latter contacts are of mutual benefit to both the defence correspondents and DPRS because it enables the correspondents to get first hand accurate information about a specific project, or a background brief on a subject which they may be considering for an article, and at the same time it provides the military with an outlet for publicity and information. In 1977 an innovation was introduced by John Ledlie, the then Deputy Chief of Public Relations, to provide more information for defence correspondents which illustrates this point. In November that year he introduced a series of regular defence press briefings under the chairmanship of the Permanent Under Secretary for Defence (Sir Frank Cooper).[7] Each session consists of a presentation on a particular topic of defence, followed by a question and answer period on that subject, and then the discussion is widened to include other aspects of defence. This idea has proved to be popular with the correspondents because not only do they receive a first hand briefing on topical subjects, but they also have the opportunity to question senior Service officers or civil servants who are specialists in that particular field. These briefings are designed to provide correspondents with advance background information on which they can base future articles, and the open question period enables them to obtain up-to-date information on newsworthy topics.

With this kind of relationship with MOD the defence correspondent is very much regarded as the oracle on defence matters and general reporters who may be required to write about the military from time to time will tend to check facts with him, or use him as a source for a contact. News editors will also rely on his expertise and may often turn to him for a contribution about a piece of news concerned with defence. An interesting example of his reliance on the defence correspondent's expertise, and of the irregular hours which this may involve, comes from BBC Radio News. At 11 pm on Sunday, 8 October 1978, the Senior News Editor received the first edition of the following morning's papers and noticed a piece in *The Daily Telegraph* which suggested that a British force consisting of a battalion, surface to air missiles and Harrier jets was going to Zambia at President Kaunda's request. He debated for a while about whether to lead with this story

---

7   These briefings are held approximately once a month.

and finally telephoned Christopher Lee, the BBC Radio Defence Correspondent at two o'clock in the morning and asked him to do a piece on this for the 7 am news bulletin on Radio 4. The newspaper article did not appear plausible to Lee for both political and military reasons, but he needed to verify the facts with his sources and that was complicated by it being in the early hours of the morning. Eventually he obtained his information from the highest source available at 3.40 am and produced a piece for the news bulletin which referred to the newspaper article but stressed that the contingent going to Zambia was only a small British Army training team due to assist the Zambians with training on the Rapier ground to air missile system. The Senior News Editor accepted Lee's article without question. Both of them knew that Lee would be 'dead' if his facts were wrong.[8]

Although the defence correspondent's expertise can often be used within a newspaper office or a broadcasting newsroom there are occasions when this is not the case. For instance, some newspapers do not employ defence correspondents at all (the *Sun*, for instance); there is a tendency not to employ them in television current affairs; and there are occasions when the defence correspondent is not available (because he is covering another story or he is abroad); or an event occurs which is so newsworthy that it requires additional reporters to cover it (*viz.* the Falklands crisis). In such circumstances non-specialists will be required to intrude into a specialist's field.

Reporting the military in action

Whenever the military is in the news it attracts a number of general reporters with little, or no, previous knowledge of the military. This is true whether we are talking about the early days of the Vietnam war, Ulster in 1969, the firemen's strike in the winter of 1977/78, or the Falklands crisis in 1982. Initially, therefore, the standard of reporting about the military is likely to vary depending upon the previous experience of the reporter, his basic knowledge of the military institution, organisation and rank structure, and any preconceptions and prejudices which the journalist may possess.

This variation in the standard of reporting is particularly relevant to the media coverage of a military campaign, especially at the beginning. One of the common characteristics of conflict, be it a major war or a street riot, is the confusion which surrounds an event immediately after it has occurred. This phenomenon makes it equally difficult for both

8 Visit to BBC Radio News, 20 November 1978 and interview with Christopher Lee, 5 December 1979.

those military officers and journalists who were not at the event to discover what actually happened. Furthermore, if both the journalists and the soldiers who took part in the action have previously experienced minimal, if any, exposure to gunfire, then there exists the classic conditions for confusion.

Such a condition existed during the Vietnam war when a 19-man Vietcong sapper group assaulted the US Embassy in Saigon in 1968 at the beginning of the Tet offensive. The attack took place in the early hours of 30 January and was initiated when the sappers blew a hole in the eight foot high wall which surrounded the complex, and killed two of the five US military police (MP) guards. They then attacked the chancery building, hitting the facade with bazooka rounds and tried to enter the front door. US reinforcements (consisting of MPs and Marine guards) arrived and a six hour intermittent gun battle ensued inside the compound, during which time a helicopter, attempting to evacuate the wounded, was driven off by ground fire. The Vietcong were all eventually killed and at sunrise the MPs outside the compound rushed the gates and the fighting ended. As this final act took place a platoon of airborne troops was landed by helicopter on the chancery roof to ensure the security of the embassy.[9]

The embassy was situated in downtown Saigon and, more significantly, within half a mile of the news bureaus. As Peter Braestrup points out in his book about the American news media coverage of the Tet offensive: 'Compared to the far larger attacks on Tan Son Nhut air base, as well as other actions in the Saigon area, the embassy fight was minor. But because of its "symbolism" and, above all, its accessibility to newsmen, it dominated the initial Tet coverage. Moreover, because of confusion and haste, the first reports made it seem that the foe had succeeded, not failed, in seizing his objective: the embassy chancery. Even as the fog cleared, corrections were slow in coming. Newsmen, this reporter included, were willing, even eager, to believe the worst. It was a classic case of journalistic reaction to surprise'.[10]

Braestrup's investigations revealed the confusions typical of war conditions. This is illustrated by his examination of the question of whether or not the Vietcong sappers actually got inside the embassy building. In particular, he explores the part played by Peter Arnett, the Associated Press (AP) correspondent, and subsequently by the AP office in New York. The situation was confused as dawn broke on 30 January with some of the newsmen (including Arnett) gathered together about 100 metres from the embassy along with some

9 The facts of this action are taken from Peter Braestrup's *Big Story*, Westview Press, Boulder Colorado 1977, p.86.
10 Ibid., p.86.;

bewildered and excited MPs, many of whom were experiencing combat for the first time. They only had a view of the top of the embassy building — nobody could see what was going on in the grounds of the compound behind the high embassy wall. Arnett later recalled that the consensus of opinion amongst the newsmen was that 'the situation was perfectly clear. Reporters were within a few yards of the fighting, as far up as we could get. After all, the MP captain did tell me with the utmost certainty when I asked him if the Vietcong were inside the embassy building: "My God, yes . . . we are taking fire from up there . . . keep your head down"'.[11]

Neither the newsmen nor the military police could see what was going on inside the compound and when the airborne troops landed by helicopter on the embassy roof it was assumed that their platoon forced the Vietcong out of the embassy building. In fact the fighting was virtually over when this force arrived and only a few minutes later the MPs broke into the compound via the front gate, closely followed by newsmen and television cameras.

Initially the AP bulletins 'attributed' reports of the Vietcong's presence in the embassy chancery,[12] but immediately prior to the deadline for the first edition for the morning newspapers in the Eastern United States the bulletins simply stated 'the facts' without any attributions:

181 VIETNAM

Saigon (AP) . . . The Vietcong seized part of the US Embassy in Saigon early Wednesday and battled American military police who tried to recapture it.

Communist Commandos penetrated the supposedly attack proof building in the climax of a combined artillery and guerrilla assault that brought limited warfare to Saigon itself . . . .[13]

When General Westmoreland visited the American Embassy after the attack, in the middle of the morning of 30 January, he stated to newsmen that the assault started at approximately 3 am with an anti-tank rocket which blasted a hole in the outer wall for the VC assault team (dressed in civilian clothes) to crawl through. They were equipped with satchel charges and demolitions in order to demolish the embassy. He further stated that there was only superficial damage to the embassy building and that MPs surrounded the area between 3 am and 5 am and then they eventually entered the compound and killed the remaining enemy.

---

11 Ibid., p.93.
12 The reports were attributed to the MPs outside the compound.
13 Ibid., p.94.

Although this account seemed plausible to Braestrup (supported by evidence from the airborne troops who said they had seen nothing, and by his own observation of the chancery doors, which were intact) it was not readily accepted by AP who, although they reported the general's account, balanced it with the earlier statement of the MP Captain. After further investigations, however, Peter Arnett eventually sent a corrective version stating that the attackers had *not* penetrated into the embassy building. But this correction was not reflected by the AP office in New York even twelve hours after that telex message was despatched. Arnett blamed this on bad editing in New York. Whatever the cause, 'as a result, in the US eastern morning newspapers, and in most of the country's other morning editions, the impression given by AP was that: (1) the Vietcong had seized the embassy itself and (2) Westmoreland was lying when he said they had not'.[14] As a postscript to this incident Braestrup observed that General Westmoreland immediately realised that Hanoi's failure to exploit surprise in the cities was a strategic mistake, and he said so when he spoke to the press in the grounds of the Embassy a few hours after it had been secured. But the listening newsmen, especially those new to combat conditions, did not believe him:

> Standing on the blood-spattered lawn of the embassy compound, as dead Vietcong sappers were being carried out, he [General Westmoreland] repeated his assurances to newsmen: 'The enemy exposed himself . . . and he suffered great casualties . . . As soon as President Thieu, with our agreement, called off the truce, American troops went on the offensive and pursued the enemy aggressively'.
>
> As Don Oberdorfer [author of *Tet!*] was later to recall, 'The reporters could hardly believe their ears. Westmoreland was standing in the ruins and saying everything was great.[15] This writer was among those who listened politely, envying the General his *sang-froid*. We walked away, shaking our heads. To the newsmen, the sapper's raid on the embassy was a dramatic, humiliating blow at the symbol of the entire US presence in Vietnam. How could Westmoreland persist in his old optimism?
>
> Later General Bruce Clarke (USA-Ret) visited Vietnam during the Tet offensive and wrote that the foe 'took the battle down around the Caravelle Hotel [headquarters for CBS and ABC] and, so, from the standpoint of the average reporter over there, it was

14 Ibid., p.98.
15 See also General William C. Westmoreland, *A Soldier Reports*, Doubleday, New York 1976, p.325.

the acorn that fell on the chicken's head and it said "The sky is falling"'.

There is no question that newsmen, especially those correspondents whose prior exposure to gunfire was minimal, were shaken.[16]

This incident demonstrates the different factors which can affect the reporting of 'the facts' and illustrates the repercussions which may result once inaccurate information is telexed across the world (in this case the American newsmen awarded a psychological victory to North Vietnam). The example also illustrates the immense importance of the newsmen's assessment of the military's credibility, and the overriding need for verification before publication. This will often conflict with the media's requirement to meet deadlines, but failure fully to investigate an incident before publication can result in dire consequences. In this case a press agency had preferred the initial account of someone who was not an eye-witness to the evidence of airborne troops who had landed on the building, to the statement of General Westmoreland (whose aide had telephoned the guard positioned in the lobby of the chancery during the battle and ascertained from him that the VC had not entered the embassy)[17] and to the visual evidence of only superficial damage to the facade of the building.

This example is not an isolated case, it is simply one which has been sufficiently well researched to illustrate the mistakes that can and have been made in reporting such incidents. As we have seen from earlier examples in this book, the same mistakes were being made 14 years later in the Falklands crisis. Initial reports of events were confused, inaccurate and therefore misleading; too often 'the facts' provided by Argentinian official sources were accepted as such without any attribution thus lending credence to Argentinian propaganda; and some of the dramatic headlines and exaggerated accounts of events served only to give the impression that a war was imminent when in fact combat of any significance was some weeks away.

The search for truth is an illusive quest at the best of times, but particularly so in the confusion of war.

Other factors which should also be taken into consideration when considering the reporting of conflict include the personal ambition of the young reporters, and the military's attitude to the news media. One of the quickest ways to make one's name in journalism is by becoming a war correspondent (as has been demonstrated by William Howard Russell in the Crimea, Winston Churchill in the Boer War, and

16 Ibid., p.141.
17 General Westmoreland, op.cit., p.324.

Julian Pettifer in Vietnam).[18] But amongst the professional objective reporters there will be some ambitious young men who may occasionally allow their personal ambition to override their journalistic duty to report the facts. The military, too, can create friction by hindering the media — either because they do not understand the newsmen's requirements or because they do not want them around to report on their activities. Alan Protheroe illustrated this most graphically when he described in *The Listener* the frustrations of trying to mount a small satellite ground station aboard one of the aircraft carriers in order to send back BBC Television News pictures during the Falklands Crisis. Despite close co-operation with expert Royal Navy Communicators and BBC Television engineers, there were some who misunderstood. One crusty RN officer said to Alan Protheroe: 'You're the chappie who wanted to put the satellite thing in the middle of the flight deck. Would've stopped us flying, y'know'.[19] One is drawn to the same conclusion as Protheroe: 'There are moments [such as this] when a long, slow pull at a stiff Scotch is the only possible response'. There are therefore many areas of potential conflict of interests between the military and the media which affect the reporting of the military 'in action' and the detailed analysis in the other chapters in Part IV have shown how often the military have been required to be employed in action (and thus be the subject of media interest, reports and comments) because of man's continual failure to solve his problems by peaceful means. This lesson of recent history serves to emphasise the requirement to improve the media's basic knowledge about the military and to make young journalists aware of the inherent problems of reporting conflict at the beginning of their careers. This is equally applicable to potential editors as it is to prospective reporters. The solution lies in education.

Conclusion

There is a requirement for all trainee journalists to receive some education on the role of the military in modern society, in the basic structure of military organisations and to become acquainted with the more frequently used terminology so that subsequently they will be better able to inform the public once they have completed their training. This requirement could be met by including 'the military' in

18 The term war correspondent is usually associated with large scale wars (such as World War II or the Vietnam war). For the basis of this study the term is used to include the media coverage of any major military conflict, including Northern Ireland and the Falklands crisis.
19 *The Listener*, 3 June 1982, p.2.

the syllabi of the various courses in journalism which are run by the appropriate bodies. This initial education could be supplemented by a subsequent liaison with the Ministry of Defence through such activities as the Editors Abroad Scheme, and occasional updating briefings given by MOD to editors and general reporters. Such a scheme would need to be initiated by MOD but should not be too difficult to arrange since it is an extension of the idea initiated in 1979 to provide regular briefings for defence correspondents. The combination of these two innovations should go a long way to improve the current knowledge which the media possess about the military and these ideas could be used as the basis for further developments in this area.

Any move to improve the education of the media about the military will inevitably require co-operation from the latter. It also presumes that such efforts to improve the comprehension of the one profession is being matched by the other. In the final chapter of this section we shall consider the education of the military about the media.

13 The Education of the Military about the Media

In the period since the Second World War the Armed Forces have been required to readjust considerably to their changing role in society. The process of adaption has not been easy because Britain herself has been redefining her position on the world stage and moving from a colonial power to a European partner. In the two decades following the Second World War the process of de-colonialisation involved the British service-man in considerable active service. These major operations included Palestine (1945–48), Malaya (1948–60), Kenya (1952–56), Cyprus (1954–59), Aden (1957–67) and Borneo (1962–66). In addition to these campaigns there were other operations which were less publicised or have simply been 'overlooked', such as the operations in Muscat and Oman (which included the defeat of the rebels by the Special Air Service in the rocky crags of Jebel Akhdar in 1959), and the sending of a British brigade to Jordan in 1958 to assist King Hussein against a threat to his throne.

This period of recent history also included the Berlin air lift (1947), the Korean War (1950–53), the Suez operation (1956), the ending of National Service in 1962, the emergence of the increasing importance to Britain of the NATO Alliance and the realities of living in the nuclear age. Therefore the British serviceman has had to cope with internal security operations, limited war, deterrence in the nuclear age, transition from a conscript to an all regular force, rapid advances in new technology — all set against a gradual reduction in size, budget and scope of operations. It is not surprising that some servicemen found it too difficult to make the necessary adjustment in such a short period. But what is often overlooked is that the postwar years saw the end of 200 years of the British Army's contribution to the establishment and defence of the British Empire. That is what made the re-orientation so difficult. And yet, despite all the difficulties associated with the re-shaping of the Armed Forces to meet the changing roles, the Services acquitted themselves surprisingly well. Correlli Barnett comments on this in his book *Britain and Her Army*:

> The two decades that followed the Second World War constituted therefore a period of painful adjustment, when all the power, wealth and empire won in the two centuries after 1690 finally vanished. It was a major turning point in British history. And just as the marches of neglected, underpaid red-coats and their thundering volleys had once marked the surge of British expansion, so the soldier in khaki-drill or battledress guarded the hesitant retreat from empire. While the politicians wavered, while authority crumbled, the soldier tried to keep order. And when at last the British had gone, from country after country, it was found that the British Army was the only British institution to leave a permanent mark — the mark of order and organisation amid a carnival of collapsing parliamentary government.[1]

The media coverage of the British military in action from 1945—67 varied considerably. The Suez landing was carried out in a blaze of publicity and news coverage (which was hardly surprising considering the political hesitation which preceded the operation), and the sinister headline 'Murder Mile' brought home to the British public the realities of the campaign against EOKA in Cyprus. In contrast the Borneo war, one of the most successful operations ever conducted by the British and Commonwealth forces, received scant news coverage although it involved 60,000 troops in 1965 (the same number as the USA had deployed in Vietnam that year). The newspaper coverage of these campaigns depended on the assessment of the cost-effectiveness and the logistics involved; a war that was being conducted on the other side of the world, and furthermore one which was considered unlikely to increase sales, would receive only superficial coverage in some papers. The logistic problems involved in covering the Borneo campaign illustrate the point. A reporter sent out to cover the war had to fly to Singapore (a 22 hour flight), then on to Kuching. Having received

---

1 Correlli Barnett, *Britain and Her Army*, Allen Lane, The Penguin Press, London 1970, p.479.

briefings at formation and brigade level he would probably go forward to one of the battalions, visit a company location and accompany a jungle foot patrol. Jungle warfare is uncomfortable, very personal and tedious. The rate of incidents in Borneo can be gauged by the statistic of 100 hours' patrolling for one contact. Therefore, unless the journalists' rare visits coincided with a major incident the reports tended to be feature articles on what conditions were like for the British troops living in the jungle. Even if the reporter happened to be in the right area when an incident occurred, he still had the problem of getting the news back to his editor in Britain in time to meet the news room's deadline. The era of satellite communication and television reporting was to change all this, but that did not become effective until Vietnam escalated into a major conflict. The notable exception to this was the Falklands crisis; however it should be remembered that the satellite communications problems were unique to that conflict and are unlikely to reoccur elsewhere.

The media's frequent failure to provide adequate news coverage of foreign affairs had a direct impact on the military. Because they were involved in operations abroad, often in remote places, military commanders were able to conduct their campaigns outside the glare of publicity. Visits from reporters were rare and therefore aroused interest amongst the military, but it was rather a curious interest in why their activities were considered to be worth reporting. There was little thought given by commanders to the effect on public opinion when making military decisions, and besides, most servicemen carried out their duties on active service assured of public support of people at home. Or so they thought.

The social revolution which started in the sixties was to involve the Armed Forces as well as many other aspects of life in Britain. By a strange quirk of history, 1968, the year of student riots in Western democracies, was the first year this century that no British soldier had been killed or wounded in action. History may well judge that year of rare peace as a key date in military annals. The following year troops were committed to Northern Ireland.

Right from the beginning, the Army's actions in Ulster were subjected to incessant news coverage and every soldier from the General Officer Commanding Northern Ireland (GOCNI) downwards, had to adjust to this new factor. Today, 13 years later, it is difficult to realise just what this meant to those soldiers serving in Northern Ireland who had recently seen action in Borneo and Aden. Although the withdrawal from Aden had been fully covered by the media, the conditions and type of operations for the servicemen were very different from the delicate job they were required to do in Ulster two years later. To illustrate this point, the last troops out of Aden in 1967 included Royal

Marines Commandos (42 and 45 Commando); in September 1969, 41 Commando Royal Marines was despatched to Northern Ireland and a number of the Marines in that unit had previously seen service in Aden.

Senior Officers realised very quickly that there was a pressing need to educate officers (and through them, the NCOs and soldiers) about the media. The importance of public opinion was acknowledged, the requirement to provide good facilities for the press through a sophisticated public relations organisation was clearly identified, and the value of television interviews was quickly realised. The effectiveness of this education has been widely praised by people both inside and outside the media and Sir Robert Mark, the then Commissioner for the Metropolitan Police, drew on the Army's example to improve the relations between the Metropolitan Police and the media.[2]

It will therefore be of value to see what the Armed Forces are taught about the media today and to discover how much emphasis is placed on this subject in the various Service colleges. Television has brought the Vietnam war, Northern Ireland, and the Falkland Islands, into the living rooms of American and British homes so what lessons have the military drawn from this experience? How much do the military really know about the media's problems, about its position in modern society, about the process of producing news, or about the editorial system? Do the military really understand the media?

Progressive education

In his book *The Soldier and Modern Society*, Lieutenant Colonel Baynes stated that one of the reasons the Army achieves good results is: 'partly because the Army continues the educational process throughout a man's service, and has a highly developed way of training him and following up each stage of his career'.[3] For officers, this educational process commences at the initial officer training colleges: the Britannia Royal Naval College, Dartmouth, the Royal Military Academy, Sandhurst and the Royal Air Force College, Cranwell. The next major step in an officer's education is selection for one of the staff colleges in his early thirties at the army rank, or equivalent, of captain or junior major to either the Royal Naval Staff College, Greenwich, the Staff College, Camberley, the Royal Air Force Staff College, Bracknell, or to a foreign staff college. Attitudes to the importance of attendance at

2   Sir Robert Mark, *In the Office of Constable*, Collins, London 1978, p.134.
3   Lieutenant Colonel J.C.M. Baynes, *The Soldier and Modern Society*, Eyre Methuen, London 1972, pp. 4—5.

these staff colleges varies to some extent between the three services, but certainly for the Army, Camberley is the stepping-stone to higher rank and selection is highly competitive. For those officers aspiring to go to the top of their profession there is the possibility of attendance in the army rank or equivalent of senior major at the National Defence College (NDC) and subsequently at the Royal College of Defence Studies (RCDS) in the army rank equivalent of colonel or brigadier.[4]

Initial training for officers

The three initial training colleges for officers vary considerably in their approach to education about the media. Dartmouth includes nothing at all about the media (not even an 'interest' lecture) and Cranwell receives only one lecture by the Command PRO. Sandhurst, on the other hand, pays some attention to this subject in its syllabi.

There are currently three main training schemes at Sandhurst for non-graduate regular officers, short service officers and graduates. All non-graduates do the 28 week Standard Military Course (SMC), the aim of which is: 'To develop the qualities of leadership and to provide the basic knowledge required by all young officers of any Arm or Service so that, after the necessary special to Arm training given by the appropriate Arm or Service, they will be fit to be a junior officer'.[5] The syllabus includes a lecture by the Director of Public Relations for the Army (DPR(A)) which is usually followed by a seminar on public relations. The programme also includes the use of closed circuit television to improve an officer's competence and powers of expression, but there is no lecture on the media. After completing the SMC, short service officers leave Sandhurst to join their regiments or corps after undergoing special to Arm training where necessary.

Regular non-graduate officers return to Sandhurst between 2½ and 4 years later, after completing regimental duties, to do a 14 week concentrated academic course. This course includes such subjects as war studies, international affairs, a study of contemporary Britain, and communications. There is a general awareness of the media

4 The educational system for officers in any of the services contains a number of variations to fit the specific requirements of an individual officer. This can vary from a degree course at University, at the Royal Naval Engineering College, Manadon or at the Royal Military College of Science, Shrivenham, to the three months' Lieutenants Greenwich Course (a course for Royal Naval Officers, Royal Marines Officers and Ministry of Defence civil servants in their mid-twenties which is designed to broaden their education and teach them basic staff work).
The survey of syllabi has been confined to those military educational establishments which are most likely to be attended by an officer as he progresses in his career. Mention of other courses has been included only when appropriate.
5 Standard Military Course, Sandhurst Syllabus, September 1977, p.vi.

throughout the syllabus which reflects the changes in society and the Army's role in that society. The present syllabus has resulted from gradual amendments since the new Sandhurst course was introduced in 1972 and the media are considered in lectures and discussions whenever appropriate (such as when discussing the problems of modern society or considering the economics of defence). Apart from the consideration of the media in general terms there are specific periods allotted for this subject: a lecture on 'The Role of the Media in Northern Ireland' which is usually given by a journalist who has reported in Ulster; the communication syllabus includes a number of television exercises; and 'crisis games' (a feature of the various courses) include media 'play' which is written into appropriate scenarios (newspapers are produced every few hours, students represent reporters, television news is transmitted at regular intervals and there is a television *Panorama* style interview at the end of each game).

It is therefore apparent that by the time a regular officer completes his training at Sandhurst he will have been made aware of the role of the media in today's society, and in the process of developing the skills of effective communication he will also have gained useful experience in television interview technique in realistic and pertinent scenarios. Indeed, the amount of time devoted to education about the media and its associated subjects reflects the importance attached to this topic by the staff at Sandhurst.

In contrast to the regular officers, however, there is a shortfall in the coverage of the media for graduates, and short service officers. But the relevant point about the short service entry is that it provides a significant percentage of the total officer entry to Sandhurst each year (approximately 50 per cent in 1982). Bearing in mind that short service officers join their regiments very soon after leaving Sandhurst, and therefore are liable to service in Northern Ireland during their short career in the Army (depending on their Arm and the unit programme), it appears illogical that less attention has been paid to their education about the media. Over the last few years there has certainly been an extension to that part of the SMC syllabus which covers this subject but it is considered that it still falls short of what is desirable.

Whereas Sandhurst may be concerned with a minor adjustment to their programme, Dartmouth and, to a lesser extent Cranwell, appear to have ignored the relevance of the media altogether. It is appreciated that both colleges run high pressure courses and there is insufficient time in the syllabus to include all the instruction that may be considered necessary; but is this the only reason for omission? Sandhurst also have programming problems but they have *made* room for the media. It is worth reflecting that a subject which is common to all three services is treated so differently at the initial colleges. Experience in Northern Ireland has naturally focused the Army's attention on the requirement but it is somewhat surprising to find that the Royal Navy and the Royal Air Force are prepared to despatch their young officers to their units with little or no instruction on the media. It is this lack of awareness of the relevance of the media which is disturbing. A lecture given by the respective Directors of Public Relations followed by a discussion is the minimum instruction required to create this awareness and a good deal more would prove beneficial, as it does at Sandhurst. Even a single lecture early in an officer's career can stimulate an informed curiosity about the media upon which he can build and develop his understanding, almost daily. The media is a powerful force in today's society and interest should be aroused at the beginning of an officer's training as part of his general education.

Staff colleges

The next relevant stage in an officer's career is attendance at one of the staff colleges. The syllabi at Greenwich, Camberley and Bracknell are similar in that they include a 'Press Day', visits to national newspapers and to television.

The Press Day at Camberley is designed to provide the opportunity for exchange of ideas between the military students and representatives of the press. To this end a number of journalists representing television, radio, national and provincial press are invited to attend. The morning is normally devoted to a series of lectures given by DPR(A) and representatives of the media, followed by a central discussion. In 1981 the speakers were Alan Protheroe, Assistant Director General of the BBC, Sir Denis Hamilton, Chairman Times Newspaper Holdings and David Fairhall, Defence Correspondent of *The Guardian*. The morning session used to be followed by further discussions in the afternoon and held in syndicate with various members of the media attending each group and the frank exchange of ideas during the afternoon seminar highlighted the value of the Press Day. The second half of the programme, however, has since been dropped, thereby devaluing the educational benefit of the day since most benefit is achieved by discussion in smaller syndicate groups. It is to be hoped that the full day will be restored to the Camberley programme as soon as possible. The Falklands crisis alone has underlined the need for the minimum of a day to be devoted to this very important subject.

Visits to national newspapers are a standard part of staff courses. They are considered part of an officer's general education, and provide him with the opportunity to observe the production of a newspaper and to talk to the editorial staff. These visits are mandatory for Camberley but voluntary for Greenwich and Bracknell. This pattern is repeated by the three colleges' attitudes to visits to television centres: Bracknell has recently commenced voluntary visits, Greenwich has arranged one voluntary visit per course to both BBC Television Centre (since 1975) and ITN (since 1976), and Camberley has arranged regular visits to the BBC and ITN since 1977. It is worth noting that visits to television are a comparatively recent innovation and the acknowledgement of the increasing importance of television is reflected by the inclusion of lectures on television techniques at Camberley (but not at Greenwich and Bracknell). Furthermore, every officer at Camberley gets practical experience of being interviewed on television, and 'PR play' is introduced into most major exercises to give officers interview experience in a realistic scenario.

Voluntary visits to Fleet Street and to television (news and current affairs) are features of the syllabi of both the National Defence College and the Royal College of Defence Studies, and both colleges include lectures and/or seminars involving eminent personalities from the media (in 1982 Dr Richard Hoggart lectured to NDC and RCDS held a media discussion which included a panel consisting of David Nicholas (ITN), Alan Protheroe (BBC), George Gale (*Daily Express*) and Peter Preston (*Guardian*)). In addition, RCDS includes a lecture on television techniques and for those who wish to pursue this further there is an opportunity for them to undergo practical television interview familiarisation.

This résumé of the syllabi of the various colleges indicates the amount of time spent on formal instruction about the media and related subjects, but it does not signify how much the media are covered in seminars and informal discussions. It would be difficult to assess how often this occurs but nevertheless this aspect should not be overlooked since discussion is at the very heart of the educational ethos of staff colleges and the media are certainly considered whenever appropriate. The other relevant characteristic of staff colleges is the requirement for student officers to produce a paper and/or a presentation on a subject of their choice. The Armed Forces and the Media has proved to be an attractive subject for some students and, indeed, in 1976 three papers were written on this topic at NDC alone. It has also attracted attention at RCDS. Since 1970 a selection of each year's papers has been published as the 'Seaford House Papers' and a number of articles have been about the military, the media and modern society. Indeed, a recent edition included Colonel C.P.R. Palmer's article on 'Public Opinion and the Armed Services'[8] which attracted the attention

8 Colonel Palmer has since been promoted to Major General.

188

of Tony Geraghty of *The Sunday Times*.[9] The papers written at NDC and RCDS have demonstrated considerable research on the part of the authors, and the RCDS papers, since they are published, have contributed to the military's knowledge about the media. It is also perhaps significant that this subject appears to become a more popular option for student officers at the more senior level.

It is evident from this review of instruction on the media carried out at the various staff colleges that those responsible for planning the curricula are aware of the need to include the media in the syllabi. It is also apparent that this subject is relatively low on the list of priorities compared with other topics more obviously relative to the military art and therefore staff colleges are only able to allocate a small percentage of the total time available to this topic. The position becomes even clearer when one considers the reduction of the total length of some staff courses which has occurred in recent years. The enforced reduction of these courses has forced a critical eye to be cast on each subject to test the justification for its retention and, indeed, when the Bracknell course was further reduced from nine to seven months in January 1975 the Press phase was dropped from the syllabus altogether. It was only reintroduced in August 1976 as a result of pressure from within the Air Force Department. Against this background how well are the staff colleges educating their officers about the media?

There is little doubt that those attending the colleges as students are very interested in the media and are fully aware of their importance. They also appear to find the coverage of the subject satisfactory; indeed, one of the students at Camberley described the 1978 Press Day as 'one of the best days of the entire course'.[10] However it was this same day which revealed the lack of understanding amongst the military of the fundamentals of the media business. There was a total of 2½ hours given over to discussion following the morning lectures and this enabled the military officers and the representatives from the media to consider areas of mutual interest in some detail. As the discussion progressed it gradually became apparent that the journalists assumed that the officers had a basic understanding of the fundamentals of the media. This was a false assumption. It inevitably led to misunderstandings during the seminars and may well be one of the contributory factors to the widespread mistrust amongst the military about the media.

These fundamentals (which were described in chapter 2) need to be understood so that the reader, viewer or listener is able to appreciate the conditions under which he receives information; and yet the

9 *The Sunday Times*, 22 October 1978.
10 Visit to the Staff College, Camberley, in November 1978.

ignorance of these facts is widespread. The case has been well put by Michael Tracey in the introduction to his book *The Production of Political Television*:

> The ubiquity of 'the box' within our everyday lives is clear and yet the most surprising fact which faces the new student of the media is the relatively sparse body of real information which one has as to the forces which shape the actions and motivations of these key institutions within our culture. Their nature, their purpose, their operations remain mysteries. At the same time, though, the formulation of theories about television and the forces that shape it abound, and everyone, from that curious aggregate the 'man in the street' to the most distinguished social theorist, is willing to offer his version of what it is that generates and influences programme-making practices. And with each and every critique the single most telling fact is that they operate from what is in effect a position of almost total ignorance.[11]

So the military are not alone in their ignorance and, indeed, they have made genuine efforts to educate themselves by, for instance, visiting newspapers and television centres. However, it is impossible to absorb the intricate details of the news process during a short visit to a newspaper or a television newsroom. For their part newspapers and television newsrooms could not possibly cope with a number of visits by two observers for a whole day (the ideal solution) as opposed to the groups of ten or so who visit for a few hours under the current arrangements. Despite the willingness on both sides to educate the military, the result is still not satisfactory because the visitors come away with only a superficial knowledge.

However the really significant point about this superficial knowledge is that the superficiality has not been fully recognised due to the limited knowledge of those responsible for planning the staff colleges' syllabi. Inevitably the instruction about the media has been based on the directing staff's memory of how the subject was covered when they were students, and on their collective experience in their dealings with the media. When they were students they received little instruction on the media; therefore there has been progress. As for their experience with the media — well, the Army's experience in Ulster has demonstrated the importance of the Press therefore the syllabi of the various colleges have tended to include a lecture by a well known media personality followed by a discussion with or without other represen-

---

11 Michael Tracey, *The Production of Political Television*, Routledge & Kegan Paul, London 1978, p.3.

tatives from the media. The similarities of the syllabi are not surprising and the exchange of ideas which results from such a format is obviously beneficial. However the results of the research for this book have shown that when officers take part in these discussions most of them have little understanding about the fundamentals of the media despite their previous educational visits and lectures.

Progressive education about the media

To illustrate the relevance of this situation it is necessary to appreciate that the vast majority of future commanding officers will be selected from the staff college students, and also to recognise the considerable responsibility which the commanding officer has for the training of the men under his command. If a commanding officer does not understand the media then there is little chance that the men under his command will, and if he does not appreciate the importance of public relations he will be unlikely to pay due attention to this matter when considering whom to appoint as unit press officer. An example of the varying attitudes by commanding officers to this subject emerged during a recent visit to Northern Ireland. One commanding officer considered this awareness of the media was second only in importance to tactical training when preparing for a tour in Ulster and that consideration of the media was a fundamental factor of his command decisions in the Province. On the other hand another battalion apparently considered public relations to be so irrelevant that the unit press officer had not even attended the unit press officers' course despite this being mandatory for all units serving in Ulster. Considerable progress has been made in educating the military about the media, most of it during the last few years and as a direct result of Northern Ireland, but as this last example illustrates the Army is a long way from standardisation, let alone the other two Services. And yet comparatively little adjustment is required to achieve the necessary progressive education about the media. If a lecture on the fundamentals of the media was delivered at Dartmouth, Sandhurst and Cranwell this would give all officers a basic understanding about the media at the beginning of their service careers.[12] Such a lecture could be given by a journalist or a civilian member of the public relations organisation of the Ministry of Defence who had a journalistic background. The introduction of this instruction would ensure that all officers, regardless of their method of entry into the Armed Forces, would receive a basic grounding in this subject

12 Such a lecture was given by the author to the Royal Marines Young Officers at the Commando Training Centre Royal Marines, Lympstone, in May 1979, and to officers under training at BRNC Dartmouth in December 1979. The experiment was considered to be a success.

191

which would form the background for any subsequent experience with the media. At present a short service officer in the Army, and any junior officer who has just completed training at Dartmouth or Cranwell, could find himself involved in an incident, or major conflict (such as the Falklands) which attracted press interest without any real understanding of how the media functions. The fact that invariably there will be a public relations representative to offer advice avoids the fundamental problem of lack of understanding. The introduction of this lecture would also enable young officers to talk to their NCOs and men with some degree of knowledge.

Such a lecture would not only educate young officers at the beginning of their career but it would also provide a good foundation from which to develop a progressive education about the media throughout their service careers. This basic knowledge, coupled with practical experience, would enable the military and the media to get far more out of their Press Days at the various colleges and also guarantee that those officers selected for command had a progressive education about the media before reaching a position of influence. In order to ensure that the education was progressive it is worth emphasising the need to include this subject on the syllabi of any other relevant courses which an officer may attend before becoming eligible for selection for staff college.

As far as the Army is concerned considerable benefit is achieved by including this subject at the Junior Division of the Staff College (JDSC) and in the Progressive Qualification Scheme (PQS) because all officers wishing to qualify for the substantive rank of captain are required to do PQS 1, and those who wish to qualify for the substantive rank of major are required to do PQS 2 and attend JDSC, regardless of whether they are subsequently selected for staff college. The PQS is designed to provide 'a logical and co-ordinated progression in the professional education and training of officers' and national and international affairs and in economic and sociological factors both in Great Britain and the world both as they affect his country and the Army'.[13] At present JDSC has a half-day session on the media which includes a lecture by DPR(A) followed by a general discussion with representatives of the press, but the PQS syllabus includes nothing directly related to the media, nor is any book about the impact of the media in today's society included in the recommended reading lists. And yet the relevance of this subject to the PQS syllabus and to an officer's general education has certainly been acknowledged by the

---

13 *The Progressive Qualification Scheme and Staff Training Handbook*, Army Code No.71065, 1976, p.1–1.

Royal Army Educational Corps (RAEC) who included a session on Defence and the Media in the Summer School in 1979.[14] The introduction of instruction about the media in the PQS syllabus would provide the essential ingredient to ensure progressive education for Army officers from Sandhurst to their selection for the rank of major.

Television techniques

'Learn to get used to it. Eels get used to skinning.' Churchill

Throughout the years the Army has gained a well deserved reputation for taking corrective action whenever a flaw has been discovered in its training or operational methods. An example of this, and very much part of the military's education about the media, is the development of television technique training.

Television equipment (for use as a training aid in the field of communications) had been installed at the Army School of Instructional Technology, Beaconsfield, for about two years when it became apparent in 1969, as a result of experience in Ulster, that there was an urgent requirement to give officers some training in television interview techniques. Beaconsfield was charged with running the courses to satisfy this requirement and the Army School of Instructional Technology has been responsible for providing most of the instruction on television techniques for the Army ever since (and for the Royal Navy since late 1973). The Television Wing at Beaconsfield is responsible for providing television technique for all who are considered to require it and within this broad guideline the training is for certain officer appointments in any batallion which serves in Northern Ireland, and is optional for senior officers in the Royal Navy and the Army. The Wing trains approximately 300 officers per year who attend either a one-day, or a 2½-day course. The aim of the course is to familiarise the student with the medium and thus prepare him for the real thing. On the one-day course each student does three interviews which are geared to his requirements (i.e. roadside interview, studio interview, etc.), and he receives advice on presentation and content. The 2½-day courses are for selected senior officers and the syllabus is more extensive. In addition to this service, the Television Wing often lecture to staff colleges, specialist courses (such as the Unit Press Officers' (UPO) Course) and visit units on location who are training for Northern Ireland. The training team also takes part in staff college and field force exercises, representing television reporters.

14 The aim of the Summer School is to update those responsible for teaching the PQS syllabus.

Television familiarisation training has also been run for the Royal Air Force at the RAF School of Education and Training Support, RAF Newton, since April 1974. Attendance on the course is not mandatory for any specific appointment but it is part of the job specification for certain Air Officer appointments and is recommended for Station Commanders. The course is also intended for other officers whose appointments may require them to appear on television (such as the team leader and the manager of the Red Arrows Aerobatic Team or the operations officer of a flying station). RAF Newton run 23 courses a year, and since 1974 approximately 600 officers have undergone this training. The one-day course is run on very similar lines to Beaconsfield.

During the last few years a considerable number of officers in the Armed Forces (particularly the Army), have benefited directly or indirectly from television techniques training. This grew out of a specific requirement: the need in Ulster for an Army spokesman to describe an event in which he, or his unit, was involved. The Army realised very quickly that this was also an excellent method of countering IRA propaganda as well as winning the sympathy of the British public. The results exceeded the Army's expectations, however, because no one had anticipated the impact on the public of confident, articulate soldiers (of whatever rank) who were able to describe an event in simple English and brief sentences. The art of communication, so vital to the military and therefore a well developed art, had reaped unexpected benefit because it was the first time that the military had communicated with the public on such a vast scale and there resulted a greater sympathy for the soldier's role in Ulster and a clearer understanding of his profession than would otherwise have been the case. The Army had established contact with the British public through the medium of television and this was an important step in the context of the military and modern society.

The significance of this step forward was acknowledged in an article which appeared in *The Economist* in 1971:

> ... No one can doubt that the soldiers in Belfast and Londonderry would find life a bit easier if they did not have to operate with television cameras watching them. Much of the work the Army has to do is hard, nasty and nervous. To be asked to explain and justify to the armchair public the way it has reacted when under fire must be irritating to say the least. . . . But the army itself accepts that, as television is the best recruiting office, soldiers must learn to live with the cameras and the microphones. Very sensibly, the army has done something to train its men to do themselves justice when being interviewed; they are told to say what they have to say shortly, straightforwardly, sticking to the

facts as they know them. No soldier is ever interviewed until his immediate superior has given permission and unless he himself is willing. The army itself believes, almost certainly rightly, that far from being subversive or damaging morale, television coverage has done it a lot of good.[15]

Television coverage of the Army's activities certainly has done it a lot of good and there has been considerable praise for the way young junior NCOs and privates have described incidents during television interviews with clarity and confidence.[16] Yet significantly these young soldiers received no training at all in television techniques! The policy of providing training for officers but not for NCOs and soldiers has been quite deliberate because it was soon realised that although some television reporters would try to extract a comment from an officer, they only expected to obtain an eye-witness account of an incident from a soldier. The realisation of these ground rules of television interviews, the fact that the soldiers came across so well on television without training, and the size of the planning problem of introducing such training have dictated the continuance of the policy.

What of the future of television training for officers? The Armed Forces have certainly learnt the importance of television, and the training techniques are as good as, if not in advance of, those employed by civilian firms. However it is perhaps significant that as the genesis for all this emerged from the Army's requirement in Ulster, so the Army has continued to lead the field. Yet even the Army does not insist on all commanding officers attending a course. Although the facilities are always available for them to use at Beaconsfield, the onus is on the commanding officer to take advantage of those facilities. Since, in all three services, a commanding officer's period just prior to taking over command is always exceptionally busy and because he is even busier whilst actually in command, he will only have time to do the preparation and courses which he believes are essential. Television interview technique familiarisation is likely to be way down on the list of priorities. Yet a ship's captain may be required to give an interview as a result of an incident at sea or an RAF Station commander may be required to talk about the continual need for his pilots to practise low flying techniques over parts of the country which include populated

15 *The Economist*, 20 November 1971, p.20.
16 Referring to this topic at a lecture to the RUSI, Dr Richard Clutterbuck said: 'You will remember the decision some while back to encourage junior ranks in the Army in Northern Ireland to talk directly into the television camera. That was one of the best things ever done. The corporal comes over loud and clear in the living room, far better than the colonel, the general or the Minister', *Ten Years of Terrorism*, RUSI 1979, p.70.

areas. The point at issue is that although very few service commanders or senior staff officers are required to give such interviews the possibility always exists and the impact of television is such that it is too important to let the service's case go by default or be spoilt by a bad performance. The latter point is particularly significant because nobody can be certain how he will fare in a television interview until he has experienced it. A television interview technique course enables him to discover this. If he does not 'come across' well on the course at least he is aware of his failing in advance and can therefore arrange for someone else to be the television spokesman. There is nothing unusual in this; indeed, it is a procedure which has been adopted by other organisations.

The call to appear on television usually comes without warning and is often associated with a controversial newsworthy incident. Such an occasion occurred when Major General Trevor Hart, then the Director of Medical Services, United Kingdom Land Forces (UKLF) found himself being interviewed both for ITN's *News at Ten* and the BBC 9 o'clock News on 26 February 1979 following the tragic incident surrounding the shooting of Trooper Edward Maggs in Belfast. Maggs had been shot dead by a colleague after he had gone berserk with a rifle and shot one junior NCO and wounded another. In his interview Major General Hart stressed the immense pressures which were placed on young NCOs and soldiers who had to make decisions on whether to open fire or not without being able to refer to their superiors. He claimed that in such circumstances the pressures were worse than in conventional war when decisions were taken by men of more senior rank, and therefore more experience, and a soldier knew who his enemy was. The General came across as a sympathetic individual who understood the soldier's dilemma. He did not gloss over the dangers but at the same time he told the public about the psychological pressures on young soldiers serving in Ulster. It was a good interview resulting from tragic circumstances which helped explain the Army's problems, satisfied the television news hunger and also educated the public. Talking about it afterwards, General Hart stressed the very brief period in which he had to prepare for the interviews and he also spoke about the 'intrusion' of television (he was interviewed by BBC in his office and by ITN in his home):

> My previous experience of television during a day at Beaconsfield adequately prepared me for the real thing. I therefore anticipated the lights and the wires around the place, I was not surprised when they re-arranged my furniture, nor was I taken aback when the director gave me instructions in my own house before the ITN interview commenced (nobody likes to be ordered around in their

own house, least of all a general!). Getting accustomed to these practicalities of the TV interview is as important as getting used to the experience of answering questions put to you by an interviewer. What one needs is training and practice.[17]

Training in television technique is rather like lifeboat drill at sea — it's a precaution. And like lifeboat drill it needs to be practised. One day spent at Beaconsfield or RAF Newton seems a small price to pay for such a precaution and the introduction of mandatory attendance for all formation commanders, commanding officers, and those appointed to certain selected staff appointments would seem a logical development from the good grounding so far achieved. Up until now it appears that the lessons from Ulster have not been fully appreciated, particularly by the Royal Navy and the RAF. Perhaps the mistakes made during the Falklands crisis (which, in many instances, were repeats of the errors made in the early days in Ulster) will now ensure that proper attention is paid to this important technique. Any serviceman interviewed on either BBC 1's 9 o'clock news or ITN's *News at Ten*, is likely to be seen by approximately 10 million people. That is certainly worth a day's training. Indeed, it would seem logical to develop progressive training for all officers at the appropriate stages in their careers.

Defence public relations staff

Any discussion about the military's education about the media would not be complete without mention of the Defence Public Relations Staff (DPRS). But before considering DPRS' contribution to education it is first necessary to take a brief look at the organisation of this department. Within the Ministry of Defence, DPRS is organised in a combination of functional and single Service branches under the Chief of Public Relations (CPR), a senior civil servant who is directly responsible to the Permanent Under Secretary of State for Defence. Each Service has its own Director (Captain RN, Brigadier and Air Commodore) who is responsible for promoting the image of his respective Service. There are also branches working through the Deputy Chief of Public Relations (DCPR) which perform a comparable task in regard to the Procurement Executive. The functional elements of DPRS are

---

17 Interview with the author, 22 June 1979. As well as the TV appearances, General Hart was also interviewed that day on the BBC Radio 4 programme *The World at One*. He had just five minutes' warning before he was on the air which illustrates the extremely short period he had to prepare for that interview.

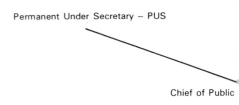

Permanent Under Secretary — PUS

Chief of Public

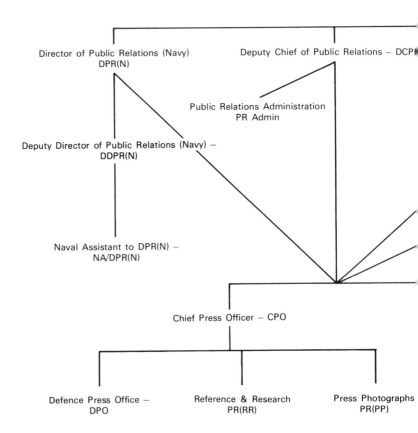

Director of Public Relations (Navy)
DPR(N)

Deputy Chief of Public Relations — DCP

Public Relations Administration
PR Admin

Deputy Director of Public Relations (Navy) —
DDPR(N)

Naval Assistant to DPR(N) —
NA/DPR(N)

Chief Press Officer — CPO

Defence Press Office —
DPO

Reference & Research
PR(RR)

Press Photographs
PR(PP)

Figure 13.1 Ministry of Defence Public Relations Staff (DPRS)
Organisation

198

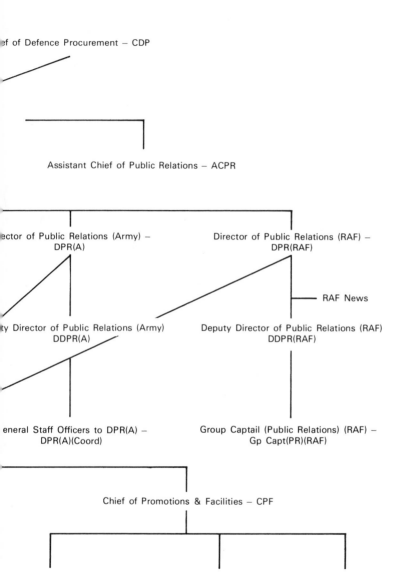

ef of Defence Procurement — CDP

Assistant Chief of Public Relations — ACPR

ector of Public Relations (Army) —
DPR(A)

Director of Public Relations (RAF) —
DPR(RAF)

RAF News

ty Director of Public Relations (Army)
DDPR(A)

Deputy Director of Public Relations (RAF)
DDPR(RAF)

eneral Staff Officers to DPR(A) —
DPR(A)(Coord)

Group Captail (Public Relations) (RAF) —
Gp Capt(PR)(RAF)

Chief of Promotions & Facilities — CPF

ce Promotions & Facilities —
DPF

Exhibitions & Publications —
DPF(Exs & Pubns)

Films —
DPF(Films)

199

responsible for handling the day-to-day news, pictures, press and broadcasting facilities on defence and multi-service subjects. (See figure 13.1 for organisation chart.)

Outside MOD there are PR staffs at most Service Commands at home and overseas and at most Army Districts and Divisions. At unit level (battalion or equivalent) the PR responsibility is either undertaken as a full time appointment or is given to a serving officer as a secondary duty. The PR staffs within MOD, and outside Whitehall down to Army District and Divisions, consist of a combination of Information Officers (civil servants, members of the Government Information Service), many of whom are former journalists or retired officers, and service officers some of whom do public relations for only one appointment of approximately two years, and others who remain in PR.

The hub of the DPRS activity within MOD is the Defence Press Office. Organised on an integrated tri-Service basis under a Chief Press Officer, it handles all questions on defence and Services matters from the British and international press and broadcasting organisation. The other major department within MOD which is relevant is the Press Facilities Section. 'Organised like the Defence Press Office on an integrated tri-Service basis it looks after the needs of Press, TV and Radio correspondents who require interviews and briefings from the Secretary of State, Ministers and senior officials, or who want to visit Defence establishments and Service Commands at home and overseas.'[18]

The three Service Directors are responsible to CPR for the administration of public relations in their respective Service and in addition each of them has become increasingly involved with the education of the military about the media. As we have seen, they all lecture to their respective staff colleges about the media, and the DPRs for the Royal Navy and the Army, or their staffs, talk about public relations to their respective Commanding Officers Designate Course, and DPR (RAF) briefs Station Commanders during the one-day briefing on public relations at MOD. These talks, together with the existence of PROs (be they civilian or Service officers) at the various formation, command and district headquarters all help to increase the awareness of the media. However by far the most important step forward in the education field has been the establishment of courses specifically designed for officers who have been selected to be Unit Press Officers (UPOs).

Once again it was the Army which took the lead — and once again the reason was Northern Ireland. For some time two members of the public relations staff at UKLF (Tony Fenn, the CPRO, and

18 *A Brief Guide to Defence Public Relations*, MOD OS 12, p.2.

Major (Retd) Onslow Dent) had been considering the idea of running a UPO's course whilst at the same time DPR(A) had been wrestling with the problem in MOD. The critical factors were the justification of the introduction of such a course and the decision about where to run it. Eventually it was decided that the PR staff at UKLF should run a 5-day pilot course at Larkhill in January 1977. This first course was attended by 27 students and was considered to be a success. As a result of this, approval was given for three courses per year to be run at UKLF with a capacity for 30 students per course.

The UPOs course is mandatory for all Army officers about to take up a public relations appointment and for all UPOs serving in units which are under orders for Northern Ireland. It is voluntary for all other UPOs and Information Officers. The course provides an excellent preparation for an officer about to become a UPO and its importance was fully recognised by John Wright when he was the Chief Public Relations Officer of UKLF: 'This course is a very important function of PR at UKLF. Perhaps one of our main functions in the future will be to create a greater awareness of PR in the Army through courses such as this'.[19] The significance of that remark lies in the considerable time it took to establish such a course in the Army (seven years after the first military involvement in Ulster), the fact that the course is still only mandatory for those undertaking PR appointments or UPOs going to Northern Ireland. This reflects the problems which Public Relations have faced in trying to educate the Army about the media and although this course is a major development there is still a faction within the Army which has yet to be convinced of the importance of such training. The Army has come a long way since officers serving in Ulster did UPO as a secondary task to their main job, but in order to capitalise on the progress which has been made it would seem logical to make attendance on this excellent course mandatory for all UPOs and information officers. Such a measure would provide the course with a guaranteed future even when the requirement for the Army to serve in Ulster no longer exists.

The need for training public relations officers has also been recognised by the Royal Navy. Since mid-1977 the PR staff of Commander-in-Chief Naval Home Command (CINCNAVHOME) have run a three-day course for PROs twice a year initially at Portsmouth, and subsequently at Greenwich. The optimum number for the course is 30 and the outline and objectives are similar to the Army's UPO course.

19 Interview with the author, 13 May 1979.

The course was designed by the Chief Public Relations Officer to CINCNAVHOME (Bob Moore), and his considerable experience in Fleet Street, and subsequently with the Metropolitan Police as press adviser to Sir Robert Mark, have ensured that the Royal Navy have a sound, practical course.[20] Attendance is still voluntary at present but there are moves to get the course accepted as part of normal training, and its future is secure.

Major stations in the RAF have full time Community Relations Officers (CROs) who are also responsible for public relations. These CROs, who are serving RAF officers, visit the RAF PR Department at MOD and at Command level on an informal basis to receive advice and training in public relations. In addition each unit has a serving RAF officer who is responsible for press liaison as a secondary task. These press liaison officers all visit the DPRS at MOD for one day for a briefing.

The introduction of these courses (particularly those run by the Royal Navy and the Army) indicates perhaps more positively than any other development the acknowledgement by the Armed Forces of the relevance of the media, and consideration is now being given to the formation of a tri-service UPO's course. It is perhaps somewhat surprising, however, that it has taken so long for the Services to recognise the requirement for such training especially as the Forces have earned a reputation for providing courses to satisfy a need. However it is just that reputation which has ensured that, once approved, the courses have provided practical and relevant instruction right from the start. The Services should reap considerable benefit from this training course in the years ahead.

Summary

In reviewing the education about the media within the military, it is evident that considerable progress has been made in recent years, but have Service officers been taught the most relevant information about the press?

The genesis of education about the media originated in the Army's experience in Northern Ireland and this Service has led the other two in the field ever since. Now the very requirement which led to the realisation that there was a gap in the Army's preparation for Ulster (i.e. indifferent performances on television interviews resulting from a lack of appreciation of the media's position in society) has dictated the

---

20 Bob Moore also introduced PR training courses to the police during his time with the Metropolitan Police Force.

approach to the education on this subject. At the beginning of the campaign the Army confidently expected the media to support them in their unenviable policing role. This belief was rooted in the past record of the media's coverage of the British Army's activities between 1945—69. But Northern Ireland was different and the Army failed to read the indicators accurately: Vietnam, the impact of television, the development of investigative journalism and, above all, the enormous dilemma faced by the media with the unprecedented problem of news coverage of events in Ulster. Desmond Taylor (late Editor, BBC News and Current Affairs), talking about the situation in 1969, described the BBC problems as follows:

> . . . Many bruises were sustained before the message got home that in Northern Ireland there was no man in the street with an ordinary opinion — each man was an amateur politician and his opinion was conditioned to advance his political cause.
>   . . . This was difficult, but containable, and could be made, with much care, to fit into the normal context of our news broadcasting as set out by our Director-General and Editor-in-Chief, Sir Charles Curran. He said:
>
>> 'We have a responsibility to provide a rationally based and balanced service of news which will enable adult people to make basic judgements about public policy in their capacity as voting citizens of a democracy.'
>
> Cool logic, and it wasn't easy to apply it in the hothouse of Ulster.[21]

Taylor then went on to describe the dilemma faced by the BBC when street rioting and the serious killing started: 'Then a new and frightening consideration made itself plain: what if the broadcasting that we did, was to increase the killing?' A special meeting of senior News and Current Affairs staff was arranged and the various views were argued out. 'We were confident of only one thing; the heavy weight of our responsibility.' Taylor's own view was that the BBC's normal policy was based on the assumption of the existence of a rational audience which was not the case in Northern Ireland at that moment, and therefore he considered that no inflammatory statement should be broadcast. 'This led another editor to say that, if my analysis was correct, we were approaching the point where normal journalistic considerations did not apply. Yet another felt that a temporary

21 Desmond Taylor, *Editorial responsibilities*, BBC 1975, pp. 9—10.

departure from normal journalistic considerations would be a small price to pay for preventing broadcasts from influencing the situation. In the end, we agreed to use reported speech rather than actuality for statements of sectarian opinion.'[22]

The Army were naturally unaware of the considerable heart searching that was going on within the BBC during those early days before the Army was deployed on the streets. But they soon became very much aware of the BBC's principle of impartiality when, later on, it reported allegations of mistaken and 'even indiscriminate' killings by soldiers:

> It did not matter whether the allegations were true or false, or even whether the people making them believed them – because they were part of the propaganda war and they had very considerable political significance. . . . Reporting these allegations raised in acute form the argument as to whether journalism should in effect be censored in order to help the authorities. We felt we must report if people in Britain, as well as Ulster, were to know and understand what was happening. Our critics suggested forcibly that we were in what amounted to a state of war, and it was our job to help the Army and not stab them in the back. . . . Our arguments carried force with the Army itself, and it initiated a policy of putting up spokesmen to give its side of the story which sustained public belief in our fairness and impartiality and did the Army a great deal of good in the process. There were many who would have stopped us, but the principle was vital. It was not just our credibility that was at stake, though that might be, it was the electorate's right to information about the conduct of their affairs.[23]

Failure to understand the media's varying attitudes and responsibilities, and the fundamental differences between newspapers, television and radio, led to expressions of righteous indignation within the Army when it was occasionally criticised for its actions. At a seminar on Terrorism and the Media organised by the Royal United Services Institute, Martin Bell, the BBC Television News correspondent, remarked: 'It will be objected that the media are not always seen to be on the Army's side. To be quite honest, we are not always on the Army's side. We are on the side of reporting the truth as we see it and as favourably as we can. We are committed to supporting the military in so far as they are acting against terrorists, but we are not committed to

22 Ibid., p.10.
23 Ibid., p.11. For a further understanding of the BBC's problems of broadcasting in Northern Ireland see also Richard Francis, *Broadcasting to a Community in Conflict – the Experience in Northern Ireland*, BBC, 1977.

supporting the military in so far as they might be in conflict with the civilian population. This presents grave problems to the reporter on the ground'.[24]

The misunderstanding of the fundamental role of the media has led to misconceptions which in turn have provided the guidelines for the educational curricula at the various Service colleges. The syllabi have concentrated on preparing the military for the face-to-face confrontation with the reporter (television roadside and studio interviews, dealing with the newspaper reporter during an exercise, etc.) without first of all explaining the fundamentals about the media business. This has bred a generation of military officers (for the other two Services have followed the Army's lead, acknowledging their greater experience in this field) who, broadly speaking, misunderstand and mistrust the media. This antagonism has not gone unnoticed by representatives of the press; as an editor of a Fleet Street newspaper remarked to the author: 'At my level I get the feeling that the military have an instinctive assumption that the press is an enemy'. A view apparently supported by one Army officer who, after a Camberley Press Day remarked that despite it being a most interesting and illuminating day he still did not trust the press.

This mistrust is likely to continue unless the education about the media is planned carefully to coincide with an officer's progression through his Service career, commencing with a proper grounding at the initial entry colleges. A firm foundation in the basic fundamentals will provide an officer with a sound basis on which to build his subsequent experiences with the media, and it should lead to a better understanding. The review of the various colleges suggests that in most cases little adjustment to the curriculum is required. What appears to be missing at present is a recognition of the dimension of the problem, resulting in no overall policy for progressive education about the media.

24 *Ten Years of Terrorism*, op.cit., p.94.

PART V

CONCLUSIONS

14 Conclusions

The military and society

This book has been about communication between the military and the media and how that relationship has in turn been affected by the rapid development in the technology of communications, and by the considerable changes which have occurred in society, and in the military, during the last two decades. But the changes during the last 20 years are as nothing to the likely changes in the next 20. If the development of the transistor changed the technology of communications, then the development of the microchip will change our whole way of life. For instance, we have yet to appreciate the implications of multi-channel and cable television or the full development of the capability of ENG (the latter is particularly relevant to military events when one considers the technical feasibility of broadcasting a conflict live via satellite). It is difficult for us to recognise when significant changes occur in society, or to realise how quickly we adapt to new conditions, except in retrospect. Any suggestion in 1967 that British troops would be deployed in a peace-keeping role within the United Kingdom in two years'time would have been almost inconceivable; and yet society soon grew accustomed to this tragic state of affairs. Similarly, nobody would have predicted in 1981 that Britain and Argentina would go to war over the Falkland Islands in 1982.

The effects of these rapid changes in society on the relationship between the military and the public are illustrated by the gap of understanding which grew after the ending of National Service. A generation has already emerged without any first hand knowledge of the Forces. Their ignorance, and the dated knowledge of those who were conscripted, have combined to produce an unrealistic and outmoded image of the military to a large part of the British public. Furthermore, in the late sixties there was a danger of alienation between the Armed Forces and society.[1] The reason that the estrangement grew no worse was largely due to the deployment of the British Army to Northern Ireland which inevitably brought the military under the full blaze of publicity due to the reporting of their 'newsworthy' actions. Northern Ireland has brought the military and the public closer together, for not only did the Army become a topical subject for news reports, current affairs programmes and newspaper articles, but this focus has led to fresh interest in the military as a whole. This has been reflected in the television documentaries and drama about modern military life, discussed in Part III, and more recently by the dramatic events in the South Atlantic.

The media have played an invaluable part in maintaining the link between the military and society and during the last ten years the focus on the military way of life, particularly by television and the press, has done much to correct the misconceptions of the past. However, it is significant that it was Northern Ireland that provided the impetus for this renewed interest in the military. It was not the result of any great initiative from within the Armed Forces. This raises the question about the capability of the Services to cope with the increasingly rapid changes in society which are anticipated in the future. Have the military learnt the right lessons from the last decade in order to prepare themselves for the future? This concluding chapter considers this important question.

The military and the media

Apart from the continuing link between the military and the defence correspondents, the news media as a whole are only interested in the Armed Forces when they are in the news. The activities of reporters and cameramen at a newsworthy event have formed the basis for the military's opinions of the media whether that event was a military

1 The problems of the Services and society (including alienation) were considered at a conference run by the Faculty of Social Sciences of Edinburgh University in May 1969. The papers read at the conference were published the following year under the title *The Armed Services and Society: Alienation, Management and Integration*, edited by J.N. Wolfe and John Erickson, University Press, Edinburgh 1970.

operation (such as the Falkland crisis), the final voyage of *HMS Ark Royal* or a regimental function covered only by the local press. The limitation of the military's horizon to this contact point with the media at a newsworthy occurrence meant that, once Northern Ireland highlighted the need for training in public relations, the instruction and syllabi were based on the experience of the face to face confrontation between the soldier and the journalist on the streets. Presumably, the recent events from the Falklands crisis will now be used as a basis for an update of the relevant syllabi and will lead to a co-ordinated tri-Service approach. As we noted in chapter 1, there has been a history of strained relations between the two professions ever since the Crimea, so it was perhaps inevitable that the curricula should reflect a 'them and us' attitude. Indeed, Alastair Burnet suggested in 1970 that it was 'natural that there should be conflict between the Armed services and journalism'.[2] But the failure to include any instruction about the mechanics of the news process has meant that the military have never really understood the media or their position in society, and as ignorance and prejudice often go hand in hand, so military suspicion of the press has remained despite the long association in Ulster (or perhaps, because of it).

In stark contrast to the attitudes of the military and media towards each other this study has revealed a previously unrecognised factor — the remarkable similarities between the characteristics of the two professions. We have noted in Part II that the newsman and the military officer consider many of the same qualities to be important in their respective professions: initiative, responsibility, professionalism, dedication, efficiency, teamwork, delegation of authority, self-discipline, forward planning and flexibility. We have also noted that both of them are liable to work long unsocial hours and that the staffs in news room and operations room are likely to be subjected to immense pressure as they wrestle with the problem of making decisions against the clock, often frustrated by incomplete information.

The study has also revealed the inadequacy of the military's education about the media despite the fact that this subject appears on the syllabi of most Service colleges. In Part IV it was suggested that the main reason for the military's mistrust of the media was the failure to appreciate the need to provide students with a thorough understanding of the mechanics and the role of the press. Prejudice and misconceptions have resulted from this ignorance. Much of the inadequacy of this education has been due to the low priority given to public relations.

---

2 Quoted in *Defence and the Mass Media*, report of a seminar held at the RUSI, 13 October 1970, p.7.

For too long it has been misunderstood by commanders and has been the poor cousin of the staff system. There is a pressing need for the Armed Forces to acknowledge the essential educational role of public relations in peacetime, and its vital importance in war.

Education of the military

It is apparent that the education of the military about the media has developed on an *ad hoc* basis with each training college deciding for itself what should be taught. In order to develop a greater awareness and better understanding of the media there would appear to be a requirement for a centrally directed progressive educational syllabus co-ordinated by DPRS. It is a common subject for all three Services and therefore the curriculum should be produced on a tri-Service basis so that the education of officers and men of all three Services is in parallel. The details of such a curriculum need to be carefully worked out by DPRS but it should include:

1 Awareness of the media's role in society to be included in training at all levels (i.e. officers, NCOs and soldiers).

2 A lecture on the basic fundamentals of the media (to include details of the news process) should be incorporated in the syllabi of all officers initial training colleges and NCO command courses. In addition, the relevant DPR should give a lecture on public relations at the appropriate new entry officer colleges to all students, including those on a short service commission.

3 Subsequent media training should be so arranged that it progressively prepares an officer for his dealings with the media at each stage in his career. This training should include lectures, discussions, television interviews technique familiarisation, visits to newspaper, radio and television news rooms. In most cases there is little amendment required to the current syllabi of the various staff colleges. What is required is the co-ordination of the separate syllabi into a progressive curriculum.

4 'The media' should be incorporated into the appropriate academic schemes for officers where this is suitable (such as the Army's Progressive Qualification scheme). Such a syllabus should be progressive and so co-ordinated that the education is linked to other instruction on the media at the various training colleges.

5 Considerable progress has already been made with regard to television familiarisation training. There is now a requirement to make this training mandatory for all formation commanders, com-

manding officers and for certain selected staff appointments. There is also a requirement to develop progressive training for all officers at the appropriate stages in their careers.

6 Public relations training should be mandatory for anyone selected to be a Unit PRO, and a PR/PI staff job.

7 Public relations 'play' should be introduced into appropriate exercises (including those at the highest level) to increase the awareness of the difficulties involved, and thus enable commanders and staff officers to learn how to cope with typical problems in realistic situations.

These recommendations are designed to increase the Services general awareness of the media and help the military to be better prepared in its future dealings with the press as a result of a better understanding of the functions of the news process, and of the role of the media in modern society.

Public relations

The organisation which must bear the brunt of any new proposals affecting the military—media relationship is the DPRS. It is already apparent that the Public Relations organisation must assume an increasing responsibility for training in the future. The success of the recently introduced courses for PROs run by the Royal Navy and the Army, the demand for places on those courses, and the difficulties of providing PR staffs with the additional manpower to carry out this important training commitment, all serve to emphasise the size of the problem which now needs to be tackled cohesively. Education is the key to a better understanding of the media and the DPRS has a vital role to play in this area.

Whatever decisions are taken about PR training in the future will probably depend upon the importance which is attached to public relations. This is the fundamental issue which lies at the heart of future developments. In the postwar years prior to 1969, military operations abroad in the pre-television satellite era attracted relatively little attention from the media, and the resulting low key attitude to publicity affected the Public Relations organisation and its reputation within the Armed Forces. That was perhaps understandable. But what is difficult to comprehend is why the status of public relations is still so low within the Services after 13 years' experience of combating terrorism in Northern Ireland. At the equivalent of brigade level and above, the importance of public relations is well understood in Ulster, and the PRO is invariably included in the inner cabinet of advisers to the respective commanders. But at unit level so much depends upon the commanding officer's understanding of the subject which in turn influences the selection of the officer chosen to be the unit PRO. As we have seen, the education about the media does not adquately prepare a future commanding officer for the realities of command in today's media dominated society, and the attitude of a number of COs stems from the image of public relations over the years. Indeed, even today, an Army officer selected for a PR appointment is more likely to receive commiserations rather than congratulations from his colleagues, particularly if he has just graduated from staff college.

The other aspect which has influenced the status of public relations is the increasing requirement for a number of high calibre civilian information officers. The requirement has always been there but it has been highlighted by the impact of the media over recent years. At all levels the military commander requires a public relations officer who is able to provide him with sound, professional advice. The commander should be able to rely on his counsel as much as he does on that provided by his operations, logistics and intelligence staff officers. In order to provide such advice PROs need to be experienced officers who have been well trained for their job. They also need to have considerable understanding of the media and be supported by a good reliable staff. Ideally the Public Relations organisation should provide worthwhile opportunities for the steady reliable officer (who arranges the facilities and processes the necessary staff work), and equally, it should attract the bright officer of above average ability who is destined to become the commander's public relations adviser. At present DPRS is not attracting enough of the highest calibre into the Information Service.

As the impact of the media is gradually being acknowledged by the Armed Forces, so the importance of the Public Relations organisation is being recognised as well. However, the speed of recognition and the acknowledgement of the importance varies within the three Services and there is even a variation of attitude within each Service. For instance, the appointments of DPR(N) and DPR(RAF) have yet to achieve the significance of DPR(A); and within the Army there is a world of difference between the importance attached to public relations in Northern Ireland compared with the attention it is given by units serving in the rest of the United Kingdom or in BAOR. Furthermore, the promotion prospects for those serving in PR appointments are not thought to be good. And yet, the facts do not support this assumption. The job, in fact, provides an exciting and stimulating challenge for an officer who has the imagination to seize upon its importance and its opportunities. It will open up a new dimension in his understanding of what really matters most in modern conflict: its effect on public opinion at home and around the world. The experience can hardly fail to develop his potential and certainly the post of DPR(A) has long been considered as a stepping stone to the top (at the time of writing the current Chief of the General Staff, Commander-in-Chief AFNORTH and Commander-in-Chief Hong Kong are all former DPR(A)s). Public relations is at least as important as any other staff function and this fact has yet to be fully accepted throughout the services. It is not enough just to appoint a good officer to the Brigadier's post as head of the Army's PR operation; no-one should reach general rank or equivalent without some first hand experience of handling the media.

The lack of consistency between the three services in their attitude to the appointment of DPR is also reflected in MOD's attitude to the appointment of CPR. Although the position of Chief of the Defence Staff (CDS) has been steadily enhanced since 1975, this has not been accompanied by an equivalent movement within the DPRS. For instance, all three service chiefs have PR advisers at one-star level, but CDS has no-one. The Falklands crisis underlined the pressing need for CDS to have PR advice available for crisis management and conflict situations from a senior military officer at the appropriate rank. In the hierarchical organisation of the MOD, for such a post to have any influence it would have to be at two-star (Assistant Chief of Defence Staff) level. This appointment could be a uniformed rotational post filled by senior officers from any of the services who had previous appropriate PR experience. This proposal would not affect the current organisation too drastically since it would still leave CPR as Head of the DPRS and available to provide PR advice on the political scene. Indeed, a case could be made for elevating his position to 3-star.

A more radical alternative to the above proposal would be to keep the appointment of CPR at 2-star level, but make it a uniformed rotational post at Assistant Chief of Defence Staff level. Whichever option is preferred, what is important is to ensure that PR advice is available to CDS from a military officer of appropriate rank. Above all else, the Falklands crisis has demonstrated the consequences of the failure to recognise this requirement up until now.

This book has drawn attention to the urgent need for further study into Public Relations within the Armed Forces. Such a study should examine the following:

1 How to improve the military's and the media's perception of DPRS.

2 How to attract more talent into DPRS to enable the service to cope with the increasing demands of the media in the future. Such

an investigation should also include a complete review of the career structure of DPRS.

3 How to provide PR advice for CDS from a military PR officer. This review should consider the alternatives of providing CDS with a 2-star PR adviser (ACDS(PI)), or converting CPR's appointment into a 2-star uniformed rotational post.

4 How to raise the prestige of PR with the Services so that it is accepted as important a staff function as operations, intelligence and logistics.

5 The co-ordination of PR training policy throughout the three Services. This proposal also incorporates the requirement to study the desirability of increasing the complement of DPRS to meet the increasing training commitment, and to investigate the feasibility of establishing a tri-Service school of PR.

6 The development within DPRS of expertise in the field of television drama.

7 Regular liaison between DPRS and the media so that personnel are kept abreast of new developments and are reminded about the realities of the news process in the press, radio and television.

8 The rapid development of communications, technology and society's increasing reliance on the news media for information means that the PR implications of command decisions need to be considered more and more. There is a requirement, therefore, to develop more awareness of this, and to anticipate these implications rather than simply reacting to the initiative of the media. In Army parlance it is a 'G' function and the inclusion of 'Public Relations' as a paragraph heading in Orders Cards aide-mémoires would be a practical first step in the right direction.

9 The continued exercising of Public Relations staff in their wartime role (this proposal will be developed further later in the chapter).

The Falklands crisis has provided a timely reminder of the importance of presenting and maintaining an accurate public image. This point has long been appreciated by the media and has now been recognised by the public. It is about time the Services reacted to this demand and carried out a detailed examination of its Public Relations to fit it for future requirements.

Education of the media

Education is a two-way process, and just as there is a requirement to improve the military's knowledge of the media, so there is a need to educate the media about the military. The lack of first-hand military experience since the ending of conscription has created a gap of understanding which has grown wider year by year and has been only marginally compensated for by events in Northern Ireland. Already, many of the television editors and producers responsible for news and current affairs programmes have no knowledge of the military and this will apply even more so to the next generation of newspaper editors. Ignorance of the military amongst those in positions of influence in the media is supplemented by the inadequate education on this subject for trainee journalists. Only three out of the nine colleges which run courses in journalism include visits to military establishments in their curricula, and there is a short-fall in the training of trainee journalists in broadcasting.

The public rely on the newspapers, radio and television for accurate information and up-to-the-minute news. Furthermore, as society has grown more complex and less homogeneous so the media have assumed an increasing educational role. As a result, the public use the media more and more to improve their knowledge of topics on which they are unable to acquire first-hand information, and they depend upon the professionalism of the journalists for accurate information and informed comment. The media, therefore, have an obligation to ensure that their trainee journalists receive a broad education so that they are well prepared to fulfil this increasingly important function.

There would appear to be a requirement for all trainee journalists to receive some instruction on the role of the military in modern society so that they will be better equipped to carry out this educational function on behalf of the public. This is particularly relevant in keeping the Services and the British people in touch with each other since, in many ways, the military ethos is at variance with the mainstream of society. Furthermore, the increasing newsworthy actions of the military are attracting more non-specialist journalists (*viz.* Vietnam, Northern Ireland and the Falklands), and the problems associated with the reporting of conflict (chapter 11) have illustrated how the public can be misinformed as a result of lack of comprehension on the part of some journalists. The initial education of trainee journalists could be supplemented by the occasional briefing given at MOD on the general outline of defence policy to editors and general reporters. This would equate to the regular briefings which are currently given at MOD to the defence correspondents. There would also be considerable merit in considering the possibility of including journalists in some staff college schemes and exercises. This proposal should be studied in detail in order to evaluate its feasibility.

The future

In a recent interview with the author, Bob Hutchinson, the Defence Correspondent of the Press Association, remarked that the public have become much more interested in defence during the last few years. This development has also been noticed by other journalists. This resurgence of interest is to be welcomed and it should be encouraged. There is a pressing need for more open debate on defence matters, particularly the strategic aspects of defence; and the media, especially television, provide the best means of communication to a woefully ill-informed public. In his article on public opinion and the Armed Services, Colonel Patrick Palmer noted that there was 'a lack of perception of modern defence needs and the changes in the structure of the Armed Forces in recent years. If the strength and virility of our democratic society rests upon a foundation of an informed and educated public opinion then in defence matters at least the foundations are firmly embedded in quicksand'.[3] He went on to highlight the disadvantage caused by the lack of an influential defence lobby and the denial of informed debate when the Ministry of Defence competed with other departments for a slice of a stagnant or declining national budget; 'it is imperative that the case for defence should not go by default because of ignorance'.[4]

At present, informed debate on defence is limited to a small select band of military officers, civil servants and those Members of Parliament, academics and journalists who are interested in defence. There has been no real attempt made in recent years to explain to the general public (as opposed to the small percentage of interested public) the complexities of modern defence, apart from the occasional television documentary. For instance, there has been no open debate about defence on television for at least ten years. It is in the country's own interest that there should be better understanding of defence issues and it is conceivable that the public's re-awakened interest may force more open debate in the future. There is a requirement for a much more imaginative approach to the whole question of promoting debate about defence and the indications are that the public may be ready for such an initiative, particularly after the recent events in the South Atlantic.

At present the attitude to the release of official information is such that the media are constantly frustrated when trying to obtain details, and serving officers are often unable to add their considerable professional knowledge to any public debate on defence for fear of

---

3 Colonel Patrick Palmer, *Public Opinion and the Armed Services*, Seaford House Papers 1977, p.81.
4 Ibid., p.82.

contravening the Official Secrets Act, or because a remark by them may be remotely construed as having political implications. In order to be of real value any public debate on defence, such as a television current affairs programme, must inevitably involve sensitive and classified information and there is no denying that this can be a tricky problem. However, the education of the public about defence issues is so important that there would now appear to be a requirement to review the attitude towards the release of official information.

The reason why all this is so important is because of the public opinion factor in any future conflict. In a lecture in 1973 about public opinion in revolutionary war, Colonel Maurice Tugwell concluded with these words:

> When historians come to study military events of the late 60s and early 70s they may conclude that the major lesson for soldiers to learn from that period was this — that if you cannot fight an enemy in a way that public opinion at home, and fair-minded opinion overseas, find tolerable, then find another enemy. To endeavour for long to conduct a campaign in the face of really hostile opinion may lose you more than just a battle.[5]

Vietnam has proved the validity of these words, the continued existence of the Army's presence in Northern Ireland is undersealed by British public opinion, and the maintenance of public support during the Falklands crisis was crucial. The importance of public support for the military in a democratic society is vital to their morale and this is true of all scales of conflict, from low-level violence to general war. It follows from this that the organisation responsible for providing the facilities for the media (from whom the public get their information) should be as well practised and prepared for their role as any other branch of the staff. Let us consider the scenario of general war in Europe and see what affect this would have on BAOR.

The implications of a European war

The world's press are so sharp at sniffing out a news story that any period of tension in Europe would result in an immediate media invasion of the Continent. BAOR would be inundated with newsmen numbering about 150 UK journalists and up to 1,000 foreign press (including German journalists, some of whom will be already in the

---

5 Colonel Maurice Tugwell, *Public Opinion in Counter-Insurgency*, lecture to the Canadian Land Forces Command and Staff College, Kingston, on 30 January 1973.

probable area of operations). The period of tension would be critical as the NATO Governments galvanised public support from their people and the Soviet Union used the freedom of the West's press to counter this with subtle propaganda. Once the war had begun the inevitable conflict between the media's incessant striving for access opposed by the military's reluctance to provide *full* access, would be aggravated by all the other demands for facilities plus the anticipated imposition of censorship. There would also probably be a conflict of interest over the media's desire for news and the inability of the military to provide detailed information for genuine security reasons. In these circumstances the news media's interpretation of events would be critical and would have a direct impact on public opinion at home.

The burden all this would place on the PR organisation in BAOR would be immense. There would be too little time to provide the additional manpower to cope with the press invasion, and therefore PR needs to be so organised in peacetime that it can move to a war footing at very short notice. The period of tension is so vital in terms of public opinion, however, that the PR has less time to prepare than other branches of the Services because it must be fully operational from the beginning of the tension period. There is therefore an urgent requirement to evaluate the whole problem in realistic exercise conditions to discover the answers to a number of pressing questions, such as: what is the manpower requirement; what are the administrative problems associated with the provision of reception areas briefing facilities, transport and accommodation for an army of pressmen; what are the escort requirements; what are the problems associated with the provision of suitable communications facilities; what about censorship; what will be the impact of ENG? The problems are immense and the indications are that the military simply have not realised the implications of the rapid changes in the media in recent years. But the media have. In its evidence to the Annan Committee in 1975, the Independent Television Companies Association (ITCA) had this to say about television war reporting:

> The increased pace of news delivery in recent years has altered in fundamental ways the nature of the daily television news programmes. In 1967 the Six Day War in the Middle East was reported first in the morning newspapers and then seen on television the same evening in reports brought to London by jet plane. Television coverage was 24 hours behind events and its role was to reinforce and give visual shape to news already known to the public. By 1973, however, satellites brought the Yom Kippur War to television screens the same day, ahead of newspapers. The

public now receives its first information as well as detailed news-film via the medium of television.[6]

But the really significant point is that the Yom Kippur War experience has already been outdated by the light-weight ENG equipment. This has been best illustrated most recently by the fact that as the Falklands War ended (with no live TV coverage) so that event was pushed into the background by the dramatic live television coverage of the seige of Beirut in July/August 1982. Television newsmen now have the facility to transmit pictures live from a battlefield bypassing any editorial process let alone military censorship. In addition, the videotape facility gives the cameraman considerable flexibility. The significance of this was highlighted in General Sir John Hackett's 'future history' about the Third World War. He describes how one of the first encounters between Soviet and US forces (in Yuogslavia) was filmed on videotape by an Italian television cameraman who then had it transmitted by satellite throughout the world: 'It was in the hands of the American networks before the White House or the Pentagon were even aware of its existence'.[7]

Almost as though by design, the Falklands crisis has come as a timely reminder of all the difficulties associated with the media coverage of a major conflict. The problems of the management of news, censorship, accuracy of news reports, provision of press facilities, access, logistics, and above all, credibility, all arose in the first few weeks of the crisis. The mistakes of Vietnam and Northern Ireland were repeated all over again. Furthermore, the conflict in the South Atlantic emphasised that the long period of relative peace prior to 1982 had not been used wisely by the military to ensure that their relationship with the media was sufficiently good to withstand the inevitable strain at the beginning of a major conflict. The Falklands crisis has highlighted the urgent require-ment for the military and the media to establish agreed guidelines for any future major conflict now, before the next crisis occurs.

Just as many military lessons will be learned from the conflict in the South Atlantic which will be applicable to any future confron-tation between NATO and the Warsaw Pact, so must the right PR lessons be learned from the media coverage of that event. Although there will be no chance of a second bite at the cherry in any future war, fate has intervened in time and exposed the pitfalls. There is still time to take remedial action.

6   ITCA, *ITV Evidence to the Annan Committee*, ITCA 1975, p.55.
7   General Sir John Hackett and others, *The Third World War*, Sidgwick and Jackson, London 1978, pp. 94—5.

Summary

Although there has been a history of mistrust between the military and the media, this study suggests that the characteristics of the two professions are surprisingly similar. Also significant is the emphasis placed on personal relations and mutual trust which was stressed again and again by both military officers and journalists during the author's period of research. Both professions inherit their myths of the past and only personal contact and education will break down the barriers of mistrust which still exist. The future of military—media relations lies in the hands of the next generation of editors and commanders who have very different attitudes and experience from the present leaders. It is hoped that this book will help to promote further study of the problem and encourage more interchange which will lead to a better understanding between the two professions.

Bibliography

Published works

Annan, Lord *Report of the Committee on the Future of Broadcasting* (London: HMSO 1977).

Barnett, Correlli *Britain and Her Army* (London: Allen Lane The Penguin Press 1970).

Baynes, Lieutenant Colonel J.C.M. *The Soldier and Modern Society* (London: Eyre Methuen 1972).

BBC *The BBC's Programme Responsibilities Towards Adolescents and Young Adults* — a study for the BBC General Advisory Council (BBC 1978); *The Task of Broadcasting News* — a study for the BBC General Advisory Council (BBC May 1976); *BBC Handbook* (BBC 1979); BBC Television Service, *Principles and Practice in Documentary Programmes* (BBC 1972); *The Public and the Programmes* (Audience Research Department Survey: BBC 1959); *Current Affairs for the Under 35s* (Audience Research Department Survey: BBC 1975); *Studies of Newsbeat on Radio 1* (Audience Research Department Survey: BBC 1974); *Play for Today* (Audience Research Department Survey: BBC 1975).

Belfast Bulletin (Belfast Workers Research Unit, Spring 1979, No.6).

Bernstein, Carl and Woodward, Bob *All the President's Men* (London: Quartet Books 1974).

Blumler, Jay G. and Katz, Elihu *The Use of Mass Communications* (London and Beverley Hills: Sage 1974).

Braestrup, Peter *Big Story* (Boulder Colorado: Westview Press 1977).

The British Media and Ireland (Campaign for Free Speech in Ireland: London 1979).

Brownrigg, Rear Admiral Sir Douglas *Indiscretions of the Naval Censor* (London: Cassell 1920).

Bryson, L. *The Communication of Ideas* (New York: Harper 1948).

Bullard, Lauriston *Famous War Correspondents* (London: Pitman 1914).

Burns, Tom *The BBC — Public Institution and Private World* (London: Macmillan 1977).

Burns, Tom 'Public Service and Private World' in Jeremy Tunstall's *Media Sociology* (London: Constable 1970).

Briggs, Asa *Sound and Vision: The History of Broadcasting in the United Kingdom*, Volume IV (Oxford: Oxford University Press 1979).

Caputo, Philip *A Rumour of War* (London: Macmillan 1977).

Charlton, Michael and Moncrieff, Anthony *Many Reasons Why* (London: Scolar Press 1978).

Clutterbuck, Dr Richard *Living with Terrorism* (London: Faber & Faber 1975); *The Media and Political Violence* (London: Macmillan 1981).

Cohen, Stanley and Young, Jock (eds) *The Manufacture of News: deviance, social problems and the mass media* (London: Constable 1973).

Curran, James 'The Impact of Television on the Audience of National Newspapers', published in Jeremy Tunstall's *Media Sociology* (London: Constable 1970).

Curran, James *The British Press: A Manifesto* (London: Macmillan 1978).

Day, Robin *Day by Day* (London: William Kimber 1975).

DeFleur, Melvin D. *Theories of Mass Communication* (New York: David McKay 1966).

Dexter, L.A. and White, D.M. *People, Society and Mass Communication* (New York: Free Press of Glencoe 1964).

Elliott, Philip 'Reporting Northern Ireland: A Study of News in Britain, Ulster and the Irish Republic' in *Ethnicity and the Media* (UNESCO 1977).

Ellul, Jacques *Propaganda: The Formation of Men's Attitudes* translated from the French by Konrad Keller and Jean Lerner (New York: Alfred Knopf 1966).

Finer, S.E. *The Man on Horseback* (Harmondsworth, Middlesex: Penguin 1976).

Fisks, John and Hartley, John *Reading Television* (London: Methuen 1978).

Fisk, Robert *The Point of No Return* (London: André Deutsch 1975).

Glasgow University Media Group *Bad News* Volume 1 (London: Routledge & Kegan Paul 1976).

Goldie, Grace Wyndham *Facing the Nation: Television and Politics 1936—76* (London: Bodley Head 1977).

Hackett, General Sir John and others *The Third World War* (London: Sidgwick and Jackson 1979).

Halloran, James D., Elliott, Philip and Murdoch, Graham *Demonstrations and Communication: a Case Study* (Harmondsworth, Middlesex: Penguin 1970).

Halloran, James D., *The Effects of Mass Communications with special reference to Television* (Leicester University Press 1964).

Herr, Michael *Dispatches* (London: Pan Books 1978).

Hill, Lord *Behind the Screen* (London: Sidgwick and Jackson 1974).

IBA, *Television and Radio 1978* (IBA Guide to Independent Television and Independent Local Radio, London: IBA 1978).

ITCA, *Evidence to the Annan Committee* (London: ITCA 1975).

Katz, Elihu *Social Research on Broadcasting: Proposals for further development* (BBC 1977).

Katz, Elihu and Lazarsfeld, P.F., *Personal Influence: the part played by the People in the flow of Mass Communications* (New York: Glencoe Free Press 1955).

Kitson, Frank *Low Intensity Operations* (London: Faber and Faber 1971).

Kitson, Frank *Bunch of Five* (London: Faber and Faber 1977).

Klapper, Joseph T. *The Effects of Mass Communication* (New York: Free Press 1960).

Knightley, Phillip *The First Casualty* (London: André Deutsch 1975).

Lapping, Brian *The Bounds of Freedom* (London: Constable 1980).

Larsen, O.N., *Violence and the Mass Media* (New York: Harper & Row 1968).

Lazarsfeld, Paul and Merton, Robert K. 'Mass Communication, Popular Taste and Original Social Action' in Lyman Bryson's *The Communication of Ideas* (New York: Cooper Square 1964).

Levy, H. Phillip *The Press Council: History, Procedure and Cases* (London: Macmillan 1967).

Lytton, Neville *The Press and the General Staff* (London: Collins 1920).

Macluhan, M. *Understanding Media* (London: Routledge & Kegan Paul 1964).

MacShane, Denis *Using the Media* (London: Pluto Press 1979).

Magnus, Philip *Kitchener* (London: John Murray 1958).

Margach, James *The Abuse of Power* (London: Star 1979).

Mark, Sir Robert *In the Office of Constable* (London: Collins 1978).

McGregor, Professor O.R. *Royal Commission on the Press* (London: HMSO 1977).

McGuire, Maria *To Take Arms* (London: Quartet Books 1973).

McQuail, Denis *Towards a Sociology of Mass Communication* (London: Cassell & Collier Macmillan 1969).

Merton, R.K. *Social Theory and Social Structure* (New York: Glencoe Free Press 1957).

Peled, Tsiyona and Katz, Elihu 'Media Functions in Wartime: The Israel Home Front in October 1973' in Jay Blumler and Elihu Katz's *The Uses of Communications* (Beverley Hills and London: Sage 1974).

Pincher, Chapman *Inside Story* (London: Sidgwick & Jackson 1978).

Ponsonby, Arthur *Falsehood in War-time* (London: George Allen & Unwin 1936).

Royal United Service Institution, *Ten Years of Terrorism* (RUSI 1979).

Schlesinger, Philip *Putting "Reality" Together — BBC News* (London: Constable 1978).

Shmid, Alex and de Graaf, Janny *Insurgent Terrorism and the Western News Media* (London: Sage 1982).

Smith, Anthony *The Politics of Information* (London: Macmillan 1978).

Steiner, G. *The People Look at Television* (New York: Alfred Knopf 1963).

Stott, Mike *Soldiers Talking, Cleanly* (London: Eyre Methuen 1978).

Thompson, Rear-Admiral George P. *Blue Pencil Admiral* (London: Sampson Low, Marston 1947).

Thompson, Sir Robert *Peace is Not at Hand* (London: Chatto & Windus 1974); *No Exit from Vietnam* (London: Chatto & Windus 1969).

Tracey, Michael *The Production of Political Television* (London: Routledge & Kegan Paul 1978).

Tunstall, Jeremy *Media Sociology* (London: Constable 1970).

Westmoreland, General William C. *A Soldier Reports* (New York: Doubleday 1976).

Whale, John *The Politics of the Media* (Glasgow: Fontana 1977).

Winchester, Simon *In Holy Terror: reporting the Ulster Troubles* (London: Faber & Faber 1974).

Wintour, Charles *Pressures on the Press* (London: André Deutsch 1972).

Wolfe, J.N. and Erickson, John *The Armed Services and Society: Alienation, Management and Integration* (Edinburgh: University Press 1970).

Wright, Charles R. *Mass Communication* (New York: Random House 1966).

Yorke, Ivor *The Techniques of Television News* (London: Focal Press 1978).

Younger, Sir Kenneth *Report of the Committee on Privacy* (Cmnd. 5012: 1972).

Published articles

Alexander, Yonah 'Terrorism, the Media and the Police' in *Police Studies*, vol.I, no.2, June 1978.

Annan, Lord 'United Kingdom: Broadcasting and Politics' in *Journal of Communication* vol.28, no.3, 1978.

Balkwill, Michael 'Broadcasting: The Guilty Men', in the *RUSI Journal* vol.124, no.1, March 1979.

Bell, Martin 'Views' in *The Listener*, 6 January 1972.

Bell, Martin 'Ulster Coverage' in *The Listener*, 5 October 1972.

Birt, John and Jay, Peter 'Can television news break the understanding barrier?', *The Times*, 22 February 1975.

Birt, John and Jay, Peter 'Television journalism: the child of an unhappy marriage between newspapers and film', *The Times*, 30 September 1975.

Birt, John and Jay, Peter 'The radical changes needed to remedy TV's bias against understanding', *The Times*, 10 October 1975.

Birt, John and Jay, Peter 'How television news can hold the mass audience', *The Times*, 2 September 1976.

Birt, John and Jay, Peter 'Why television news is in danger of becoming an anti-social force', *The Times*, 3 September 1976.

Browne, Vincent 'There will be no more ceasefires until the end', in *Magill*, August 1978.

Cockerell, Michael 'Turmoil behind the The Times', in *The Spectator*, 9 December 1978.

Cooper, Brigadier G.L.C. 'Some Aspects of Conflict in Ulster' in *British Army Review*, vol.43, April 1973.

Crozier, S.F. 'The Press and the Army' in *Army Quarterly*, vol.68, no.2, July 1954.

Curran, Sir Charles 'Should we televise our enemies' in *The Listener*, 20 June 1974.

Curran, Sir Charles 'The BBC's policy on Northern Ireland' in *The Listener*, 18 November 1976.

Ford, Air Commodore G.H. 'Protest, Violence and Conflict: Some Observations on the Role of Television' in the *Seaford House Papers*, 1974.

Hart, Colonel T.S. 'Likely Changes in English Society over the next two decades and the Possible Effects on the British Army', in the *Seaford House Papers*, 1973.

Hofstetter, C. Richard and Moore, David W. 'Watching TV News and Supporting the Military' in *Armed Forces and Society*, vol.5, no.2, February 1979.

Hoggart, Simon, 'The Army PR men in Ulster' in *New Society*, 11 October 1973.

Howard, Anthony 'Behind the Bureaucratic Curtain' in *The New York Times Magazine*, 23 October 1966.

Janowitz, Morris 'The Study of Mass Communication' in the *International Encyclopedia of the Social Sciences*, vol.3, 1968.

Katz, Elihu and Foulkes, David 'On the Use of the Mass Media as "Escape": Clarification of a Concept' in *Public Opinion Quarterly*, no.26, 1962.

Katz, Elihu 'The Two-Step Flow of Communication: An up-to-date report on an Hypothesis' in *Public Opinion Quarterly*, no.21, 1957.

Kennedy, Colonel William V. 'It takes more than talent to cover a War' in *Army*, July 1978.

Kornhouser, William 'Mass Society' in *International Encyclopedia of the Social Sciences*, vol.10, 1978.

McCann, Eamonn 'The British Press and Northern Ireland' in *The British Press and Northern Ireland* (Northern Ireland Socialist Research Centre, Pluto Press, London 1971).

McCormack, Colonel J.V. 'The Army and the Press in War' in the *RUSI Journal*, vol.98, 1953.

Money, W.J. 'Do we need a new model army?' in the *Sociological Review*, vol.23, no.23, August 1975.

Mullady, Major Brian 'The Military Implications of Public Opinion' in *Air University Review*, May/June 1978.

Palmer, Colonel C.P.R. 'Public Opinion and the Armed Services' in the *Seaford House Papers*, 1977.

Paulu, Burton 'United Kingdom: Quality With Control' in *Journal of Communication*, vol.28, no.3, 1978.

Paxmen, Jeremy 'Reporting Failure in Ulster' in *The Listener*, 5 October 1978.

Protheroe, Alan 'Why we have lost the information war' in *The Listener*, 3 June 1982.

Reed, David 'Northern Ireland's Agony Without End' in *Reader's Digest* (US edition), January 1982.

Reynolds, Michael 'The War Correspondent's Job' in *Army Quarterly*, vol.59, no.2, January 1950.

Scott-Barrett, Brigadier D.W. 'The Media, Conflict and the Armed Services' in the *Seaford House Papers*, 1970.

Sheppard, Major E.W. 'The Military Correspondent' in *Army Quarterly*, vol.53, no.2, January 1952.

Sheppard, S.T. 'In Memorium: William Howard Russell' in *The United Service Magazine* no.940, March 1907.

Sullivan, A.E. 'Getting the Story, Some Facts about War Correspondents' in *Army Quarterly*, vol.81, no.2, January 1961.

Terraine, John 'A Comfortless Mythology' in *The Times Saturday Review*, 11 November 1978.

Towle, Philip 'The Debate on Wartime Censorship in Britain 1902—14' in *War and Society: a Yearbook of Military History*, 1975.

Tuchman, Gaye 'Objectivity as Strategic Ritual: An Examination of Newsmen's Notions of Objectivity' in the *American Journal of Sociology*, no.77, 1972.

Tuchman, Gaye 'Making News by Doing Work: Routinizing the Unexpected' in the *American Journal of Sociology*, no.79, 1973.

UK Public Record Office, WO 28/131.

Wain, Christopher 'Rebirth of the IRA' in *The Listener*, 7 June 1979.

Wain, Christopher 'Television Reporting of Military Operations — A Personal View' in the *RUSI Journal*, March 1974.

Waller, Brigadier R.P. 'The Soul of An Army' in *Army Quarterly*, vol.53, no.2, January 1947.

Lectures and seminars

Buchan, Alastair *Conflict and Communication* (the University of Essex Noel Buxton Lecture 2 March 1971; Longman for the University of Essex 1971).

Francis, Richard *Broadcasting to a Community in Conflict — the Experience in Northern Ireland* (lecture at the Royal Institute of International Affairs, Chatham House, 22 February 1977; BBC 1977).

Gwynne, H.A. *The Press in War* (lecture at the RUSI 5 November 1913; *Journal of the RUSI*, vol.58, 1913).

Institute for the Study of Conflict *Television and Conflict* (Seminar 21—23 April 1978 (ISC Special Report, November 1978).

Murdoch, Graham *Fabricating Fictions: Approaches to the Study of Television Drama Production* (lecture given at the proceedings of the Prix Italia Symposium at Bologna in 1976. Later published in *Organisation and Creativity in Television*; Turin Editizioni, RA1, 1977).

Newby, Howard *Radio, Television and the Arts* (lunch-time lecture at Broadcasting House, 15 January 1976; BBC 1976).

Royal United Service Institution Seminar on *Defence and the Mass Media* held on 13 October 1970 (RUSI 1970).

Swann, Sir Michael *On Disliking the Media* (lecture at the University of Salford, 7 November 1978; BBC 1978).

Swann, Sir Michael *The Responsibility of the Governors* (lunch-time lecture at Broadcasting House, 29 October 1974; BBC 1974).

Swann, Sir Michael *Society in Rough Water* (University of Leicester Convocation Lecture, 6 May 1975; BBC 1975).

Taylor, Desmond *Editorial Responsibilities* (lunch-time lecture at the BBC, November 1975; BBC 1975).

Tugwell, Colonel Maurice *Public Opinion in Counter-Insurgency* (lecture to the Canadian Land Forces Command and Staff College, Kingston, 30 January 1973).

Military publications

A Brief Guide to Defence Public Relations (MOD OS 12).

The Progressive Qualification Scheme and Staff Training Handbook (Army Code No 71065, 1976).

Standard Military Course, Sandhurst Syllabus (September 1977).

Visor (edition 274), 6 July 1979.

Unpublished works

Blumler, Jay G. *The Intervention of Television in British Politics: A research paper for the Committee on the Future of Broadcasting* (University of Leeds, 1975).

Cable-Alexander, Major Patrick *The Media and the American Involvement in Vietnam* (paper produced at NDC Latimer, 1976).

Edmonds, Wing-Commander K.R. *The Military and the Media* (paper produced at NDC Latimer, March 1975).

Evans, Major I.D. *Public Relations Practice Within the Army* (paper produced at NDC Latimer, 1976).

Ewbank, Alison T. *News Diffusion: A Study of the Diffusion of News about the Events on Sunday, 30 January 1972, which led to loss of life in connection with the procession in Londonderry, Northern Ireland on that day* (Centre for Television Research, University of Leeds, November 1973).

Hollis, Richard *Vanishing Army* BBC 2 'Play of the Week' broadcast on 29 November 1978 (unpublished script).

Hudlestone, F.J. *Use of Newspapers to the Enemy Intelligence Service* concocted for the DMI by the Librarian of the General Staff Section, War Office Library, 21 May 1917.

Palmer, Andrew *The Public Presentation and Discussion of Defence Questions: The Way Ahead* (paper produced at RCDS, 1978).

Tugwell, Brigadier Maurice *Revolutionary Propaganda and Possible Counter-Measures* (Defence Fellowship Thesis 1976—77).

Newspapers and periodicals

Daily Express 18 August 1974.

Daily Mail 8 May 1981, 9 May 1981, 3 April 1982.

Daily Telegraph 8 October 1976, 6 December 1978, 10 December 1978, 27 February 1979, 5 March 1979, 19 June 1979, 5 July 1979, 14 July 1979, 31 July 1979, 31 January 1980, 4 January 1982.

Economist 20 November 1971.

Financial Times 13 October 1976.

Foreign News January 1969.

Guardian 20 December 1971, 4 April 1979.

Observer 18 August 1974, 4 March 1979, 24 January 1982, 9 May 1982.

Sunday Express 24 October 1981.

Sunday Times 16 July 1978, 13 August 1978, 22 October 1978, 26 November 1978, 21 March 1982, 4 April 1982.

The Times 5 August 1974, 16 August 1974, 28 February 1975, 30 September 1975, 1 October 1975, 24 February 1976, 27 February 1976, 17 July 1981, 25 March 1982, 27 May 1982, 22 July 1982.

Index

238

News (cont.)
153, 178, 182; home, 15—16,
31—2, 43—4, 46—7, 53; lists,
31—2, 38, 44—8, 50, 53, 61;
management of the, x—xi,
38, 112, 120, 128—9, 156,
161, 221; manufacturing the,
22—4, 54, 120, 124, 131;
misinformation *see* News,
management of; 'off the
record' interviews, 17, 152,
161—2, 164, 173, 180, 217;
problems of reporting the, 8,
11, 13—14, 16, 21, 23—9,
31—9, 42—3, 45, 47—55,
61—3, 65—8, 114, 131—2,
136, 139, 149, 152—3, 157,
162—3, 211; advertising ,
26, 31, 38—9; competition,
26, 45—6; format, 50—2;
legal, 24—6, 32, 37, 53,
139; strains of, 11, 13—14,
23, 26, 34, 36—8, 42, 61—
3, 67, 173—4, 211; tech-
nical, 21, 26—9, 34, 49,
157, 162—3; time and space
strictures of, 11, 13, 16,
23—5, 31—9, 43, 45, 47—
55, 61—2, 65—8, 114, 131—
2, 136, 149, 156, 176, 211;
process of, xi—xiii, 8, 11, 23,
29—64, 116, 163, 184,
212—3, 216; press, xii—xiii,
8, 11, 23, 29—41, 64, 216;
radio, xii—xiii, 8, 11, 23,
29, 58—64, 216; television,
xii—xiii, 8, 11, 23, 29, 42—
57, 64, 216;
role of, 57, 147; selection of,
13, 15—19, 29, 31—2, 34—5,
38—9, 43—9, 50—5, 60—2,
113—8, 121—122, 129, 136,
158, 176—7; sensationalism,
22—4, 53, 69, 114—21, 125,

127—8, 136—7, 145—6, 150,
159, 178; sources of, xi, 13,
15—18, 24, 36, 39—41, 47,
53—5, 60—61, 66, 111—2,
119—20, 155—7, 163—74;
speculation, xi, 41, 128—9,
141—2, 155, 158, 161;
v. Current affairs, 13—14,
22—7, 57, 59—60;
see also Armed conflict, Censorship, Editors, Editorial
control, Journalists, Media,
New technology, Press, Propaganda, Radio and Television
News Agencies, 15—16, 34—5,
47, 52, 54, 66, 147, 165
News at 5.45 see ITN
News at Ten see ITN
Newsbeat (BBC Radio News
Programme), 59
News Film Agency, 16
Newsmen *see* Journalists
Newsnight (BBC TV News and
Current Affairs Programme),
22, 65, 158
Newspapers *see* Press
New Officers (BBC TV *Panorama*
Special Programme), 74—9,
83, 86—8, 91
New technology, 7, 15—16, 26—
9, 34—5, 45—6, 51—2, 55, 67,
80, 110, 115, 135, 162—3,
167, 179, 181, 183, 185, 209,
213, 220—1; *see also* Military
and Television
New York Daily News, 145—6
New York Times, 110, 112
Nicholas, David (Editor of ITN),
14, 66—7, 152, 188
Nine o'clock News (BBC TV
News Programme) *see* Tele-
vision
Northcliffe, Lord, 14

Press (cont.)
problems of reporting news in the, 11, 13, 14, 21, 23–9, 31–9, 66, 136; competition, 26; libel, 24–6, 32, 37; new technology, 26–9, 34–5; strains of, 11, 13–14, 23, 26, 34, 36–8; time and space, strictures of, 11, 13, 23–5, 31–9, 66, 136;

production of the, 30–41; selection of news, 17, 19, 32, 34–5, 38–9, 117; sensationalism, 115, 117–8, 127–8; 'spiked', 117, 119

see also Editors, Editorial control, Journalists, Media, News, Radio and Television
Press Association (PA), 15, 162, 218
Preston, Peter (Editor of the Guardian), 188
Pringle, Lieutenant General Sir Steuart (Commandant General of the Royal Marines), 125–6
Progressive Qualification Scheme (PQS), 192–3, 212 see also British Army
Propaganda, x, 4, 14, 19, 54, 112–4, 120–21, 124–9, 131–50, 155–6, 159, 162–3, 177–8, 204, 220; countering, 126–9, 159, 162, 194

see also Argentina, Armed conflict, Censorship, IRA, Media, News, Northern Ireland and Vietnam War
Protheroe, Alan (Assistant Director General of the BBC), x–xi, 14, 18, 26, 53, 56–7, 147, 154, 179, 187–8

Public, education about defence, 7–8, 59, 71, 78, 85–91, 98–9, 103–4, 194, 196, 219; knowledge of media, 13–14, 19–24, 27–9, 35, 38, 42–3, 50, 53, 55, 57, 60, 68, 91, 99, 150, 156, 190, 217; of the military, 4, 7, 8, 68, 85–9, 91, 97, 99, 104–5, 167, 209–10, 218–9; opinion on defence matters, 110, 113–6, 121, 125, 127, 137, 146–7, 158, 164, 183–4, 215, 218–20

see also Armed conflict, Media, Military, Press, Radio and Television
Public Relations, 16, 61, 83, 88, 96, 98
Public School (BBC TV Documentary), 73
Purdie, John (TV Producer of Sailor), 79–83, 85–7

Radio, drama, 93; local, 15–16, 169
News, accuracy of, 59, 61, 163, 174; advantages of, 58–9, 163–4; analysis, 21–2, 60; and current affairs, 58–64 see also News and Television; as source of information, 60; balance, 20, 60;

BBC, 11, 13, 15–16, 18, 22, 38, 58–64, 128, 163, 165, 167, 169–70, 173–74, 197; expansion of, 58–60; impartiality see BBC

bulletins, length of, 16, 21, 58–62; critics of, 58, distortion, 61; editorial and